Resilience Enhancement in Social Work Practice

Roberta Greene • Nancy Greene • Connie Corley
Editors

Resilience Enhancement in Social Work Practice

Anti-Oppressive Social Work Skills and Techniques

Springer

Editors
Roberta Greene
Steve Hicks School of Social Work
The University of Texas at Austin
Austin, TX, USA

Nancy Greene
Ethelyn R. Strong School of Social Work
Norfolk State University
Norfolk, VA, USA

Connie Corley
Fielding Graduate University
Santa Barbara, CA, USA

ISBN 978-3-031-38517-9 ISBN 978-3-031-38518-6 (eBook)
https://doi.org/10.1007/978-3-031-38518-6

This Springer imprint is published by the registered company Springer Nature Switzerland AG
The registered company address is: Gewerbestrasse 11, 6330 Cham, Switzerland

Paper in this product is recyclable.

Foreword

Older Adult Services/Clinical Social Worker, Jewish Family Service of Greater Dallas, Dallas, TX, USA

The text *Resilience Enhancement in Social Work Practice: Anti-Oppressive Social Work Skills and Techniques* cannot come at a better time. Client difficulties that challenge social workers are getting increasingly complex as people around the globe experience inordinate stressors due to violence in their communities, civil unrest, environmental disruption, and social and economic inequality.

As a sequel to *A Resilience-Enhancing Stress Model: A Social Work Multisystemic Practice Approach* (Greene et al., 2022), the current text deepens readers' resilience-enhancing skill sets so they can more effectively serve clients and constituencies who are trying to overcome difficult life transitions and challenging environmental demands. In addition, the resilience-enhancing stress model described in this text has been used earlier (Greene et al., 2019) with diverse individuals, families, groups, organizations, and communities in various social work practice settings.

The text offers contemporary practice strategies that can supplement courses in human behavior that take a developmental life span approach. Furthermore, the text is appropriate for preparing generalist practitioners serving diverse populations and settings. Most important, the text underscores the Council on Social Work Education's (2022) *Educational Policy and Accreditation Standards*, which mandate that students engage in anti-racism, diversity, and inclusion in social work practice. Included are chapters that articulate anti-oppressive practice strategies, the role of cultural diversity in resilient social functioning, and processes for countering human rights violations during life transitions.

Harriet L. Cohen

References

Council on Social Work Education. (2022). *Educational policy and accreditation standards*. Retrieved September 22, 2022, from https://www.cswe.org/getmedia/94471c42-13b8-493b-9041-b30f48533d64/2022-EPAS.pdf

Greene, R. R., Wright, M., Herring, M., Wright, T., & Dubus, N. (2019). *Human behavior theory and social work practice with marginalized oppressed populations*. Routledge.

Greene, R., Dubus, N., & Greene, N. (2022). *A resilience-enhancing stress model: A social work multisystemic practice approach*. Springer.

Preface

As a professor of social work for over 50 years, I have strived to write textbook content that reflects the context and needs of contemporary times. Because this text goes to press at a time of pronounced civil strife and the demanding aftermath of the COVID-19 pandemic, the effort to write subject matter relevant to clients' difficulties has become an even greater challenge.

The resilience-enhancing stress model (RESM) was originally developed and continues to be expanded to provide social workers with the knowledge and skills to help clients during times of distress. Therefore, my co-authors and I have attempted to select current client and constituency issues that address the inordinate stress of difficult life course transitions and challenging environmental demands including school shootings and the opioid epidemic. At the same time, it applies a person-environment perspective that is broad enough to offer skills to ameliorate problems that might be more every day but painful concerns.

When writing the text first began, the Council on Social Work Education's Educational Policy Statement (CSWE, EPAS) was under review. The approved 2022 revision mandated that students engage in anti-racism, diversity, and inclusion in social work practice (CSWE, 2022). This curriculum design magnified the impetus for text authors to explore content related to the anti-oppressive approach to social work practice embedded in the resilience-enhancing stress model. We hope the readers find the emphasis on the connection between culture, individual concerns, and societal power structures and institutions a useful and essential perspective on their approach to social work practice.

Austin, TX, USA Roberta Greene

Reference

Council on Social Work Education. (2022). *Educational policy and accreditation standards.* Retrieved September 22, 2022, from https://www.cswe.org/getmedia/94471c42-13b8-493b-9041-b30f48533d64/2022-EPAS.pdf

Contents

List of Figures

List of Tables

About the Editors

Roberta Greene, PhD, MSW, professor emerita, was the Louis and Ann Wolens Centennial Chair in Gerontology and Social Welfare at the University of Texas at Austin. Prior to that, she was dean of social work at Indiana University. Dr. Greene has a wide range of practice experience, including clinical practice, clinical supervision, policy, administrative, and research expertise. She is an NASW Pioneer, known for her advocacy work on nursing home reform. She was the 2015 recipient of the Knee/Whitman Outstanding Achievement Award, which recognizes significant impacts on national health, public policy, and/or professional standards. Dr. Greene has served on the Council on Social Work Education's Educational Policy Commission. A Fellow of the Gerontological Society of America, she has conducted significant research on resilience among Holocaust survivors. A prolific author, she has authored 21 books and 6 of which are on resilience. Others include *A Handbook of Human Behavior in the Social Environment* (Aldine Transaction Press, 2017), *Caregiving and Care Sharing: A Life Course Perspective* (NASW Press, 2014), and *Human Behavior Theory and Social Work Practice with Marginalized Oppressed Populations* (Routledge, 2019).

Nancy Greene, DSW, MSW, MA, has a master of social work from the University of Texas at Austin and a master of arts from Nova Southeastern University in Fort Lauderdale, Florida. Her doctorate is from the University of Southern California. She is a licensed clinical social worker who has practiced in home healthcare and hospice. She has taught for Tulane University, Grand Canyon University, and Johnson C. Smith University in North Carolina. He is currently an assistant professor in the Norfolk State University School of Social Work, where she teaches human behavior in the social environment and practice methods.

Connie Corley, PhD, MSW, MA, has a long history in the fields of gerontology and geriatrics as a graduate of the University of Michigan, Ann Arbor. She cocreated the doctoral concentration in creative longevity and wisdom in the School of Leadership Studies at Fielding Graduate University and is professor emeritus at California State University, Los Angeles. A Fellow of the Gerontological Society of America and the Academy for Gerontology in Higher Education, she has engaged in multiple programs as a mentor and leader in curriculum development and cofounded and directed a lifelong learning program in Los Angeles for more than 10 years. The author of numerous peer-reviewed publications and coeditor of *Resilience: Navigating Challenges of Modern Life* (with Marie Sonnet, PhD; Fielding University Press, 2019), her recent work focuses on creativity in later life (emerging from a national study of resilience in Holocaust survivors led by Roberta Greene, PhD) and intergenerational/intercultural mutual mentoring. She created the podcast *LOVE GOES VIRAL* to offer support during the COVID-19 pandemic and beyond (www.lovegoesviral.org) and was cohost and producer of *EXPERIENCE TALKS* on Pacifica station KPFK-FM in Los Angeles for more than a decade.

About the Contributors

Jackie Bartell, MS, has a bachelor of arts in psychology from the University of Rochester (1983) and a master of science in developmental disabilities from the University of Rochester (1985). She has certifications in special education K–12, secondary social studies 9–12, and K–2 elementary education. She has worked in the field of special education for more than 35 years, working with special needs children and adults in a variety of settings, including both private and public schools, as well as consulting with families in their homes. As an experienced trainer, she has helped more than 1,000 professionals and parents both in the United States and around the world learn the DIRFloortime model.

Lizzi Cummings, MSW, LCSW, is the manager of clinical excellence and training in the Department of Social Work and Community Health of Rush University Medical Center in Chicago. Lizzi is also the senior manager of training and site engagement with the Center for Health and Social Care Integration (CHaSCI), providing clinical and training support to health systems and community-based organizations across the nation as they implement CHaSCI Care Models. In addition to working at Rush, Lizzi is the secretary for the Society for Social Work Leadership in Health Care–Illinois Chapter. Lizzi holds a master of social work from DePaul University in Chicago, Illinois, and a bachelor of arts in psychology from DePauw University in Greencastle, Indiana.

Adrian Du Plessis van Breda, PhD, MSW, is a professor of social work at the University of Johannesburg in South Africa. His research centers on the resilience processes that facilitate young people's transition from care to adulthood. He is well published in the international literature on resilience and leaving care. He is a coeditor of the forthcoming book *Living on the Edge: Innovative Research on Leaving Care and Transitions to Adulthood* (Policy Press) and editor of the *Southern African Journal of Social Work and Social Development*.

Abbreviations

AOP	anti-oppressive practice
ASD	autism spectrum disorder
CCYC	child and youth care center
CHaSCI	Center for Health and Social Care Integration
CSWE	Council on Social Work Education
DC-Cam	Documentation Center of Cambodia
DIR	Developmental, Individual-differences, and Relationship-based
ECCC	Extraordinary Chambers in the Courts of Cambodia
GBTSA	Girls and Boys Town South Africa
MDS	Minimum Data Set
MS	muscular dystrophy
NAACP	National Association for the Advancement of Colored People
NASW	National Association of Social Workers
NEET	not in employment, education, or training
NICWA	National Indian Child Welfare Association
P-E	person–environment
RESM	resilience-enhancing stress model
RSA	Republic of South Africa
UNHCR	United Nations High Commissioner for Refugees

Chapter 1
Introducing the Resilience-Enhancing Stress Model

Roberta Greene, Nancy Greene, and Connie Corley

Learning Objectives
This chapter introduces the resilience-enhancing stress model (RESM), an anti-oppressive human behavior approach to serve clients and constituencies who are facing stress associated with life transitions, challenging environmental demands, or adverse critical events. On completing this chapter, you should better understand how life transitions can challenge client and constituency resilient functioning and what the theory base of the RESM suggests can be done to resist risks. You should be prepared to answer the following questions:

- In what ways does social work practice focus on the wellness of people and their environments?
- Why can life transitions present challenges?
- How do strategies from each theory in the RESM contribute to enhancing resilience?

1.1 The Need for the RESM

The concept of resilience has increasingly been used to define mission statements (see, e.g., the mission statement of the American Red Cross at www.redcross.org/about-us/who-we-are/mission-and-values), shape program design (World Bank Operations Evaluation Department, 2005), and plan intervention strategies

R. Greene (✉)
Steve Hicks School of Social Work, The University of Texas at Austin, Austin, TX, USA
e-mail: rgreene@utexas.edu

N. Greene
Ethelyn R. Strong School of Social Work, Norfolk State University, Norfolk, VA, USA
e-mail: nagreene@nsu.edu

C. Corley
Fielding Graduate University, Santa Barbara, CA, USA
e-mail: conniecorleyphd@gmail.com

R. Greene et al. (eds.), *Resilience Enhancement in Social Work Practice*,
https://doi.org/10.1007/978-3-031-38518-6_1

(Meredith et al., 2011). The popularity of resilience as a concept can be traced to the recognition that it is appropriate for helping people during difficult, complex times (Greene, 2007; Greene et al., 2019). Namely, understanding resilience can help today's social workers and their clients mutually explore and seek solutions for "the complexity of personal and social relationships, and the continuing historical challenges of the times" (Lifton, 1993/1999, p. 28).

The complexity of difficulties that social workers now face is getting increased attention in the design of health and human services programs. Scholars and journalists have pointed out that people around the globe are experiencing increased stressors due to civil unrest and environmental disruption. For example, a study by Lebrasseur et al. (2021) brought to light the fact that older adults experienced a reduced quality of life and increased depression at the height of the COVID-19 pandemic. In addition, in 2022 Congresswomen Gwen Moore and Barbara Lee, members of the Congressional Social Work Caucus, introduced legislation to increase students' access to school social workers to address the growing need for school-based mental health services, which was heightened by school closings during the COVID-19 pandemic (Moore, 2022; see Chap. 2). The following overview of the RESM describes how its knowledge base can inform the needs of such contemporary social work practice. Social workers can use the enriched RESM proactive skill base also presented here to increase their capacity to assist their clients and constituencies.

1.2 The Professional Use of Self: Practitioner Readiness for Applying the RESM

The readiness of today's social workers to apply the RESM can be tested by increased societal disruption and civil unrest. Contemporary practice requires skills in listening to cocreated narratives—a collaborative process for defining problems and contracting with individuals, families, groups, organizations, and communities on mutually agreed-on goals. Becoming conversant with the underpinnings of risk and resilience research and human behavior can be helpful in this regard.

1.2.1 Learning About Research on Risk and Resilience

Three Waves of Resilience Research Advances in research have been instrumental in changing the way in which resilience is defined and in turn how social workers apply the term in practice. This progression was summarized by Richardson (2002), who proposed that resilience research has gone through three waves. The first wave explored personal characteristics such as optimism that help people continue to function despite adversity. In this wave, educators and mental health professionals created programs, in particular for children, that fostered the development of individual character traits. The second wave, emphasized today, examines the processes of retaining or maintaining resiliency by pursuing adaptive solutions. The third wave, also still ongoing, studies factors that contribute to people's growth and transformation following adversity, such as children's engagement in art during the war in Ukraine (see, e.g., Save the Children's Healing and Education Through the Arts program at https://www.savethechildren.org/us/what-we-do/protection/healing-and-education-through-the-arts).

Research-Informed Social Work Practice The RESM is a research-informed approach to social work practice. Therefore, a knowledge of the research background of risk and resilience theory offers a starting point for social work practice with the model. Early risk and resilience researchers sought to explain a differential developmental response to risk, namely, why some children were able to withstand high levels of adversity better than others. Research revealed that children who had person–environment protective factors to bolster their resilience also had more effective social functioning. Over the years, research findings have been used to plan various school-based resilience programs and other resilience-based interventions for children and youth (Begun, 1993; Benard, 1997).

Lifton (1967/1991), an early researcher who examined resilience in adults, began his work interviewing survivors of the bombing of Hiroshima following World War II. His research helped mental health practitioners understand how people remain resilient despite living through the trauma of inordinately stressful times. More recent research has called clinicians' and educators' attention to the need to understand resilience at multiple systems levels (Masten, 2014; Ungar, 2005). Key milestones in the research are summarized in Table 1.1.

Table 1.1 Milestones: resilience research, theory, and practice

Time frame	Major theorist(s)	Theoretical view	Major theme	Concepts adopted for practice
1972	Chestang	Environments as hostile or nurturing	Living in a dual society	Reduce dissonance between nurturing and hostile environments
1971–1982	Werner & Smith	Differential response to adversity	Overcoming risks	Bolster protective factors as a means of prevention
1987	Rutter	Natural adaptation to daily risk	Attending to the balance between risks and protection	Reduce risks and foster protection to enhance adaptation
1991	Garmezy	Functional competence	Exploring resilience at individual, family, and institutional levels	Develop client skills and secure resources to increase competence
1967–1999	Lifton	Protean self	Living in uncertain times	Learn to live with ambiguity and remain grounded
2005–2011	Ungar	Systems navigation	Charting cultural pathways	Remove societal barriers in a cultural context
2004–2014	Masten	Adaptive systems	Targeting assets and resources	Promote competence at multiple system levels

1.2.2 Comprehending Human Behavior

In addition to familiarity with the research background of the RESM, practitioner readiness to apply the model necessitates a knowledge of human behavior theory. That is, one of the basic premises of social work practice is that practitioners should "apply knowledge of human behavior and the social environment, person-in-environment, and other multidisciplinary theoretical frameworks to engage [assess, intervene with, and evaluate their] clients and constituencies" (Council on Social Work Education, 2015, p. 9). Basic theoretical assumptions related to social functioning are described below.

Problems in Living Resilience is an individual's or social system's ability to respond to stressful or risk-laden events and retain competent functioning. According to Strumpfer (2002), the process of "resiling" starts when someone perceives an environmental challenge or threat. In this sense, people do not have (ongoing) resilience but manifest it as they try to meet demanding environmental situations that interrupt social functioning. Stated another way, social work practice is conducted with the goal of reducing the stress of events that interrupt individual, family, and community functioning by addressing problems in living (Germain & Gitterman, 1996).

Normative Versus Nonnormative Development To understand the sources of stress that set resilience in motion, social workers need to address the transitions that occur across a person's life span. Two theoretical frameworks address the trajectory of change or developmental timing during people's lives: the *life-stage approach*, which suggests that all people pass through common, normative age-graded markers known as developmental stages or milestones; and the *life course perspective*, which argues that the timing of a person's life events is idiosyncratic to that individual and associated with that person's historical and cultural context (Greene, 2012). The RESM subscribes to the life course perspective as a means of individualizing the person-centered model to fit a particular person in a certain situational context.

In addition, the RESM addresses the development of families, groups, and communities, which involves changes in systemic patterns of communication, organization, and belief systems over time. Such change is usually a natural reconstruction of members' roles or the division of labor as the social system progresses over time in their respective environments.

Role Theory Role theory provides a set of constructs that social workers can use to understand human behavior as a pattern of reciprocal relationships marked by a set of culturally specific attitudes, beliefs, values, and expectations about how people should conduct themselves in a particular situation. Roles are an element of individuals' behavior as they interact in a social system. In other words, individuals are connected to social systems through the roles they occupy in them (Longres, 1997).

Person–Environment During the RESM helping process, social workers can choose change strategies aimed at the individual, the environment, or both. The intent is to select interventions that support, enhance, and promote client competence (Masten, 2014). To use the RESM effectively, practitioners should first become familiar with the human behavior frameworks that provide an understanding of resilience as a developmental process that is linked to demonstrated competence, or the learned capacity to interact positively with the environment (Greene, 2014; Masten, 1994).

Developmental Turning Points Research on naturally occurring resilience suggests that there are critical windows of opportunity for people to make changes in their social functioning, especially when developmental processes, context, and available opportunities converge to provide an opening (Masten, 2014). Substantial and enduring change during turning points in life course development often occurs during periods of transition, such as when one enters school or the workforce or begins to form a family. These events are characterized by the assumption that people create or modify social roles as changes in context emerge.

1.3 The RESM: A Metatheory

The RESM, which consists of risk and resilience theory, ecological theory, systems theory, and narrative theory, was synthesized as a culturally sound metatheory for serving diverse populations under stress (Greene et al., 2019). A "metatheory is concerned … with the study of theories, theorists, communities of theorists, as well as with the larger intellectual and social context of theories and theorists" (Ritzer, 1988, p. 188). A metatheory, a means of explaining and predicting phenomena, can assist social workers in planning assessment and intervention processes (Newman & Newman, 2005). That is, it is helpful for organizing and understanding client and constituency data during the helping process.

1.3.1 Risk and Resilience Theory

Central Focus

Risk and resilience theory suggests that when people are undergoing a transitional life event, protective factors may or may not adequately shield them from risk. When protective factors are effective at shielding a person from the negative effects of stress, that person may be said to be resilient.

RESM principles suggest that clients and social workers use the process of narrative cocreation to identify and reduce risks and to uncover and foster protective factors. This process requires the use of skills that foster clients' self-awareness and thus promotes their functional capacity within their special cultural context.

The RESM encompasses issues of diversity and social, economic, and environmental justice within the helping process (Greene et al., 2019). To address diversity, social workers should become conversant with the intersectionality of multiple factors that characterize and shape the human experience and are critical to the formation of identity (Crenshaw, 1993). The concept of intersectionality specifies that

> the dimensions of diversity are understood as the intersectionality of multiple factors including but not limited to age, class, color, culture, disability and ability, ethnicity, gender, gender identity and expression, immigration status, marital status, political ideology, race, religion/spirituality, sex, sexual orientation, and tribal sovereign status. (Council on Social Work Education, 2015, p. 7)

Terms

- *Transitional event.* An occurrence that requires growth in a person's basic life assumptions and response to stress.
- *Risks.* Influences that increase the probability of stress worsening.
- *Protective factors.* Events and conditions that shield individuals from risk and enhance resilience.
- *Resilience.* A person's or system's effective functioning during or following a life transition.

Assumptions

- Stress varies from individual to individual, family to family, community to community, and country to country.
- People's varying responses to stress are precipitated by such risks as personal or family life transitions, political and economic disruptions, disturbing historical events, and troubling environmental pressures (Germain & Gitterman, 1996).
- Protective factors shield people and the systems in which they interact from adverse reactions to stress.

1.3.2 Ecological Theory

Central Focus

Ecological concepts in the RESM emphasize a person-in-environment perspective. That is, ecological theory calls for the social worker to apply theory and skills that address a life course developmental perspective at multiple systems levels, especially during times of life transition. Moreover, it requires that social workers examine whether people have equal access to environmental opportunities (Germain & Gitterman, 1996).

Terms

- *Chronosystem.* The sociocultural, historical, and political factors that characterize the time and place in which a person or system develops.
- *Competence.* A person's or system's successful history of transactions with the environment.

- *Life course.* The development or timing of life events within a social, cultural, and historical context.
- *Macrosystem.* The overarching social context or patterns of a given society.
- *Mesosystem.* The linkages and processes that occur between two or more settings containing the (developing) person.
- *Microsystem.* The pattern of activities and roles and interpersonal face-to-face relations in an immediate setting.

Assumptions

- People demonstrate resilience at multiple system levels (macro, meso, and micro levels).
- Resilience is associated with the availability of resources as well as social, economic, and environmental circumstances that are equitable.

1.3.3 Systems Theory

Central Focus

The development of systems is informed by general systems theory, which suggests that social workers conceptualize living systems as a unified whole (von Bertalanffy, 1968). Practitioners focus on the patterns of people's interactions in and between social systems. The understanding of communication, organization, and belief systems that emerges creates a family narrative related to the ways in which social institutions support the family's social functioning. That is, systems thinking is used by the social worker to make an assessment and intervention plan that reconstructs the family system's response to stress or risks (Buckley, 1968).

Terms

- *Belief system.* The collective worldview of members of a social system.
- *Communication.* The flow of information between and among system members and between and among systems.
- *Organization.* The way in which system members work together or establish patterns that achieve the system's goals.
- *Reconstruction.* A method of rewriting a family story in a less problem-laden, more positive manner.
- *System.* A complex, dynamic unit composed of people in mutual interaction.

Assumptions

- Stress is a natural part of daily life in social systems.
- Stress may be more acute during times of life transition and challenging environmental demands.
- Resilient systems balance risk and protective factors to maintain functioning.
- A social system that has been disrupted by high-level stress strives to keep its balance by reconstructing itself, becoming "more differentiated or complex" (Buckley, 1968, p. 494).

1.3.4 Narrative Theory

Central Focus
Narrative theory is the methodological base of the RESM. A narrative approach views skillful conversations between clients and social workers as the core of the helping process. By cocreating clients' or constituencies' narratives, social workers gather data about client concerns and reflect on the complexity, uncertainty, and ambiguity that are part of everyday life experiences (Bhabha, 1994/2007).

Terms
- *Narrative.* An account of events as perceived by the narrator(s).
- *Meaning-making.* Peoples' appraisal of life events.
- *Externalization.* Attributing stressors to influences outside oneself or one's community (White & Epston, 1990).
- *Reconstruction.* Rearranging a system's patterns of communication, organization, and belief systems to rewrite a more positive narrative.

Assumptions
- Telling a narrative allows people to organize and make sense of their experiences.
- New meanings of events are realized as narratives are told, deconstructed, and reconstructed.
- A positive reconstruction of stressful events contributes to people's resilience as well as their functional ability.

Using a cocreated narrative in health care to learn about needs for psychosocial care is a well-known technique in the United Kingdom and Ireland and is now being applied more often in the United States to address inequities in health care (Pallai & Tran, 2019). This helping process is illustrated in the practice example in Box 1.1, in which hospital social worker Joan is meeting with Marcia to prepare her to go home (also see Chap. 6). (Hospital-to-home programs are designed to give some patients acute care at home rather than in the hospital.)

Box 1.1: Practice Example: Transitioning from Hospital to Home
A hospital health care team chose Marcia as a candidate for its hospital-to-home program as a means of recovering from a heart monitor surgically installed that morning. Joan combined her skills in traditional resource allocation with a resilience-enhancing narrative interview to learn about Marcia's needs for psychosocial health care. Joan met with Marcia to learn how she might fare during her transition home and to hopefully reduce her risk of being readmitted to the hospital.

1.4 Phases of the RESM

1.4.1 Engagement as Relationship Building

Engagement occurs when the social worker and client work together to explicitly discuss the purposes of the helping process. This encompasses applying reflective listening in a trusting relationship.

Joan: Hello. I am Joan, the discharge facilitator. I'm here to get to know you and talk about what you think about going home.
Marcia: I just don't know. I feel like I am on another planet.
Joan: That is why I am here. Patients usually feel that way after surgery. I hope to sit with you and sort things out so you can go home with what you need. Do you think you can help me by describing yourself? What kind of person would you say you are?
Marcia: Well, I am usually a type A!
Joan: I am too. What does that mean to you? Can you say more?
Marcia: I usually keep things well organized.

1.4.2 Assessment as Narrative Coconstruction

The narrative is the source of the client data that are used by social workers and clients to coconstruct a tailored assessment of the client's life events. By listening for themes in the narrative interview, clients and social workers uncover issues related to the presenting concerns and pursue new meanings and solutions. In short, risks, protective factors, and processes related to resilience are explored.

Joan: So you are always on time and well organized?
Marcia: Yes! I think I am.
Joan: That will be helpful in our hospital-to-home program. If you like, we can make a chart of what services you might need.
Marcia: Yes, I don't want health care people all over the place! Oh, excuse me. I didn't mean to offend you.
Joan: You didn't at all. It is great that you are telling me what you like. Will you have other people around?
Marcia: Yes, my niece, Molly, lives with me, but she is in college. I love having her around, but she needs to be able to study.
Joan: Should we see what she thinks about your coming home?
Marcia: She is very outspoken, like me. So we will know soon.

1.4.3 Intervention as Deconstruction and Reconstruction of Narratives

Marcia's assessment profile led to an intervention plan that involved developing new meaning(s) about home care. The goal was to reframe Marcia's narrative so she could take more positive control of her life. Marcia and her social worker Joan were able to write a plan for the transition from hospital to home that allowed Marcia to set personal boundaries and goals and take part in her own care.

1.4.4 Evaluation as Collaborative Progress Review

Evaluation is a mutual appraisal of the progress made during the helping process. How well was the purpose of the RESM—to reduce or eliminate risks and stress, to enhance protective factors, and to support resilience—achieved? The envisioned outcome is for clients to gain a better perception of their competent daily functioning. Marcia and Joan's final interview illustrates Marcia's readiness to move on to a positive future at home.

Joan: I see you're going home today. Did you get all our information about care and how it will be scheduled?

Marcia: Yes, I think I did. I hope I didn't forget something.

Joan: Don't worry. I will be transitioning with you and will make at least one home visit. Maybe I will get to meet your niece.

Marcia: We can try and set a time.

1.5 Summary and Conclusion

This chapter discussed the central focus, terms, and assumptions of the theoretical base of the RESM. The metatheory was discussed as a means of helping alleviate problems of living and building on clients' natural resilience.

Summary of Learning Outcomes
Keep in mind the following:

- Social workers can apply human behavior theory to inform their practice.
- Social workers can synthesize various theories to construct a practice approach.

Discussion Questions

1. What accounts for the growing use of risk and resilience theory?
2. Why may social work services be needed during times of life transition?

Chapter Exercise

Write a one-page reflection paper on how Joan used the RESM to prepare Marcia to go home.

Glossary

Assessment An examination of a cocreated tailored story of critical events.

Engagement The formation of a safe relationship in the third space.

Evaluation A consideration of whether client issues have been resolved or stress has been reduced.

Intervention The deconstruction and reconstruction of client narratives.

Life course perspective A perspective that views life events as idiosyncratic to an individual.

Life-stage approach An approach that acknowledges that people pass through common, age-graded developmental markers.

Nonnormative development Individual development within a specific historical and cultural context.

Normative development The expected MAINSTREAM timing of life events.

Problems in living Everyday tensions.

Research-informed Describing a theoretical approach based on research studies.

References

Begun, A. (1993). Human behavior and the social environment: The vulnerability, risk, and resilience model. *Journal of Social Work Education, 29*(1), 26–35.

Benard, B. (1997). *Turning it around for all youth: From risk to resilience*. Retrieved June 14, 2022, from https://files.eric.ed.gov/fulltext/ED412309.pdf

Bhabha, H. (2007). *The location of culture*. Routledge. (Original work published 1994).

Buckley, W. (1968). Society as a complex adaptive system. In W. Buckley (Ed.), *Modern systems research for the behavioral scientist* (pp. 490–511). Aldine.

Chestang, L. (1972). *Character development in a hostile environment (Occasional Paper No. 3)*. University of Chicago, School of Social Service Administration.

Council on Social Work Education. (2015). *Educational policy and accreditation standards*.

Crenshaw, K. (1993). Mapping the margins: Intersectionality, identity politics, and violence against women of color. *Stanford Law Review, 43*(6), 1241–1299.

Garmezy, N. (1991). Resilience in children's adaptation to negative life events and stressed environments. *Pediatric Annals, 20*(9), 459–466.
Germain, C. B., & Gitterman, A. (1996). *The life model of social work: Advances in theory and practice*. Columbia University Press.
Greene, R. R. (2007). *Social work practice: A risk and resilience perspective*. Brooks/Cole.
Greene, R. R. (2012). *Resiliency theory: An integrated framework for practice, research, and policy* (2nd ed.). NASW Press.
Greene, R. R. (2014). Resilience as effective functional capacity: An ecological stress model. *Journal of Human Behavior in the Social Environment, 24*(8), 937–950.
Greene, R. R., Wright, M., Herring, M., Wright, T., & Dubus, N. (2019). *Human behavior theory and social work practice with marginalized oppressed populations*. Routledge.
Lebrasseur, A., Fortin-Bédard, N., Lettre, J., Raymond, E., Bussières, E.-L., Lapierre, N., Faieta, J., Vincent, C., Duchesne, L., Ouellet, M.-C., Gagnon, E., Tourigny, A., Lamontagne, M.-È., & Routhier, F. (2021). Impact of the Covid-19 pandemic on older adults: Rapid review. *JMIR Aging, 4*(2), 264–274.
Lifton, R. J. (1991). *Death in life: Survivors of Hiroshima*. University of North Carolina Press. (Original work published 1967).
Lifton, R. J. (1999). *The protean self: Human resilience in an age of fragmentation*. University of Chicago Press. (Original work published 1993).
Longres, J. (1997). Is it feasible to teach HBSE from a strengths perspective, in contrast to one emphasizing limitations and weaknesses? In M. Bloom (Ed.), *Controversial issues in human behavior in the social environment* (pp. 16–33). Allyn & Bacon.
Masten, A. (1994). Resilience in individual development: Successful adaptation despite risk and adversity. In M. C. Wang & E. W. Gordon (Eds.), *Educational resilience in inner-city America: Challenges and prospects* (pp. 3–25). Erlbaum.
Masten, A. S. (2014). Global perspectives on resilience in children and youth. *Child Development, 85*(1), 6–20.
Meredith, L. S., Sherbourne, C. D., Gaillot, S. J., Hansell, L., Ritschard, H. V., Parker, A. M., & Wrenn, G. (2011). Promoting psychological resilience in the U.S. military. *Rand Health Quarterly, 1*(2), 2. Retrieved June 14, 2022, from https://www.ncbi.nlm.nih.gov/pmc/articles/PMC4945176/
Moore, G. (2022, March 11). Congresswoman Gwen Moore and Congresswoman Barbara Lee introduce legislation to increase access to school social workers to address growing need for school-based mental health services among young people. Retrieved June 14, 2022, from https://gwenmoore.house.gov/news/documentsingle.aspx?DocumentID=4966
Newman, B. M., & Newman, P. R. (2005). *Development through life: A psychosocial approach* (8th ed.). Brooks/Cole.
Pallai, E., & Tran, K. (2019). Narrative health: Using story to explore definitions of health and address bias in health care. *The Permanente Journal, 23*, 18–052. Retrieved June 14, 2022, from https://www.ncbi.nlm.nih.gov/pmc/articles/PMC6380479/
Richardson, G. E. (2002). Metatheory of resilience and resiliency. *Journal of Clinical Psychology, 58*(3), 307–321.
Ritzer, G. (1988). Sociological metatheory: A defense of a subfield by a delineation of its parameters. *Sociological Theory, 6*(2), 187–200.
Rutter, M. (1987). Psychosocial resilience and protective mechanisms. *American Journal of Orthopsychiatry, 57*(3), 316–331.
Strumpfer, D. J. W. (2002, September). *A different way of viewing adult resilience* [Paper presentation]. 34th international congress on military medicine, Sun City, Northwest Province, South Africa.
Ungar, M. (2005). *Handbook for working with children and youth: Pathways to resilience across cultures and contexts*. Sage.
von Bertalanffy, L. (1968). *General system theory*. Braziller.

Werner, E., & Smith, R. (1982). *Vulnerable, but invincible: A longitudinal study of resilient children and youth*. McGraw-Hill.
White, M., & Epston, D. (1990). *Narrative means to therapeutic ends*. Norton.
World Bank Operations Evaluation Department. (2005, January 10). *Lessons from natural disasters and emergency reconstruction*. Retrieved June 14, 2022, from http://www.china-up.com:8080/international/case/case/924.pdf

Supplemental References

Anderson, H., & Goolishian, H. A. (1988). Human systems as linguistic systems. *Family Process, 27*(4), 371–393.
Anderson, H., & Goolishian, H. (1992). The client is the expert: A not-knowing approach to therapy. In S. McNamee & K. J. Gergen (Eds.), *Therapy as social construction* (pp. 25–39). Sage.
Dean, R. G., & Fleck-Henderson, A. (1992). Teaching clinical theory and practice through a constructivist lens. *Journal of Teaching in Social Work, 6*(1), 3–20.
Genero, N. P. (1998). Culture, resiliency, and mutual psychological development. In H. I. McCubbin, E. A. Thompson, A. I. Thompson, & J. E. Fromer (Eds.), *Resiliency in Native American and immigrant families* (pp. 31–48). Sage.
Greene, R., Dubus, N., & Greene, N. (2022). *A resilience-enhancing stress model: A social work multisystemic practice approach*. Springer.
Grotberg, E. H. (1995, September 27–30). *The international resilience project: Research, application, and policy* [Paper presentation]. Simposio Internecinal Stress e Valencia, Lisbon, Portugal.
Karls, J., Lowery, C., Mattaini, M., & Wandrei, K. (1997). The use of the PIE (person-in-environment) system in social work education. *Journal of Social Work Education, 33*(1), 49–59.
Kuhn, T. (1970). *The structure of scientific revolutions*. University of Chicago Press.
Laird, J. (1993). Introduction. In J. Laird (Ed.), *Revisioning social work education: A social constructionist approach* (pp. 1–10). Haworth Press.
Longres, J. F. (1990). *Human behavior in the social environment*. Peacock.
National Association of Social Workers. (2018). *NASW code of ethics*.
Schiele, J. H. (1996). Afrocentricity: An emerging paradigm in social work practice. *Social Work, 41*(3), 284–294.
Schon, D. (1983). *The reflective practitioner*. Basic Books.
van Breda, A. (2018). Developmental social casework: A process model. *International Social Work, 6*(1), 66–78.
Wakefield, J. C. (1996). Does social work need the eco-systems perspective? [Part 1]. *Social Service Review, 70*(1), 1–32.
Weick, A. (1993). Reconstructing social work education. In J. Laird (Ed.), *Revisioning social work education: A social constructionist approach* (pp. 11–30). Haworth Press.

Chapter 2
The Resilience-Enhancing Stress Model: Articulating Anti-Oppressive Practice

Roberta Greene, Nancy Greene, and Connie Corley

Learning Objectives
This chapter introduces anti-oppressive practice (AOP) as a core feature of the resilience-enhancing stress model (RESM). On completing this chapter, you should be prepared to answer the following questions:

- How does a person–environment (P-E) perspective set the boundaries for anti-oppressive social work practice?
- How does the use of an integrated traditional, RESM, and anti-oppressive skill base help clients and constituencies face difficult life transitions?

Chapter 1 reviewed the theoretical base of the RESM. This chapter initiates discussion of the anti-oppressive approach to social work practice that is embedded in the RESM. AOP is characterized by a resistance to the systemic mechanisms of societal oppression and discrimination. Chapters 3 and 4 augment this focus on the AOP methodology with a discussion of cultural diversity and human rights. Taken together these various ideas can actualize the "the search for a proper and helpful [micro to macro] fit between client, social worker, and theory of intervention" (Turner, 1996, p. 35).

R. Greene (✉)
Steve Hicks School of Social Work, The University of Texas at Austin, Austin, TX, USA
e-mail: rgreene@utexas.edu

N. Greene
Ethelyn R. Strong School of Social Work, Norfolk State University, Norfolk, VA, USA
e-mail: nagreene@nsu.edu

C. Corley
Fielding Graduate University, Santa Barbara, CA, USA
e-mail: conniecorleyphd@gmail.com

R. Greene et al. (eds.), *Resilience Enhancement in Social Work Practice*,
https://doi.org/10.1007/978-3-031-38518-6_2

2.1 AOP: A P-E Perspective

Social workers' search for proper interventions has had a mixed history, with practitioners in the field vacillating between strategies that emphasize internal change and those that emphasize societal change. Interventions that give sufficient attention to macrolevel issues that address societal inequities and oppression have been given short shrift (Specht & Courtney, 1994). Such interventions highlight the long-standing adage recognized in the RESM that "the personal is political"—which means that there is an inevitable connection between individual concerns and societal power structures and institutions (Van Den Bergh & Cooper, 1986, p. 9).

The assumption that personal issues are intertwined with political ones is established in AOP and necessitates that social workers use a P-E perspective to configure their practice, providing a perspective on how individuals and social systems interact. That is, the P-E perspective is central to the anti-oppressive approach to practice in the RESM because it directs social workers' attention to the multiple systems that influence a client's social functioning. By attending to the totality of a client's or constituency's micro- to macrolevel space, social workers can avoid establishing a false dichotomy between proximal (close by) and distal (far away) factors that influence people's lives.

At the same time, the P-E perspective is so broad in scope that the RESM emphasizes 10 P-E dimensions to help social workers organize assessment information about risk and protection acquired in the helping process. Two of these P-E dimensions with strong connections to anti-oppressive social work practice—effects of strong cultural identity and ties and effects of human rights violations—are elaborated on in Chaps. 3 and 4.

2.2 The Need for Anti-Oppressive Social Work Measures

The COVID-19 pandemic brought increased attention to long-standing systemic inequities in the United States. These inequities call for social workers to critically examine how they use theory and their readiness to "engage in strategies to eliminate oppressive structural barriers" (Council on Social Work Education [CSWE], 2022, p. 9). This urgency was underscored in a 2022 editorial in *Social Work*:

> Our time is one of challenge and conflict, with a syndemic of concatenated crises—COVID-19, racism, chronic health disparities, structurally unjust systems, a failing economy where people are differentially vulnerable and have differential access to resources and goods, with a government that is fissured ideologically and willing to suppress the voices and votes of the vulnerable. (Scheyett, 2022, p. 101)

To meet these crises, the RESM has adopted explicit practice strategies and skills that incorporate concepts related to diversity, oppression, culture, and human rights within its helping process (Chaps. 3 and 4). This central point of view suggests that the focus of professional practice is clients' and constituencies' lived experiences (CSWE, 2022) and that social workers need to engage in practice that addresses both clients' personal distress as well as their exclusion from or limited participation in social institutions.

2.3 Articulating Anti-Oppressive Social Work Practice

2.3.1 Central Focus

As stated previously, AOP is based on the understanding that human development occurs not only through a person's independent activities but also through complex reciprocal interactions between the person and others and between person in environment (Bronfenbrenner & Morris, 1998).

The notion that social work practice can be strengthened by using client experiences and activist skills to achieve social change can be traced primarily to Bertha Reynolds, a medical doctor, community worker, and social work educator who strove to eliminate poverty and racism (Reynolds, 1935). Although AOP has been an arm of the profession since its early days, practitioners have not always given attention to clients' access to resources or their right to exercise influence, power, or control over the conditions in which they live. By referring to theory and skills in the RESM and the literature on AOP, social workers can expand the narrative interview, making it even more responsive to societal inequities. That is, clients and social workers can collaborate in a helping process that emphasizes how to resist discriminatory stress.

2.3.2 Terms

- *Anti-oppressive practice (AOP).* An umbrella term for a practice stance social workers can take to resist or confront discrimination and the domination of mainstream discourse.
- *Anti-racism.* An active value stance social workers assume to identify and oppose racism.
- *Discriminatory stress.* The toll people feel due to the strain of bigotry or prejudice.
- *Microaggressions.* Indignities that communicate hostile, derogatory, or otherwise negative prejudicial insults.
- *Bullying.* Recurring aggressiveness that can cause distress to the recipient.

2.3.3 *Assumptions*

The social work literature underscores the profession's compatibility with the AOP tenet to counter social inequities in practice (Baines, 2011). For example, the most recent *Educational Policy and Accreditation Standards* call for social workers to understand that racism and oppression shape human experiences and influence practice at the individual, family, group, organizational, and community levels and in policy and research. Moreover, helping professionals must understand the pervasive impact of White supremacy and privilege (CSWE, 2022, p. 9).

In a similar vein, key assumptions of AOP also include the following:

- Social workers address oppression associated with societal prejudices.
- Social workers use techniques to counter inequities.
- Social workers focus on power abuses in their practice (Baines, 2011).
- Social workers recognize that personal issues may stem from structural or systemic discrimination.
- Social workers understand that diversity is defined as the intersectionality of people's social statuses (Crenshaw, 1993).

2.4 The Systemic Nature of Oppression: Examples From Multisystemic Practice

The practice examples in this section shed light on multisystemic AOP. The example in Box 2.1 speaks to policy practice that involves legislative advocacy. Social workers engaged in legislative advocacy attempt to "influence policy formulation,

Box 2.1: Practice Example: Addressing Hate Crimes Through Legislation

It is no secret that Social Workers wear many hats. And often, we wear multiple at the same time. The NASW-SC Chapter is no exception. As educators and advocates for not only our profession, but for our clients, and our communities it is the mission of this chapter to continue all the important work that Social Workers before us have started. Whether in-person with politicians asking tough questions and finding ways to reach across the aisle, or virtually in trainings that help to enhance the knowledge of our professionals empower them to do their best work, we will continue to focus on key legislation and topics to improve the lives of ALL with equity and compassion. We don't believe there is one answer to solve the issues we face; we believe there are many answers. And those focus on Medicaid Expansion, Reproductive Healthcare Decisions, and Social Justice issues. We are not in the business of picking one over the other, we are in the business of uplifting ALL South Carolinians.

NASW-SC Chapter

analysis, implementation, and evaluation within their practice settings" (CSWE, 2022, pp. 10–11). The purpose is to bring about legislative change that enables people's greater participation in society.

In addition to social workers working on behalf of state-level anti-oppressive initiatives, many universities provide diversity and inclusion programs. As seen in the practice example in Box 2.2, Rochelle, a social worker employed by the university, talked with students in her orientation workshop about their experiences of feeling different and their involvement in incidents of social injustice. The brief narratives in this chapter reveal how students in the group got on the path to more resilient social functioning. In addition, listening to and reflecting on one another's narratives created connections between group members.

Box 2.2: Practice Example: Transitioning from the Barrio to the University

Roberto came from a border town near Mexico known for its cultural events. Unfortunately, the area was extremely impoverished, and a vast number of residents lived in highly segregated ghettos or barrios, some in homes without running water.

Roberto graduated from high school in the top 10 in his class and won a scholarship to the state university. As a first-year college student, he was transitioning from living with his family in the barrio to living in a large dormitory on campus.

While attending a majority-White charter high school, Roberto had experienced far too many microaggressions that had belittled his Latinx culture. Consequently, he was leery about moving away from his family and community support systems.

Roberto decided to take advantage of university resources that encouraged students to engage in diversity and inclusion, including a welcome to campus workshop. Rochelle, a social work faculty member assigned to the diversity center, led the new student orientation.

2.5 RESM Social Work, AOP, and Roberto

2.5.1 Engagement

Rochelle was facilitating a one-time student orientation group. She needed to quickly engage the students, establish trust, be transparent, and clarify the agenda. Furthermore, members of the group needed to collaborate with her to establish a third-space relationship in which all voices were heard. The purpose of the diversity center—to promote social justice and inclusion—was spelled out in a welcome kit containing pertinent readings and campus resources and was shared with group members beforehand. It was hoped that this would assist the group in becoming a well-functioning unit that would accomplish its purpose. Rochelle began the workshop by imparting the idea that each student was a valued and respected member of the group. She also traced or mapped students' negative life influences and began to turn them around.

Rochelle: Welcome everyone. Did you get the resource and reading list I sent? The kit is intended to let you know that the university is committed to creating an inclusive campus environment. Is it too soon to have any questions?
Roberto: I wondered if I would feel comfortable talking in a group.
Juan: I did too.
Rochelle: It may help to introduce ourselves. I could go first if no one else wants to.
Ashley: What kind of things would we say?
Rochelle: I was going to say that I was the first in my family to attend a university. I now work at one.
Juan: I am also the first.
Roberto: Me too. I thought I would be the only one.
Ashley: I do not like to stand out.
Rochelle: So? What is it okay to say?
Andrew: I know I want to make good grades. But I do not want to worry about whether I fit in.
Stanley: I was worried too. I was afraid I would be picked on because I am Black.
Rochelle: That is what the diversity center is all about—helping students feel they can fit in. We run workshops throughout the semester and have a drop-in-anytime policy.

2.5.1.1 Practice Example Analysis: Steps Taken

Rochelle drew on the hesitancy expressed in the group. She hoped members could learn from one another about some of their challenges, in particular "just fitting in." Rochelle was also aware that some group members had previously faced oppression in their daily lives. During their brief conversation, students learned about one another's struggles. They also began to become aware of not only risks they might face on campus but also protective factors that might shield them from discriminatory stress.

2.5.2 Assessment

Rochelle helped group members cocreate a narrative about how they perceived their sense of inclusion in society. Themes revealed by the data indicated what needed to be done to arrive at a more positive group narrative.

Rochelle: I think just about everyone has experienced or witnessed how someone is made to feel they do not fit in.

Andrew: Yes, I certainly have. I sometimes wonder what, if anything, I can do about it.
Stanley: Yeah, I don't want to just look the other way anymore.
Ashley: My high school had an antibullying program. I learned a lot about the roots of discrimination.
Rochelle: One of the diversity center workshops will be on that topic.
Roberto: I think I might go to that.
Stanley: I'll see you there.

2.5.3 *Intervention*

When the students began to understand the structural roots of discrimination, they started to externalize the problem and avoid self-blame. They also became more empowered to function as causal agents, making choices on their own behalf (Solomon, 1976). Roberto and Stanley followed up by attending the antibullying workshop. They collaborated with other students to create a flyer they distributed to all the university dormitories. The flyer said the following:

- Bullies are not wanted here.
- Bullies go home.
- Bullies are cowards.
- Bullies move out of my way.

2.5.3.1 Practice Example Analysis: Steps Taken

Although the RESM is sensitive to diversity and issues of social, economic, and environmental justice, AOP skills and techniques add a more strategic dimension to confront systemic discrimination. Resistance to systemic discrimination is integrated into narrative interviews as practitioners help clients and constituencies appraise life events and establish meaning. This enables externalization of the problem (e.g., "I don't fit in" becomes "Bullies are not welcome here").

2.5.4 *Evaluation*

Students evaluated the antibullying workshop using a short Likert survey. They were also asked to suggest topics for future workshops.

2.6 Constructing a RESM Anti-Oppressive Skill Base

The anti-oppressive skill base used in the practice example of Roberta was derived from three major theoretical sources: traditional social work theory, the RESM (risk and resilience theory), and the coaching literature.

2.6.1 *Traditional Skills*

In addition to skills such as empathy, traditional social work skills incorporated into the RESM might include Freud's (1956) widely known practice skill of interpreting clients' feelings to expand their self-awareness and Rogers's (1957) cardinal principle that an effective interview involves establishing rapport with clients.

2.6.2 *The RESM (Risk and Resilience Theory)*

The RESM (risk and resilience theory) emphasizes skills that help people overcome stressors associated with adversity and become competent, resilient adults. The use of skills that help clients reduce risks and identify and bolster protective factors such as family, new-found friendships, and other social supports is key to client assessment and intervention. Social workers emphasize skills that reflect the importance of making and maintaining connections or relationships with others.

2.6.3 *Coaching Skills*

Coaching skills are directive. These may include asking probing questions and giving homework assignments. Coaching skills are used to develop client self-awareness, help clients identify their choices, and help them find their own solutions. Coaching assists clients and social workers in creating an action plan composed of goals that are based on an awareness of how more resilient social functioning can be attained. Summaries of traditional, RESM, and anti-oppressive skills and techniques and sample practitioner statements appear in Tables 2.1 and 2.2.

2.7 Four Phases of the RESM Interview

The practice example in Box 2.3 shows how Ms. Martin, a school social worker, integrated AOP skills into RESM practice.

Box 2.3: Practice Example: Transitioning from Loss After a School Shooting

Alberta had just enrolled as a middle school student when she experienced a school shooting. After 2 months of group counseling and the creation of a memorial for students, Alberta still felt anxious. When her anxiety negatively impacted her ability to complete her schoolwork, her English teacher referred her to the school social worker, Ms. Martin. As they coconstructed Alberta's narrative, Ms. Martin learned that Alberta's close friend, Jennifer, had been killed in the school shooting. Alberta said she felt like not enough had been done to remember her friend.

Table 2.1 Integrated interview skills: theoretical foundation

Time frame	Theorist(s)	Concepts adopted for practice
1956	Freud	Develop client self-awareness
1957	Rogers	Hold clients in unconditional positive regard
1979, 1987	Antonovsky	Appraise life events to establish their meaning
2007	White	Map clients' negative life influences to externalize their problem and prevent self-blame
1982–1992	Werner & Smith	Bolster protective factors to support resilience
2002	Barrera & Corso	Respect and understand client voices to create a third space
2011	Ungar	Teach clients to navigate their environments to obtain resources

Table 2.2 Anti-oppressive practice skills

RESM practice skill	Practitioner statement
Hold clients in unconditional positive regard	"I respect what you want to do."
Display warmth and genuine concern	"Could we do this together?"
Respect and understand client voices to create a third space	"What each of what you say fits the situation."
Create anchored understanding	"I hope I understand what you are saying. Tell me more."
Map clients' negative life influences	"Can we trace where this all began?"
Identify and bolster protective factors to support resilience	"What you said sounds helpful. Do you want to do it again?"
Appraise life events to establish their meaning	"It sounds like you are getting on top of this. Can you tell me more?"
Externalize clients' problem and prevent self-blame	"This seems to involve a glitch in the system. What do you think?"
Assist clients in overcoming oppression	"Are you telling me that this was unfair?"
Teach clients to navigate their environments to obtain resources	"Have you found what you need on campus?"

Note. RESM resilience-enhancing stress model

2.7.1 Engagement: Forming a Third-Space Relationship

Forming a third-space relationship involves orienting clients and constituencies to how they can overcome their difficulties. To get a positive start, social workers may apply the familiar traditional social work skills of empathy (understanding another's point of view), genuineness (showing one's true self), and warmth (feeling received).

The RESM practice skill of anchored understanding also comes into play from the outset. Creating anchored understanding involves recognizing the (third) space that others occupy. In other words, social workers function as explorers of another's point of view. Ms. Martin was able to learn that Alberta believed that more needed to be done to memorialize her friend and the others who were killed during the shooting.

Ms. Martin applied attending skills to show Alberta that she was interested in her loss. She acknowledged that she could not possibly know how the school shooting had made Alberta feel. Ms. Martin said, "I realize you don't know me well yet. But I hope we can eventually get to know each other well enough to talk about Jennifer." Ms. Martin conveyed the idea that just because Jennifer had been lost in the shooting did not mean she was forgotten: "What memories of Jennifer will stay with you? I am sure there are times you will never forget."

2.7.2 Assessment: Cocreating a Narrative

Cocreating a narrative involves skills for exploring a client's or constituency's life through storytelling. Narratives are cocreated when social workers use the skill of open curiosity, asking questions or giving prompts to elicit client difficulties and workable solutions. The creation of a narrative reveals what oppressive experiences are of concern to the client and synthesizes them into an assessment profile. As the social worker and client use skills to cocreate and reflect on an emancipatory narrative, themes emerge, eventually forming a plot. This in turn is the source of the data needed in assessment and intervention planning that leads to resistance to societal injustices. (See Chap. 5, "The Resilience-Enhancing Stress Model: A Practice Overview and Guide," for the 10 research-informed P-E dimensions, which can be used to organize assessments and intervention planning.)

2.7.3 Intervention: Deconstructing and Reconstructing Narratives

Intervention necessitates engaging in appraisal and meaning-making, during which social workers and clients generate new ideas to rewrite oppressive, problem-laden narratives (Antonovsky, 1979). Ms. Martin said, "I'd like to better understand what happened so we can begin to make some sense of what students did on that terrible day." In addition, she asked Alberta whether she would complete a coaching assignment to help her better understand and articulate her anxiety. Alberta was asked to write a short paper on diverse memorial practices. She then was asked to share it with the school's grief counseling group for discussion.

In short, to deconstruct and reconstruct a narrative, social workers use AOP skills that help clients better understand and map the personal life situations or environmental factors that affect their equal participation in society. By mapping or visualizing their past negative and future positive life influences, clients are better able to rewrite their negative stories and enhance their resilience (White, 2007). (The RESM practice overview and guide in Chap. 5 offers tools social workers can use to map client influences on resilient social functioning.)

2.7.4 Evaluation: Collaboratively Reviewing Progress

During the evaluation or collaborative progress review, social workers and clients explore what actions and goals were set and which ones were met effectively. (Table 5.2 in Chap. 5 presents questions related to such an evaluation.)

2.8 Summary and Conclusion

There are many similarities among traditional, RESM, and AOP skills. All contribute to the RESM. Dissimilarities in skills may come down to differences in emphasis: AOP highlights skills that promote social change at the structural and institutional levels, whereas coaching principles emphasize individual change, with clients setting goals and making choices. The social worker's mission is to address both. It is the responsibility of practitioners to build their own personal social work practice skill set and apply it to the situation of a particular client or constituency.

Summary of Learning Outcomes
Keep in mind the following:

- Social workers can collaborate with clients to reimagine their stories.
- Social workers can foster client diversity and inclusion.
- Social workers can encourage a client's participation in society.

Discussion Questions

1. What benefits do you think can be gained by merging the RESM and AOP skills?
2. What benefits do you think can be gained by combining the RESM and coaching skills?

Chapter Exercise
Write a one-page reflection paper on the skills you would use to mitigate the negative response to the school shooting among Alberta and her community.

Glossary

Anchored understanding Recognition of the ideas of others.

Coaching A method of helping that develops client self-awareness, decision-making, and goal setting.

Institutional inequity Individual discrimination connected to societal structures and institutions.

Intersectionality The overlap of societal characteristics or statuses.

Lived experience Knowledge gained through undergoing certain events.

Person–environment perspective A perspective that recognizes how individuals and their environments mutually influence one another.

Structural barriers Impediments that systematically block marginalized groups from obtaining opportunities and resources.

Third-space relationship A relationship that involves an acceptance of clients' ideas.

Transitions Life changes and events.

White supremacy The belief that people with white skin are superior to people of other races and should have more power.

References

Antonovsky, A. (1979). *Health, stress, and coping*. Jossey-Bass.

Antonovsky, A. (1987). *Unraveling the mystery of health: How people manage stress and stay well*. Jossey-Bass.

Baines, D. (2011). *Doing anti-oppressive practice*. Fernwood.

Barrera, I., & Corso, R. (2002). Cultural competency as skilled dialogue. *Topics in Early Childhood Special Education, 22*(2), 103–113.

Bronfenbrenner, U., & Morris, P. A. (1998). The ecology of developmental processes. In W. Damon & R. M. Lerner (Eds.), *Handbook of child psychology: Theoretical models of human development* (pp. 993–1028). Wiley.

Council on Social Work Education. (2022). *Educational policy and accreditation standards*. Retrieved September 22, 2022, from https://www.cswe.org/getmedia/94471c42-13b8-493b-9041-b30f48533d64/2022-EPAS.pdf

Crenshaw, K. (1993). Mapping the margins: Intersectionality, identity politics, and violence against women of color. *Stanford Law Review, 43*(6), 1241–1299.

Freud, S. (1956). On psychotherapy. In *Collected papers* (Vol. 1, pp. 256–268). Hogarth.

Reynolds, B. C. (1935). Rethinking social casework. *Family, 16*, 230–237.

Rogers, C. R. (1957). The necessary and sufficient condition of therapeutic personality change. *Journal of Consulting Psychology, 21*(2), 95–103.

Scheyett, A. (2022). The time is right for social work. *Social Work, 67*(2), 101–103. https://doi.org/10.1093/sw/swac010

Solomon, B. B. (1976). *Black empowerment: Social work in oppressed communities*. Columbia University Press.

Specht, H., & Courtney, M. (1994). *Unfaithful angels: How social work abandoned its mission*. Free Press.

Turner, F. (1996). *Social work treatment* (4th ed.). Free Press.

Ungar, M. (2011). *Counseling in challenging contexts: Working with individuals and families across clinical and community settings*. Brooks/Cole.

Van Den Bergh, N., & Cooper, L. B. (Eds.). (1986). *Feminist visions for social work*. NASW Press.

Werner, E., & Smith, R. (1982). *Vulnerable but invincible: A longitudinal study of resilient children and youth*. McGraw-Hill.

Werner, E., & Smith, R. (1992). *Overcoming the odds: High risk children from birth to adulthood*. Cornell University Press.

White, M. (2007). *Mapping of narrative practice*. Norton.

Supplemental References

Earl, T. R. (2005). Response to Greene 2001, Redefining social work. *Journal of Human Behavior in the Social Environment, 11*(1), 55–61.

Flynn, D. (2005). What's wrong with rights? Rethinking human rights and responsibilities. *Australian Social Work, 58*(3), 244–256.

Greene, R. R. (2005). Redefining social work for the new millennium. *Journal of Human Behavior in the Social Environment, 11*(1), 37–54. https://doi.org/10.1300/J137v11n01_03

Greene, R. R., Cohen, H., Wright, M., Dubus, N., Wright, T., & Greene, N. (2021). *Geriatric practice with older adults: A resilience-enhancing guide*. NASW Press.

Grotberg, E. H. (1995, September 27–30). *The international resilience project: Research, application, and policy* [Paper presentation]. Simposio Internecinal Stress e Valencia, Lisbon, Portugal.

International Coaching Federation. (2020). *ICF code of ethics*. Retrieved June 15, 2022, https://coachfederation.org/code-of-ethics

National Association of Social Workers. (n.d.). *Read the code of ethics*. Retrieved May 5, 2022, from https://www.socialworkers.org/About/Ethics/Code-of-Ethics/Code-of-Ethics-English

Swigonski, M. E. (1996). Challenging privilege through Africentric social work practice. *Social Work, 4*(2), 153–161.

Van Den Bergh, N. (1995). Feminist social work practice: Where have we been … where are we going? In N. Van Den Bergh (Ed.), *Feminist practice in the 21st century* (pp. xi–xxxix). National Association of Social Workers.

Wexler, L. M., DiFluvio, G., & Burke, T. K. (2009). Resilience and marginalized youth: Making a case for personal and collective meaning-making as part of resilience research in public health. *Social Science and Medicine, 69*(4), 565–570.

Supplemental References: Coaching

Allen, K. (2013). A framework for family life coaching. *International Coaching Psychology Review, 8*(1), 72–79.

American Psychological Association. (2016). *Stress in America: The impact of discrimination*. American Psychological Association.

Hartman, A., & Laird, J. (1983). *Family-centered social work practice*. Free Press.
International Coaching Federation. (n.d.). *Coaching FAQs*. Retrieved August 15, 2022, from http://www.coachfederation.org/need/landing.cfm?ItemNumber=978&navItemNumber=567.
Ives, Y. (2008). What is "coaching"? An exploration of conflicting paradigms. *International Journal of Evidence Based Coaching and Mentoring, 6*(2), 100–113.
Ives, Y. (2012). What is relationship coaching? *International Journal of Evidence Based Coaching and Mentoring, 10*(2), 88–99.
McGoldrick, M., & Carter, B. (2001). Advances in coaching: Family therapy with one person. *Journal of Marital and Family Therapy, 27*(3), 281–300.
Parker, P., Kram, K. E., & Hall, D. T. (2012). Exploring risk factors in peer coaching: A multilevel approach. *Journal of Applied Behavioral Science, 49*(3), 361–387.
Specht, H., & Courtney, M. (1994). *Unfaithful angels: How social work has abandoned its mission*. Free Press.
Theeboom, T., Beersma, B., & van Vianen, A. E. M. (2013). Does coaching work? A metaanalysis on the effects of coaching on individual outcome levels in an organizational context. *Journal of Positive Psychology, 9*(1), 1–18.

Chapter 3
Exploring the Role of Cultural Diversity in Resilient Social Functioning: Theory and Skills

Roberta Greene, Nancy Greene, and Connie Corley

Learning Objectives
This chapter highlights major skills and techniques needed to conduct a RESM culturally sound anti-oppressive narrative interview. On completing this chapter, you should be better able to attend to culture as a protective factor during engagement, assessment, intervention, and evaluation processes with clients and constituencies. You should be prepared to answer the following questions:

- What is culture?
- How does culture act as a protective factor?
- What cultural factors are key to the narrative interview process?

The RESM is a human behavior and practice model that explains resilient functioning in individuals and among social systems across time (Greene, 2014). The model is designed to guide culturally sound anti-oppressive social work practice with and on behalf of diverse individuals, families, groups, organizations, and communities.

This chapter is intended to assist social workers in the process of individualizing the cultural contexts of clients and constituencies. Although more research is needed, studies document that people who have strong links with their cultures are better able to respond to hardships (Cohen et al., 2006; Cross et al., 2000; Greene, 2015; Wexler, 2009). Being a member of a cultural group offers people opportunities to support resiliency through social connectedness and positive mutual

R. Greene (✉)
Steve Hicks School of Social Work, The University of Texas at Austin, Austin, TX, USA
e-mail: rgreene@utexas.edu

N. Greene
Ethelyn R. Strong School of Social Work, Norfolk State University, Norfolk, VA, USA
e-mail: nagreene@nsu.edu

C. Corley
Fielding Graduate University, Santa Barbara, CA, USA
e-mail: conniecorleyphd@gmail.com

R. Greene et al. (eds.), *Resilience Enhancement in Social Work Practice*,
https://doi.org/10.1007/978-3-031-38518-6_3

experiences. Cultural affiliations also can contribute to people's collective memories and historical continuity (Nagel, 1994; Yates & Youniss, 1996). In fact, the transmission of cultural values has been said to lay the foundation for people's resilience (Substance Abuse and Mental Health Services Administration, 2022).

The chapter describes why a RESM narrative interview requires practitioners to understand that resilience looks both the same and different within and between various populations (Ungar, 2013). Said another way, the conditions that bolster resilient functioning may differ according to a client's social positionality, life contexts, and culture (Kirmayer et al., 2011; Schoon, 2006).

3.1 Identifying Culture as a Protective Factor

As US society grows increasingly diverse and polarized by civil strife, there is a greater need for social workers to give attention to protective factors that contribute to a positive cultural climate. Such factors encompass person–environment exchanges that bolster resilient functioning, including social connectedness, through family and friends and social cohesiveness through interconnected communities. The practice example in Box 3.1 continued from Chap. 2 illuminates how a social worker who attended to a client's culture and community context remediated loss.

Box 3.1: Practice Example: Exploring Grief, Culture, and Faith Traditions

Following an attack by a school shooter, Alberta, a middle school student, was anxious and not completing homework assignments. She was referred to Ms. Martin, the school social worker, who recognized that recovering from loss was both a personal and collective process. Consequently, Ms. Martin began her meetings with the recognition that Alberta's anxiety resulted from the loss of her friend as well as the negative school climate following the shooting.

3.2 Culture and Resilience-Enhancing Practice Skills

Social workers can use several skills in their interviews to uncover cultural content. These include exhibiting cultural competence, cultural humility, and cultural soundness.

3.2.1 Differentiating Cultural Competence

To be culturally competent, social workers must give consistent attention to mastering and applying the knowledge, attitudes, and skills needed to intentionally address culture in the social work helping process. The concept of cultural competence assumes that the more knowledge social workers obtain about another culture, the more cultural competency skills they will display in practice. Therefore, Ms. Martin focused on how she could gain further knowledge of cultural practices that help people overcome grief.

3.2.2 Defining Cultural Humility

Social workers who display cultural humility recognize the limitations of their cultural knowledge. Therefore, they use practice skills to learn about the cultural practices of their clients and constituencies. That is, social workers who exhibit skills related to cultural humility take an interpersonal stance with clients that is other oriented and that addresses power imbalances in the helping process (Stubbe, 2020). They also emphasize their own *lifelong learning*—a process of striving to increase one's proficiency in knowledge, attitudes, and skills (Council on Social Work Education, 2022). Note how Ms. Martin acknowledged her need to learn more about her students' cultural practices.

3.2.3 Delineating Cultural Soundness

Being culturally sound requires that social workers recognize that they and their clients have been socialized into their own cultures, which consist of local knowledge and beliefs about how to best engage in problem resolution. Therefore, differences around problem resolution and client-specific sociocultural and historical information need to be recognized during the helping process. As illustrated in Box 3.2, Ms. Martin solicited feedback from students to achieve this goal.

Box 3.2: Skill Box: Culture and Resilience-Enhancing Practice

Skill	Practitioner statement
Cultural competence	"I am reading about the healing traditions among our students."
Cultural humility	"I need to learn more from our students about their grief and healing traditions."
Cultural soundness	"I understand you may want to tell me about what might help you get on the road to recovery after the school shooting."

3.3 Engagement: Forming a Third-Space Relationship

3.3.1 Establishing a Third-Space Relationship

Social workers engaged in a third-space relationship use skilled dialogue to learn about each client's story across diverse cultural parameters (Barrera & Corso, 2002). To ensure that multiple voices are heard, the practitioner may use a variety of skills to create a third-space relationship. The *third space* is a secure zone in which multiple truths can be heard. In other words, it is a client–social worker collaboration or safe place in which narratives are cocreated. As can be seen in the practice example in Box 3.3, students displayed skillful dialogue in a talking circle as they cocreated their group narrative.

3.3.2 Achieving Anchored Understanding

Anchored understanding is another skill social workers use to comprehend the (third) space that others occupy. Social workers accomplish this by facilitating the exploration of the culture of an individual as well as multiple points of view. Practitioners use attending skills to show interest in clients ("I really want to know about that") and active listening skills to clarify statements ("I think I understand this. Am I right?").

3.4 Assessment: Cocreating a Narrative

3.4.1 Gathering Client Data

Before developing a mutual plan to promote resilience, social workers need to appreciate that the narrative is a source of client assessment data. A *narrative* is a story or a client or constituency account of a series of connected events ("Narrative", 2022). It is composed of multiple threads woven together into a plot that comprises the person's or group's interpretation of life events.

The skill of *open curiosity*, or asking pointed questions, can be used to shape conversations with clients to gather the data ("I am interested in your thoughts about how this works"). The goal is to maximize information about the client's or constituency's singular (cultural) situation. That is, as seen in the practice example in Box 3.3, the social worker used prompts to shape scattered events into a coherent culturally specific story on which they could reflect.

Box 3.3: Practice Example: From the Personal to the Collective

Alberta completed her coaching homework assignment to learn about cross-cultural traditions and rituals for dealing with grief, accepting an invitation to present her findings to the school's bereavement counseling group. As the school social worker, Ms. Martin was asked to lead a discussion following Alberta's paper presentation. Ms. Martin realized that improving the collective school climate after the loss necessitated adopting a whole-school, systemic approach that could promote resilience (Carmel, 2021).

Ms. Martin chose to use a talking circle, which stems from the traditions of the Indigenous people of North America, to create a third space. Talking circles are a conversational technique in which members of a group sit in a circle and take turns talking and listening to one another. They are a means of communicating that give participants opportunities to share and contribute within the group. Talking circles also equalize participants' power relationships. The purpose is to create a space in which positive interpersonal connections are made. This can be particularly useful when talking about difficult topics. Participants sit in a circle and a feather or other object is passed from one participant to the next to establish who is the next to speak (Winters, n.d.).

Talking Circle: Grief and Culturally Based Grief Rituals

Ms. Martin: Thank you Alberta. That was a wonderful paper presentation. Thanks for inviting me to lead the group discussion. We are going to use an ancient way of holding a group discussion that was created by Indigenous Americans called a talking circle. Has anyone heard of it?

Roger: I have. We get to sit in a circle and take turns talking. Do you have a feather to pass along to each of us?

Ms. Martin: Yes, I do. The only other rule is not to interrupt each other. Let's sit in a circle and see who wants to go first. We are going to discuss what ceremonies or memorials following various tragedies you have attended or want to describe.

Steve: Can I start?

Ms. Martin: Okay. Here is the feather. When you are through, give it to the person next to you. Anyone who doesn't want to talk should just pass the feather to the person sitting next to them.

Steve: I got to go. My family went to New York City, and I got to go! The 9/11 memorial was awesome. The names of everyone who died were on a wall near the water pool. There are so many lights. They even have the remains of the airplane that was shot down. It's called Ground Zero! The memorial candles were beautiful.

(continued)

Box 3.3 (continued)

Tanya:	Well, my Aunt Norma's homecoming ceremony was conducted to let her father go home to heaven. That idea came when the slaves were forced to come to America. Aunt Norma held the homecoming at our church so we could hear the Bible readings and gospel songs. She said her father went to a better place.
Rosie:	I pass! It's too sad.
Marion:	I saw on TV that the Parkland School shooting was memorialized for 6 weeks when people from the community placed flowers and teddy bears outside the school. My Jewish friend said they designed a virtual cemetery called the Star of David Memorial Gardens.
Ms. Martin:	Thank you all for sharing. What do you think comes next?
Alberta:	Maybe our school group can come up with something we can do.
Roger:	That should be our next meeting.

3.4.2 *Attending to Local Language and Worldview*

Language The United States is home to many people of different national origins, some of whom have limited English proficiency. But rich, varied experiences are expressed in their narratives. At the same time, an insufficient number of professionals are equipped to speak various languages. Because of this, linguistic minorities may be denied services, experience delays in service delivery, or undergo inaccurate assessment (Gonzalez, 2006). Furthermore, a study of the utilization mental health care patterns of 3000 Mexican American older adults found that knowing where to find a specialty mental health provider increased the likelihood of service use (Gonzalez, 2006).

However, innovations to overcome language barriers are currently being tried. For example, an English teacher at Sullivan High, a Chicago high school with one of the largest refugee populations, is using Google Translate to reach her students. Also, the school's social worker has collaborated with a well-settled immigrant who speaks fluent English to translate group discussions.

Worldview *Worldviews* are collective systems of meaning created during a family or community group developmental pathway (Barber, 2008). Over time, positive and negative interactions form a belief system based on the group's rules, ideals, and values. These beliefs are often reflected in the group's grand narrative.

3.4.3 Learning About Help-Seeking Patterns

So as not to create distance between the professional and the client during social work encounters, social workers need to understand how help-seeking behaviors differ from culture to culture. To try and prevent dissonance, practitioners can use a conceptual framework created by James Green (1998) to examine help-seeking behaviors that are based on a minority client's cultural knowledge, idiosyncratic experiences, and ideas about illness and treatment.

Green contended that the client–provider relationship is a cross-cultural experience that consists of the *client culture* and the *professional subculture*. Consequently, practitioners need to be aware that problem recognition happens when clients notice that a change has occurred in their usual social functioning. Clients then label their problem based on their own knowledge, which comes from their everyday experience, their cultural beliefs, and feedback from their social network (including their families, friends, and other community members). Help may be sought from local Indigenous help providers in the client community, who often shape the decision of whether to utilize formal health or social services. If formal mainstream services are used, it is important for social workers to learn about clients' cultural help-seeking pathways and how they define or label their difficulties so this information can inform the helping process.

3.4.4 Mapping Person–Environment Influences

During a client assessment, social workers and clients coconstruct an overarching picture of the clients' life events. They map the multiple layers of social systems in which the clients interact, exploring the various person–environment dimensions related to risk and protection that have shaped their lives.

From this person–environment perspective, culture is a feature of daily living that is based on relationships and not on individual action as such. In other words, culture is a phenomenon that emerges from interactions among the members of a group that can contribute to the maintenance of resilience.

3.5 Intervention: Reconstructing Narratives

3.5.1 Establishing Cultural Meaning

As with all phases of helping, RESM interventions should be congruent with the client's cultural values and goals. Culture, a form of shared beliefs and ideas, affords people a chance to collectively construe the meaning of critical life events. That is, personal and community-based meaning-making emerges through human interaction (Bruner, 1987) that can be tapped during the social work helping process.

3.5.2 Reconstructing Narratives

RESM interventions are based on a construction and reconstruction of a client's or constituency's narrative. This means that clients need to understand that a problem or distress may occur when they create a negative self-story. Meaning-making and externalization are two important skills to use in reconstructing negative client narratives into asset-based stories.

3.5.3 Actualizing Meaning-Making

Appraisal Clients may seek help when their world ceases to make sense. An appraisal of meaning begins when clients ask themselves whether they can handle a difficult life situation. The social worker may say, "I'd like to understand how that happened" or "What do you think it means?"

Meaning-Making Meaning-making involves clients realizing whether a stressor is "comprehensible (structured, predictable, and explicable), manageable (resources are available to meet demands), and meaningful (challenges, worthy of investment and engagement)" (Antonovsky, 1987, p. 31). Meaning-making can occur when social workers encourage clients to reveal, reflect on, and appraise the connotation, significance, or implications of a critical event (Greene et al., 2019). Engaging in this process helps clients and constituencies discover environmental supports or protective factors that can reduce or shield them from risk. This idea was best captured by Saleebey (1994), who said the following:

> Two essential characteristics of the human condition important for social work practitioners to remember are (1) human beings build themselves into the world by creating meaning, and (2) culture gives meaning to action by situating underlying states in an interpretive system. Practice is an intersection where the meanings of the worker (theories), the client (stories and narratives), and culture (myths, rituals, and themes) meet. Social workers must open themselves up to clients' constructions of their individual and collective worlds. The major vehicles for this are stories, narratives, and myths. (p. 351)

3.5.4 Externalizing

Actualizing meaning-making involves externalizing a problem. Externalizing a problem or difficulty requires that the client or constituency look outside themselves for the possible sources of distress as well as solutions. In the practice example in Box 3.4, Alberta's anxiety was reduced as Ms. Martin helped her connect to others and oppose gun violence. A dictionary of related skills appears in Table 3.1.

Box 3.4: Practice Example: Group Members Begin to Heal

Ms. Martin:	How did your meeting with the memorial planning committee go?
Alberta:	I think we are on to something. We may hold an event at the Boys and Girls Club and invite people from the community.
Ms. Martin:	Do you think some parents will want to come?
Alberta:	My parents are attending and so are John's.
Ms. Martin:	Sounds like more voices will be heard. What will be the goals? What will someone get from attending?
Alberta:	Oh, do you mean learn something or feel better?
Ms. Martin:	Those are good choices.
Alberta:	Maybe some will want to lobby for gun control.
Ms. Martin:	Why not see what the others think?

Table 3.1 Narrative interview skills for culturally diverse practice

Learning why the client sought help. Understanding why the client may have originally asked for the social worker's help. "Why did you come to see me? What can we work on together?"
Acknowledging diversity. Recognizing the client's or family's belief system or worldview. "I hear you saying that your (family) traditions of grieving are important to you."
Individualizing the client's social identity. Addressing social, political, and historical content in the client's life (course). "I hear you have experienced several influential events during your lifetime. Are any more important now than others?"
Joining in group action. Collaborating with individuals and community groups to redress a problem. "It sounds like your group members really care to work with others. What are your goals?"
Promoting positive cultural identity. Learning about and supporting cultural protective factors. "It sounds like your values and traditions are helping you along the way. Am I right?"
Strengthening social supports. Identifying, bolstering, and affirming interpersonal or community relatedness. "It sounds like the group has been important to you. What is next on the agenda?"
Transitioning into new roles. Facilitating clients' capacity to carry out new behaviors as they interact with others. "I see you are doing new things lately. How is it going?"

3.5.4.1 Practice Example Analysis: Externalization and Narrative Reconstruction

The school planning committee decided to invite community members to a meeting to establish multiple goals for a memorial day for victims of the school shooting to be held at the Boys and Girls Club. Group members chose to create a portable picture wall of the children who were shot and killed during the attack on the school. The plan was to take the memorial wall to the town council and state legislature as a form of protest when gun laws and regulations were going to be debated. That is, the group members engaged in a process of activism, taking up a cause or joining with others to enact change.

This process of activism externalized the problem, which helped members of the group realize that the source of the difficulty of the school shooting was outside themselves and lay with the proliferation of ownership of assault weapons. In short, externalizing the problem was a process of not accepting gun violence as normal and reconstructing the problem-laden story.

3.6 Evaluation: Appraising Progress

When Alberta and Ms. Martin mutually evaluated the helping process, they agreed that they had achieved two major goals: reducing Alberta's anxiety and mobilizing the community. They were excited that the activism of taking the picture wall to the state legislature had made the local newspaper.

3.7 Summary and Conclusion

This chapter described culture as a protective factor that has both personal and collective meanings. In addition, it emphasized the fact that social workers and clients can collaborate as agents of change to make resilient life transitions.

Summary of Learning Outcomes
Keep in mind the following:

- Social workers can ensure that all voices are understood, respected, and heard in the third-space relationship.
- Social workers can collaborate with clients to discover and build on cultural protective factors or strengths.
- Social workers and clients can find culturally sound meaning in difficult life events.
- Social workers can mobilize individual and community activism.
- Social workers and clients evaluate progress in meeting identified goals based on clients' or constituencies' values.

Discussion Questions
1. Differentiate cultural competence, cultural humility, and cultural soundness.
2. Explain why culture is a protective factor.

Chapter Exercise
Write a one-page essay on which one of your cultural beliefs would best help you through a life transition following a tragic event.

Glossary

Client culture A client's everyday experience.
Culture The way of life of a group.
Diversity Differences in life experiences and social positions.
Externalization A process in which clients' source of distress is placed outside themselves.
Grief traditions Rituals that recognize loss within a faith tradition.
Individualization The process of tailoring the helping context to a specific client.
Mapping person–environment fit Exploring clients' or constituencies' place in their surroundings.
Oppression A process that diminishes the rights of others through the abuse of power.
Professional subculture Professional norms and language.
Talking circle A way of conversing in which group members sit in a circle and take turns talking and listening to one another.

References

Antonovsky, A. (1987). *Unraveling the mystery of health: How people manage stress and stay well.* Jossey-Bass.

Barber, B. (2008). Contrasting portraits of war: Youth's varied experiences with political violence in Bosnia and Palestine. *International Journal of Behavioral Development, 32*(4), 298–309.

Barrera, I., & Corso, R. M. (2002). Cultural competency as skilled dialogue. *Topics in Early Childhood Special Education, 22*(2), 103–113.

Bruner, J. (1987). Life as narrative. *Social Research, 54*(1), 11–32.

Carmel, C. (2021). A transactional, whole-school approach to resilience. In M. Ungar (Ed.), *Multisystemic resilience* (pp. 220–236). Oxford University Press. https://doi.org/10.1093/oso/9780190095888.003.001

Cohen, H., Greene, R. R., Lee, Y., Gonzalez, J. G., & Evans, M. (2006). Older adults who overcame oppression. *Families in Society, 87*(1), 35–49.

Council on Social Work Education. (2022). *Educational policy and accreditation standards.* Retrieved September 22, 2022, from https://www.cswe.org/getmedia/94471c42-13b8-493b-9041-b30f48533d64/2022-EPAS.pdf

Cross, S. E., Bacon, P. L., & Morris, M. L. (2000). The relational-interdependent self-construal and relationships. *Journal of Personality and Social Psychology, 78*(4), 791–808.

Gonzalez, J. (2006). Older Latinos and mental health services: Understanding access barriers. In R. R. Greene (Ed.), *Contemporary issues in life care (pp. 73–93).* Haworth Press.

Green, J. W. (1998). *Cultural awareness in the human services: A multi-ethnic approach* (3rd ed.) Pearson.

Greene, R. R. (2014). Resilience as effective functional capacity: An ecological stress model. *Journal of Human Behavior in the Social Environment, 24*(8), 937–950.
Greene, R. R. (2015). Resilience and healing among Cambodian survivors of the Khmer Rouge regime. *Journal of Evidence-Informed Social Work, 12*(6), 579–587.
Greene, R. R., Wright, M., Herring, M., Wright, T., & Dubus, N. (2019). *Human behavior theory and social work practice with marginalized oppressed populations*. Routledge.
Kirmayer, L. J., Dandeneau, S., Marshall, E., Phillips, M. K., & Williamson, K. J. (2011). Rethinking resilience from Indigenous perspectives. *The Canadian Journal of Psychiatry, 56*(2), 84–91. https://doi.org/10.1177/070674371105600203
Nagel, J. (1994). Constructing ethnicity: Creating and recreating ethnic identity and culture. *Social Problems, 41*(1), 152–176.
Narrative. (2022). Retrieved September 27, 2022, from https://www.collinsdictionary.com/dictionary/english/narrative
Saleebey, D. (1994). Culture, theory, and narrative: The intersection of meaning in practice. *Social Work, 39*(4), 351–359.
Schoon, I. (2006). *Risk and resilience: Adaptations in changing times*. Cambridge University Press.
Stubbe, D. E. (2020). Practicing cultural competence and cultural humility in the care of diverse patients. *Focus, 18*(1), 49–51. https://doi.org/10.1176/appi.focus.20190041
Substance Abuse and Mental Health Services Administration. (2022). Risk and protective factors.
Ungar, M. (2013). Resilience, trauma, context, and culture. *Journal of Trauma, Violence, & Abuse, 14*(3), 255–266.
Wexler, L. (2009). The importance of identity, history, and culture in the wellbeing of in Indigenous youth. *Journal of the History of Childhood and Youth, 2*(2), 267–276.
Winters, A. (n.d.). *Using talking circles in the classroom*. Retrieved September 27, 2022, from www.heartland.edu/documents/idc/talkingcircleclassroom.pdf
Yates, M., & Youniss, J. (1996). Community service and political-moral identity in adolescents. *Journal of Research on Adolescence, 6*(3), 271–284.

Supplemental References

Bohanon, J. P. (2005). *The talking circle: A perspective in culturally appropriate group work with indigenous peoples*. Retrieved May 8, 2023, from https://www.se.edu/international-student/wp-content/uploads/sites/85/2019/09/Proceedings-2005-Bohanon.pdf
Bonanno, G. A. (2004). Loss, trauma, and human resilience: Have we underestimated the human capacity to thrive after extremely aversive events? *American Psychologist, 59*(1), 20–28. https://doi.org/10.1037/0003-066X.59.1.20
Garbarino, J. (1982). Sociocultural risk: Dangers to competence. In C. B. Kopp & J. B. Krakow (Eds.), *The child: Development in a social context (pp. 630–685)*. Addison-Wesley.
Gubrium, J. (1993). Speaking of life: Horizons of meaning for nursing home residents. Aldine de Gruyter.
Henson, M., Sabo, S., Trujillo, A., & Teufel-Shone, N. (2017). Identifying protective factors to promote health in American Indian and Alaska Native adolescents: A literature review. *Journal of Primary Prevention, 38*(1–2), 5–26. https://doi.org/10.1007/s10935-016-0455-2
Kearney, A. (2014). *Cultural wounding, healing, and emerging ethnicities*. Springer.
LaFromboise, T., Coleman, H. L. K., & Gerton, J. (1993). Psychological impact of biculturalism: Evidence and theory. *Psychological Bulletin, 114*(3), 395–412.
Nasim, A., Fernander, A., Townsend, T. G., Corona, R., & Belgrave, F. Z. (2011). Cultural protective factors for community risks and substance use among rural African American adolescents. *Journal of Ethnicity in Substance Abuse, 10*(4), 316–336. https://doi.org/10.1080/15332640.2011.623510

Ponterotto, J. G., & Casas, J. M. (1991). Handbook of racial/ethnic minority counseling research. Charles C Thomas.

Saleebey, D. (2012). The strengths perspective in social work practice. Pearson.

Schriver, J. (2019). *Human behavior and the social environment: Shifting paradigms in essential knowledge for social work practice* (7th ed.) Pearson.

Ungar, M. (2021). Modeling multisystemic resilience. In M. Ungar (Ed.), *Multisystemic resilience (pp. 6–31)*. Oxford University Press.

Vega, W. A., Kolody, B., Aguilar-Gaxiola, S., Alderete, E., Catalano, R., & Caraveo-Anduaga, J. (1998). Lifetime prevalence of DSM-III-R psychiatric disorders among urban and rural Mexican Americans in California. *Archives of General Psychiatry, 55*(9), 771–778. https://doi.org/10.1001/archpsyc.55.9.771

Wexler, L., Chandler, M., Gone, J. P., Cwik, M., Kirmayer, L. J., LaFromboise, T., Brockie, T., O'Keefe, V., Walkup, J., & Allen, J. (2015). Advancing suicide prevention research with rural American Indian and Alaska Native populations. *American Journal of Public Health, 105*(5), 891–899.

Wexler, L. M., DiFluvio, G., & Burke, T. K. (2009). Resilience and marginalized youth: Making a case for personal and collective meaning-making as part of resilience research in public health. *Social Science and Medicine, 69*(4), 565–570.

Whiteshield, R. (2001). Historical trauma response. *The Circle: News from an American Indian Perspective, 22*(1), 7–8.

Chapter 4
Countering Human Rights Violations During Life Transitions

Roberta Greene, Nancy Greene, and Connie Corley

Learning Objectives
This chapter discusses concepts related to human rights embedded in the resilience-enhancing stress model (RESM) of social work practice. It illustrates how interventions to combat societal inequities and exclusion can ameliorate clients' and constituencies' distress and increase their capacity to maintain resilience at multiple systems levels. On completing this chapter, you should better understand how human rights abuses challenge client and constituency resilient social functioning and what can be done to resist these risks. You should be prepared to answer the following questions:

- How do human rights violations affect clients at all systems levels?
- What can social workers do to further clients' capacity to become part of an inclusive society?
- How can historical trauma be ameliorated at the family and societal levels?

This chapter continues the discussion of anti-oppressive practice strategies, specifically those related to a global human rights perspective. It discusses practice skills and techniques embedded in the RESM that bolster people's human rights and foster their recovery from discriminatory stress.

The first practice example illustrates how a social worker helped a new immigrant family build on their natural resilience and avoid historical trauma as they were forced to flee their homeland and transition to life in the United States. The second describes how interventions at the societal and family levels by the staff of a

R. Greene (✉)
Steve Hicks School of Social Work, The University of Texas at Austin, Austin, TX, USA
e-mail: rgreene@utexas.edu

N. Greene
Ethelyn R. Strong School of Social Work, Norfolk State University, Norfolk, VA, USA
e-mail: nagreene@nsu.edu

C. Corley
Fielding Graduate University, Santa Barbara, CA, USA
e-mail: conniecorleyphd@gmail.com

R. Greene et al. (eds.), *Resilience Enhancement in Social Work Practice*,
https://doi.org/10.1007/978-3-031-38518-6_4

Cambodian nongovernmental organization ameliorated historical trauma caused by years of genocide and civil war.

4.1 A Historical Global Human Rights Perspective

In 1948, in response to the atrocities of the Nazi regime during World War II, the international members of the United Nations developed the Universal Declaration of Human Rights. Thirty human rights were identified and defined as universally accepted and indivisible. These rights, which appear in Table 4.1, provide an overview of human rights people are entitled to that may be revealed as client narratives are cocreated.

4.1.1 Establishing Refugee Status

In 1950 the United Nations took another step in supporting human rights by establishing the office of the United Nations High Commissioner for Refugees (UNHCR), which helps forced migrants resettle. The UNHCR makes a provision for migrants—whom it recognizes as having been forced to flee their homelands because of fear of persecution—to be officially declared refugees. The UNHCR and designated agencies in the host country provide 1 year of support to help these refugees obtain housing, health care, education, and employment (UNHCR, 2017).

4.1.2 Resisting Marginalization

A human rights perspective in social work practice strengthens its anti-oppressive approach. The need for refugee resettlement has reached crisis proportions. In 2021, for the first time on record, the number of people globally who were forced to relocate to flee conflict, violence, and persecution surpassed 90 million (UNHCR, 2021). Without proper services, these people face a stressful future living on the margins or edges of society.

Marginalized people are members of social groups that are stigmatized and devalued by mainstream society. Marginalized people may remain invisible unless social workers make a particular effort to draw attention to the issues they experience in their lives. When social workers use strategies to reduce human rights violations, they can help to create more inclusive environments for everyone (see Box 4.1).

Table 4.1 Summary of United Nations' Declaration of Human Rights

Article 1	All human beings are born free and equal in dignity and rights. They are endowed with reason and conscience and should act towards one another in a spirit of brotherhood.
Article 2	Everyone is entitled to all the rights and freedoms set forth in this Declaration, without distinction of any kind.
Article 3	Everyone has the right to life, liberty and security of person.
Article 4	No one shall be held in slavery or servitude; slavery and the slave trade shall be prohibited in all their forms.
Article 5	No one shall be subjected to torture or to cruel, inhuman or degrading treatment or punishment.
Article 6	Everyone has the right to recognition everywhere as a person before the law.
Article 7	All are equal before the law and are entitled without any discrimination to equal protection of the law.
Article 8	Everyone has the right to an effective remedy by the competent national tribunals for acts violating the fundamental rights granted him by the constitution or by law.
Article 9	No one shall be subjected to arbitrary arrest, detention or exile.
Article 10	Everyone is entitled in full equality to a fair and public hearing by an independent and impartial tribunal, in the determination of his rights and obligations and of any criminal charge against him.
Article 11	Everyone charged with a penal offence has the right to be presumed innocent until proved guilty according to law in a public trial at which he has had all the guarantees necessary for his defence.
Article 12	No one shall be subjected to arbitrary interference with his privacy, family, home or correspondence, nor to attacks upon his honour and reputation.
Article 13	Everyone has the right to freedom of movement and residence within the borders of each state.
Article 14	Everyone has the right to seek and to enjoy in other countries asylum from persecution.
Article 15	Everyone has the right to a nationality.
Article 16	Men and women of full age, without any limitation due to race, nationality or religion, have the right to marry and to found a family.
Article 17	Everyone has the right to own property alone as well as in association with others. No one shall be arbitrarily deprived of his property.
Article 18	Everyone has the right to freedom of thought, conscience and religion; this right includes freedom to change his religion or belief, and freedom, either alone or in community with others and in public or private, to manifest his religion or belief in teaching, practice, worship and observance.
Article 19	Everyone has the right to freedom of opinion and expression; this right includes freedom to hold opinions without interference and to seek, receive and impart information and ideas through any media and regardless of frontiers.
Article 20	Everyone has the right to freedom of peaceful assembly and association.
Article 21	Everyone has the right to take part in the government of his country, directly or through freely chosen representatives.
Article 22	Everyone, as a member of society, has the right to social security and is entitled to realization, through national effort and international co-operation and in accordance with the organization and resources of each State, of the economic, social and cultural rights indispensable for his dignity and the free development of his personality.

(continued)

Table 4.1 (continued)

Article 23	Everyone has the right to work, to free choice of employment, to just and favourable conditions of work and to protection against unemployment.
Article 24	Everyone has the right to rest and leisure, including reasonable limitation of working hours and periodic holidays with pay.
Article 25	Everyone has the right to a standard of living adequate for the health and well-being of himself and of his family, including food, clothing, housing and medical care and necessary social services, and the right to security in the event of unemployment, sickness, disability, widowhood, old age or other lack of livelihood in circumstances beyond his control.
Article 26	Everyone has the right to education.
Article 27	Everyone has the right freely to participate in the cultural life of the community, to enjoy the arts and to share in scientific advancement and its benefits.
Article 28	Everyone is entitled to a social and international order in which the rights and freedoms set forth in this Declaration can be fully realized.
Article 29	Everyone has duties to the community in which alone the free and full development of his personality is possible.
Article 30	Nothing in this Declaration may be interpreted as implying for any State, group or person any right to engage in any activity or to perform any act aimed at the destruction of any of the rights and freedoms set forth herein.

Note. Excerpted from United Nations (1948)

Box 4.1: Taking a Human Rights Self-Check
When I meet with clients, I will

- Learn about their history of oppression.
- Help raise their consciousness about their rights as members of society.
- Discover how institutionalized discriminatory policies impact their lives.
- Encourage activities that equalize their participation and inclusion in society.
- Help them access the goods and services to which they are entitled.
- Promote their capacity to influence social institutions when the need arises.

4.1.3 Applying Human Behavior Terms

Social workers' understanding and application of major theoretical frameworks and human behavior terms associated with refugee resettlement can help them assist clients in making a positive transition to living in their new environments. Serving diverse clients as they attempt to live resilient lives in a new country begins with helping them take the steps needed to live a resilient life in a different society. The following terms provide social workers with a departure point for such practice.

- *Societal power and privilege*: Power is the relative ability to control or influence others. These power inequities may be institutionalized in societal institutions.

The term *White privilege* was coined in the United States to describe White supremacy or the attitudes of those who have a disproportionate influence on or direct the behaviors of others (McIntosh, 1988; Van Soest & Garcia, 2022). The extent to which White privilege influences our clients varies from person to person and community to community and is best understood through client assessment.

- *Powerlessness*: Powerlessness is people's sense that they do not control their own destiny. This concept speaks to the idea that privilege is embedded in institutions and needs to be redressed at the system level. According to a seminal statement by Pinderhughes (1989), the cycle of powerlessness can be circular and hinders families "from meeting the needs of their members and from organizing the community so that it can provide them with more support" (p. 332). In other words, people who are powerless are at risk for having less access to systemically limited social, economic, and political resources. Therefore, formal refugee resettlement programs encompass activities that help refugees obtain basic housing, education, and employment services.
- *Ethnosystems*: Refugees who resettle in the United States come from around the globe. Solomon (1976) originated the term *ethnosystems* to explain variations in a group's cultural patterns, social organization, language, communication, and degree of power. Because of these shared system's elements many refugee families feel comfortable seeking out members of their ethnic community for support.
- *Dual perspective*: The concept of the dual perspective assumes that all people are a part of two systems: the smaller system of their immediate environment and the larger societal system. Social workers need to consciously and systematically use a dual perspective to address differences in the values, attitudes, and behaviors of both the minority ethnic and mainstream cultures (Chestang, 1972; Norton, 1978). This is most helpful as refugee families transition to life in the United States and acquire a blend of new and old cultural forms.
- *Bicultural*: The term *bicultural*, which is closely aligned with the idea of the dual perspective, describes a person who has integrated two cultural forms. When there is dissonance between cultural forms, as may be the case when a refugee family first arrives in the United States, these differences are best addressed in the helping process.

Table 4.2 lists authors who have produced seminal landmark resources that have given direction to anti-oppressive social work practice efforts.

4.2 Practitioner Readiness: Infusing Human Rights Content in the RESM

Many people who have faced human rights violations and have been forced to leave their home countries have found or are still seeking asylum in the United States. The practice example in Box 4.2 involves the Awan family, who resettled to the United

Table 4.2 Seminal anti-oppression frameworks

1.	Brave Heart, M. Y. H., & DeBruyn, L. (1998). The American Indian holocaust: Healing historical unresolved grief. *American Indian and Alaska Native Mental Health Research*, 8(2), 56–78.
	Maria Brave Heart, MSW, introduced the concept of historical trauma in clinical social work with Indigenous peoples. As she came to understand the experiences of Holocaust survivors in the mid-1980s, Brave Heart recognized the generations of tribal nation children like those from the Lakota tribe, who had been forced to move away from their families and elders who were their culture bearers to attend boarding schools in the belief that they should be taught to embrace mainstream culture. This practice began in 1892 and did not end until 2007. At the height of this practice, the federal government ran more than 400 such schools.
2.	Chestang, L. (1972). *Character development in a hostile environment* (Occasional Paper No. 3). University of Chicago, School of Social Service Administration.
	Research by Leon Chestang, PhD., MSW, led him to call attention to the way in which the environment can be detrimental to the development of the self. He suggested that *social injustice*, or the denial of legal rights, and *societal inconsistency*, or the double standard for Black people and Whites and the disparity between societal ideals and actions, can lead to prejudicial conditions.
3.	Cross, T. L., Earle, K., Solie, H. E-H., & Manness, K. (2000). *Systems of care: Promising practices in children's mental health, 2000 series: Vol. 1. Cultural strengths and challenges in implementing a system of care model in American Indian communities*. American Institutes for Research, Center for Effective Collaboration and Practice.
	Terry Cross, MSW, a child welfare worker and member of the Seneca Nation, spearheaded the conceptualization of a relational self-concept. From the relational self point of view, organizational change depends on people's personal bonds with significant others as they form an organizational collective. As president of the National Indian Child Welfare Association, Cross established a program to empower communities and create child systems of care congruent with local practices.
4.	Hopps, J. G. (1982). Oppression based on color. *Social Work*, 27(1), 3–5.
	June Hopps, PhD, MSW, contended that the term *minority group* was too vague and was applied inconsistently. She suggested that the term *people of color* was better for addressing people who are oppressed because of their skin color. She also proposed that social workers examine and address the needs of specific client ethnic groups.
5.	McIntosh, P. (1988). *White privilege and male privilege: A personal account of coming to see correspondences through work in women's studies (1988)*. Retrieved September 28, 2022, from http://www.collegeart.org/pdf/diversity/white-privilege-and-male-privilege.pdf
	Peggy McIntosh, PhD a women's studies professor, coined the term *White privilege* to describe the disparity between race and genders about what can be claimed as a life advantage. She wrote an account of personal experiences that she thought allowed her to be in a position of privilege, including renting or purchasing housing in an area in which she wanted to live and arranging to protect her children most of the time from people who might not like them. McIntosh's idea that privilege places people at the center of political, economic, and social power has been integrated into social work curriculum and practice.
6.	Norton, D. G. (1978). *The dual perspective: Inclusion of ethnic minority content in social work curriculum*. Council on Social Work Education.
	Dolores Norton MSW, PhD and colleagues argued for social work methods and human behavior courses to move away from a Eurocentric perspective and incorporate more substance on what she termed *ethnic minority content*. Norton and colleagues' work on the dual perspective was designed to make the social work curriculum more inclusive. It also was intended to help practitioners understand how clients may struggle living in two cultural worlds.

(continued)

Table 4.2 (continued)

7.	Pinderhughes, E. B. (1983). Empowerment for our clients and for ourselves. *Social Casework*, 64(6), 331–338.
	Pinderhughes, E. (1989). *Understanding race, ethnicity, and power: The key to efficacy in clinical practice*. Free Press.
	Elaine Pinderhughes MSWwas a leader in cross-cultural clinical practice. She suggested that cross-cultural social work requires practitioners to be self-aware and to reflect on their values.
8.	Solomon, B. (1976). *Black empowerment*. Columbia University.
	Barbara Solomon's PhD., MSW book on Black empowerment provided a conceptual foundation for the social work empowerment movement. She proposed that social workers should collaborate with clients and constituencies to take a more active role as social change agents.

Box 4.2: Practice Example: Refugees, Stress, and Resettlement
Carlos, a social worker at Lutheran Family Services, assisted the Awan family, who had just arrived from Afghanistan. The family was composed of Mr. and Mrs. Awan, their son Omar (age 12), and their daughter Maira (age 8). Carlos wondered what risks the family could face as they adjusted to a different culture and transitioned to a new intercultural environment in the United States. He was aware that, if not addressed in the helping process, acculturation stress—stress associated with learning new cultural ideas and practices—could jeopardize the family's natural resilient functioning (Berry et al., 2002). Therefore, Carlos met biweekly with the Awan family to tackle potential difficulties and identify protective factors that could shield them from adverse stress.

States from Afghanistan. For Carlos, the social worker, to effectively infuse content that addresses human rights into his anti-oppressive RESM practice, he had to make an intentional effort to explore and ameliorate any human rights abuses uncovered during the helping process. In this way, the Awan family could be more assured that they were becoming full members of society and improving their capacity to lead more resilient functioning lives.

4.3 Engagement

4.3.1 Establishing Trust and Anchored Understanding

Carlos first had to establish trust in his third-space relationship with the Awan family. He hoped to gain an anchored understanding of their situation, which required hearing all voices in the family. His first task was to put the family somewhat at ease.

4.3.2 *Actualizing the Third Space*

Actualizing a third-space relationship can benefit from using the skills of open curiosity, realigning power, reciprocity, responsiveness, and respect (see Box 4.3). Carlos carried out these skills by asking about how successfully the Awan family had met or overcome past obstacles. The Awan family told Carlos that when they had been forced to flee Afghanistan, they had faced many difficulties. Mr. Awan and Omar proudly recalled their "service" on the night patrol in the potentially dangerous refugee camp while they awaited resettlement. The entire family then praised the resettlement volunteers for helping them get acclimated in their wonderful safe neighborhood. Maira said, "I have even made a friend next door."

Box 4.3: Skill Box: Human Rights RESM Engagement Skills

Skill	Definition	Practitioner statement
Open curiosity	Showing a strong interest in knowing	"I am interested in your thoughts about how this all fits together."
Realigning power	Acknowledging that the client and social worker are collaborators in the helping process	"I have learned a lot from what you have told me about your journey to the United States. It is good to be more informed."
Reciprocity	Collaborating in the helping relationship	"I really don't have all the answers. We can find them together."
Respect	Acknowledging diverse perspectives and staying with the tension	"Thank you for sharing difficult experiences with me."
Responsiveness	Being willing to not know for sure where the dialogue will continue	"I don't fully understand yet. Can you tell me more?"

4.3.2.1 Practice Example Analysis: Steps Taken

During the first 6 months of their resettlement, the Awan family's meetings with Carlos turned to issues that arose as they attempted to acculturate, a process of change that necessitates balancing two cultures. For example, because of Mr. Awan's employment as an English translator, the Awan family had held a relatively high status in Afghanistan. They wondered whether they would ever regain such a position in the United States. Moreover, Mrs. Awan was unsure whether she could continue to prepare food for Muslim holidays.

4.4 Assessment: Cocreating a Narrative

4.4.1 Uncovering Clients' and Constituencies' Historical Trauma

Refugee family narratives are the source of assessment data that can reveal how the family has handled past risks or discriminatory stress. Box 4.4 defines additional practice skills Carlos used to identify ways in which the Awan family addressed human rights abuses and resisted living at the margins of society.

Box 4.4: Skill Box: Human Rights and Resilience-Enhancing Practice Skills

Skill	Definition	Practitioner statement
Identifying human rights abuses	Strategizing with clients about resisting unjust interpersonal or institutional actions	"Do you think any of the experiences you have had limited your opportunity?"
Separating from the margin	Expanding a client's perception of choice	"Can we think about ways to get your family in a better situation?"

Experiencing Conflict In 2004 the International Federation of Red Cross and Red Crescent Societies published the *World Disasters Report*, which said that Afghan children were being raised in an environment of chronic conflict. However, the report went on to state that most children learn resilience strategies from their parents and from teachers in school (Alameldeen & Cakan, 2021). The report concluded that the Afghan people were sure that children who had such resilient qualities would be affected by violence but not permanently scarred by it (UNHCR, 2023).

Exploring Historical Trauma *Historical trauma* is prolonged chronic stress brought about by multiple losses and/or oppression across generations, including genocide, slavery, and forced relocation (Brave Heart & Deschenie, 2006). Members of several US ethnic groups continue to experience trauma caused by past adverse critical events. For example, African Americans were forcibly moved to the United States as slaves. Some Jewish Americans are survivors of the Nazi Holocaust of World War II, during which six million people died in concentration camps. Children of Indigenous Americans were forcibly moved to US-sponsored boarding schools, and Japanese Americans were placed in concentration camps during World War II. Box 4.5 explores the Awan's family's journey as they fled Afghanistan to renew their life in the United States.

Box 4.5: Practice Example: A Family Envisions Change

Carlos:	Moving to a new country can bring about change, both good and bad. Do you think you are ready to think about that?
Mr. Awan:	I am not sure. Some of us like it better than others.
Carlos:	In my experience that is common in a family of four.
Maira:	Yes, I hope my father gets used to my going over to other girlfriends' homes alone—everyone does it! I am planning to get permission to do a sleepover!
Omar:	I don't get a hard time when I go out to play soccer.
Maira:	But you are a boy and played soccer in Afghanistan.
Mrs. Awan:	I am having to adjust to what children can do here in the United States.
Mr. Awan:	You get to do most of what you did at home in Afghanistan. Now that you have been driven to the halal [permissible Muslim food] grocery store I know you are happy following Islamic dietary rules.
Carlos:	Mr. Awan, from what you just said, I am wondering what you miss about your old home and what you don't like about your new one?
Mr. Awan:	That's easy. I once had a job I liked as an English translator. But I now know my family and I are safe. I can sleep at night.
Mrs. Awan:	And you are not always on edge.
Omar:	You don't even yell as much!
Maira:	Only at me—if I stay at my friends' houses too late.
Mr. Awan:	I guess it all comes down to not being afraid?
Carlos:	At our next meeting do you want to let me know what marks on resettlement you give to one another and to the family as a whole?
Mr. Awan:	Maybe by then that job interview will come through. I would also very much appreciate getting transportation to the mosque. It is many miles from our home.
Carlos:	I know our volunteer coordinator is working on that.

4.4.1.1 Practice Example Analysis: Steps Taken

Given the Awan family's immigration status, Carlos explored issues of human rights abuses that could perpetuate historical trauma. The family's grand narrative was the source of these assessment data. To counter the possibility of experiencing historical trauma, Carlos wanted to help the Awan family strengthen their emerging ability to live in two different worlds. At the same time, he hoped they would learn that it was alright that some of their values and rules for behaviors were in a dynamic state of flux.

Carlos listened for narrative themes that could reveal how the family unit was responding to stress. Carlos came to understand that the Awan family was flexible in maintaining and modifying family rules. Based on feedback from the family, Carlos concluded that there seemed to be no long-term traumatic effects of their prolonged journey to the United States. However, he left the door open for the family to return to the agency.

4.4.2 *Using Assessment Tools*

Following a critical life event such as a relocation, a wide range of risks and protective factors could either exacerbate or ameliorate a family's distress. Assessment required that Carlos and the Awan family uncover ways to further enhance the family's natural resiliency. Risk factors were person–environment factors that could cause an adverse reaction to stress, whereas protective factors could shield the Awan family from adversity and bolster their resilient functioning.

4.4.3 *Creating an Assessment Profile: Balancing Risk and Protection*

An assessment profile is a summary of information about person–environment risk and protective factors gathered during the cocreation of the family narrative. The major potential risk factors disclosed during the Awan family assessment were disruptions in the positionality or social status of the family and a hope for acceptance from the majority US culture. At the same time, major protective factors were the family members' connectedness to one another and the social supports they received from their faith community. Carlos's assessment concluded that the Awan family was able to modify their family rules as they made some adjustments to US child-raising customs. They also retained religious cultural practices that sustained them in their new environment.

4.5 Intervention: Coaching to Reconstruct Family Patterns

Interventions for the Awan family were intended to bolster their natural capacity to respond well to stress. Carlos gave the family coaching assignments and believed they could use this homework to make progress on their own.

4.5.1 *Coaching the Family*

Carlos gave the Awan family a homework coaching assignment to discuss changes in family roles and rules experienced since living in the United States. Mr. and Mrs. Awan reported that they had become less strict about knowing the children's whereabouts now that their neighborhood seemed safe.

4.5.2 *Coaching for Employment*

Another coaching intervention was a role play by Carlos and Mr. Awan of an employment interview. The role play was instrumental in helping Mr. Awan secure employment that was in keeping with his aspirations for a bright future in the United States.

4.6 Evaluation: Rating the Family's Progress

The Awan family reflected on the progress they had made in meeting personal and environmental demands around resettlement. They all shared their ideas with Carlos at their last meeting (see Box 4.6).

Box 4.6: Practice Example: Last Meeting

Carlos:	Welcome to our last meeting. Any lingering concerns?
Mr. Awan:	Some days I wonder if we will be real Americans.
Omar:	You worry too much.
Mrs. Awan:	I think we have done a lot to settle in.
Carlos:	Can you tell me about your best accomplishments moving to the United States?
Mr. Awan:	I have a job I like and can purchase what we need.
Mrs. Awan:	I made friends who care about halal foods.
Omar:	I am now on the soccer team. They really take care of one another.
Maira:	I got to do a sleepover. It was fun!
Carlos:	If difficulties come up, remember, I am always here!
Maira:	You bet.

4.7 Societal Resilience: Systemic Interventions

This first section of this chapter offered an understanding of how a family's micro-level resilience was challenged after they were forced to move from one society to another. This section explores how risk and disruption at the macrolevel of Cambodian society affected all. The staff of the Documentation Center of Cambodia (DC-Cam) continue to make efforts to accomplish transformational resilient change in the aftermath of genocide by the Khmer Rouge regime and civil war in Cambodia (see Box 4.7).

4.7.1 Assessing the Cambodian Genocide: Narrative

According to survivors, the regime sought to achieve its aim by depriving all Cambodians of their basic rights (Dy, 2007). People who did not comply were put into labor camps or forced into military service (Andrews, 2012). Famine and starvation were rampant (DeFalco et al., 2013).

The historical grand narrative obtained from survivors of the genocide and civil war was used to help DC-Cam staff develop means to mitigate the effects of human rights abuses and historical trauma. The most prevailing theme in the grand narrative was the difficulty of losing a loved one. Most study participants wanted to find

Box 4.7: Grand Narrative: Healing and Resilience
The communist Khmer Rouge regime ruled Cambodia from 1976 to 1979. The party aim was to force Cambodians to abandon all Western capitalist ideas and become an agricultural, collectivist society. As a result of their oppressive policies, 1.7–2 million Cambodians, or 21% of the country's population, died from 1975 to 1979 (Men, 2012). These atrocities did not end until 1991, when the constitutional Kingdom of Cambodia was restored.

The human rights abuses committed over several decades further exacerbated structural inequalities and created advantages for some people at the expense of others, leading to entire cross-sections of society being marginalized, exploited, or otherwise vulnerable to a variety of risks. A social work educator conducted a qualitative study of healing and resilience among Cambodian survivors of the communist Khmer Rouge regime (Greene, 2015). She analyzed 30 stories of survivors who had lost family members to the regime that were published in the DC-Cam journal. A constant comparison data analysis was conducted to code the data and assign them to emergent categories and themes (Creswell, 1998; Miles et al., 2019). The revelation of themes allowed for the construction of the survivors' grand narrative. The grand narrative documented the survivors' resilience despite their extreme inordinate stress (Greene, 2015).

out what had happened to a deceased relative to honor them, find meaning, and come to closure. Participants also acknowledged the connection between personal feelings of resilience and public support. For example, BP said the following:

> Without the Documentation Center of Cambodia researching [my background], I would not have known the whereabouts of my deceased relatives. More importantly, I would like to express my deep thank to the Documentation Center of Cambodia. I am so lucky. I didn't know how to deal with my lost; I wanted to talk but had no chance.

4.7.2 Responding to the Cambodian Genocide and Civil War

Ever since Cambodia arose from decades of civil war, the in-debt nation has been challenged by a widespread need for psychological and physical health care. According to the Asian Development Bank (2022), more than 17% of Cambodians live below the poverty line. Vulnerable populations are more likely to live in unhygienic environments and less likely to have the resources they need to ensure a healthy quality of life. Although the Cambodian government has made efforts to construct symbolic memorial sites to provide a degree of public healing, the meeting of recovery needs has largely fallen to nongovernmental organizations.

4.7.3 Intervening to Enhance Resilience

4.7.3.1 International Initiatives

In 1994 the United States was one of the first countries to undertake recovery efforts in Cambodia. The then President Bill Clinton signed the Cambodian Genocide Justice Act, which provided for research on and the collection of information about war crimes. To aid in this recovery effort, Yale University's Genocide Studies Program founded DC-Cam, whose mission is to improve the welfare of Cambodian survivors and to document and seek justice for the atrocities committed by the communist Khmer Rouge regime (https://dccam.org/homepage).

4.7.3.2 Social Welfare Interventions

Given the magnitude of human rights abuses around the globe, it is important for social workers to understand techniques that can support resilience at the societal level. Social workers need to extend their skill base to include techniques that bolster a society's social and economic infrastructure across various community networks. This is akin to a public health approach that promotes care at multiple localities and is consistent with a resilience-enhancing social work approach that explores and supports systemic, ecological interventions.

Societal resilience calls for interventions that decrease inequality and expand inclusiveness (Haavik, 2020). DC-Cam staff conduct several societal-level resilience-enhancing interventions that fall under this rubric:

- Educational intergenerational enterprises provide textbooks and teacher training to share experiences from the Khmer Rouge historical period with the next generations of Cambodian students. Older survivors share their stories with children and youth.
- DC-Cam health initiatives sponsor public health forums to obtain survivors' stories as health information is disseminated.
- The collected narratives have been continuously used along with laser technology and forensics to reunite survivors with yet unclaimed remains of relatives who were interrogated, tortured, and killed during the Khmer Rouge regime.
- Data collected by DC-Cam have been shared with the United Nations–sponsored trial Extraordinary Chambers in the Courts of Cambodia (ECCC) to prosecute war criminals for crimes committed during the genocide and civil war.
- DC-Cam staff enlisted survivors to act as civil parties who had the right to testify in the ECCC tribunal involving the trial of Duch, the head of a prison where many victims of the Khmer Rouge regime were killed. The tribunal is currently approaching the end of its work, and DC-Cam staff are advocating for a renewed effort to provide more health care services for the aging group of survivors.

4.8 Summary and Conclusion

The chapter has described the use of the narrative as a method of assessment and intervention in anti-oppressive RESM social work practice. The Awan family described a worldview that expressed their wish to become US citizens. The survivors of the Cambodian genocide who acted as civil parties at the ECCC spoke about a sense of reconciliation and the belief that they could do something to come to closure around their relatives' deaths. These examples offer an understanding of how resilience is fostered through psychosocial care at the individual, family, and societal levels.

Summary of Learning Outcomes
Keep in mind the following:

- Social workers can collaborate with clients to make resettlement a resilient life transition.
- Social workers partner and network with various agencies to contribute to societal resilience.
- Social work services can help clients and constituencies begin to heal from historical trauma.

Discussion Questions

1. How is the Universal Declaration of Human Rights still pertinent today?
2. Would you consider yourself bicultural? Explain.
3. How would you coach clients who are living in a dual society?

Chapter Exercise

Write a one-page reflection paper on U.S. House Bill 40 on reparations for slavery. (See Coates, 2015.)

Glossary

Civil party A witness at a trial.

Constant comparison A process of analyzing data by sorting and grouping the data according to characteristics or attributes.

Genocide The intention to kill or destroy a national, ethnic, racial, or religious group.

Historical trauma Prolonged chronic stress brought about by multiple losses across generations.

Human rights People's universally accepted and indivisible entitlements.

Marginalization A process of stigmatizing and devaluing social groups by mainstream society; marginalized groups have less access to goods and services.

Refugees People forced to flee their homelands because of fear of persecution, officially declared as such by the United Nations.

Social welfare intervention An intervention that acts to bolster a society's social and economic infrastructure across various community networks.

Societal resilience intervention An intervention that works to decrease inequality and increase inclusiveness.

Systemic intervention The disruption of macrolevel institutional barriers.

References

Alameldeen, A., & Cakan, Z. (2021, September). What is a resilient community? *Academia Letters*, Article 3615. https://doi.org/10.20935/AL3615

Andrews, K. D. (2012, May 28). *Ny Kan, brother of Son Sen, testifies before the ECCC*. Retrieved September 28, 2022, from https://cambodiatribunal.org/2012/05/28/ny-kan-brother-of-son-sen-testifies-before-the-eccc/

Asian Development Bank. (2022). *Asian Development Bank*. Retrieved May 5, 2023, from https://www.adb.org

Berry, J. W., Poortinga, Y. H., Segall, M. H., & Dasen, P. R. (2002). *Cross-cultural psychology: Research and applications* (2nd ed.). Cambridge University Press.

Brave Heart, M. Y. H., & Deschenie, T. (2006). Resource guide: Historical trauma and post-colonial stress in American Indian populations. *Tribal College Journal, 17*(3), 24–27.
Chestang, L. (1972). *Character development in a hostile environment*. (Occasional Paper No. 3). University of Chicago, School of Social Service Administration.
Coates, T. (2015). *Between the world and me*. Spiegel & Grau.
Creswell, J. W. (1998). *Qualitative inquiry and research design: Choosing among five traditions*. Sage.
DeFalco, R. C., Pechet, M., & Dalin, L. (2013). *Episode 2: Famine and excess mortality in democratic Kampuchea*. Voices of Genocide Survivors (VoG): Famine in Democratic Kampuchea and Case 002 at the ECCC. Available at https://dccam.org/radio-3
Dy, K. (2007). *A history of democratic Kampuchea (1975–1979)*. Documentation Center of Cambodia.
Greene, R. R. (2015). Resilience and healing among Cambodian survivors of the Khmer Rouge regime. *Journal of Evidence-Informed Social Work, 12*(6), 579–587.
Haavik, T. (2020). Societal resilience: Clarifying the concept and upscaling the scope. *Safety Science, 132*, Article 104964. https://doi.org/10.1016/j.ssci.2020.104964
McIntosh, P. (1988). *White privilege and male privilege: A personal account of coming to see correspondences through work in women's studies*. (Working Paper No. 189). Center for Research on Women, Wellesley College.
Men, L. (2012, February). *I wonder how Duch would feel if one of his sons or daughters were brought into Tuol Sleng? Searching for the Truth*. Retrieved September 28, 2022, from https://khmernews.wordpress.com/2012/03/19/i-wonder-how-duch-would-feel-if-one-of-his-sons-or-daughters-were-brought-into-tuol-sleng/
Miles, M. B., Huberman, A. M., & Saldaña, J. (2019). *Qualitative data analysis: A methods sourcebook* (4th ed.).
Norton, D. (1978). *The dual perspective: Inclusion of ethnic minority content in the social work curriculum*. Council on Social Work Education.
Pinderhughes, E. B. (1989). *Understanding race, ethnicity, and power: The key to efficacy in clinical practice*. Free Press.
Solomon, B. B. (1976). *Black empowerment: Social work in oppressed communities*. Columbia University Press.
United Nations. (1948). *Universal Declaration of Human Rights*. http://www.un.org/en/documents/udhr/
United Nations High Commissioner for Refugees. (2017). *UN system and the rule of law*. Retrieved May 1, 2023, from https://www.un.org/ruleoflaw/un-and-the-rule-of-law/
United Nations High Commissioner for Refugees. (2021). *Global report 2021*. Retrieved May 5, 2023, from https://reporting.unhcr.org/globalreport2021
United Nations High Commissioner for Refugees. (2023). *International organizations*. Retrieved May 5, 2023, from https://www.unhcr.org/about-unhcr/our-partners/un-and-international-institutions/international-organizations-1
Van Soest, D., & Garcia, B. (2022). *Diversity education for social justice: Mastering teaching skills* (2nd ed.). Council on Social Work Education.

Supplemental References

Aponte, H. J. (1994). *Bread and spirit: Therapy with the new poor*. Norton.
Aptheker, H. (2006). *Nat Turner's slave rebellion*. Dover.
Devore, W., & Schlesinger, E. G. (2012). *Ethnic-sensitive social work practice* (5th ed.). Pearson.
DuBois, W. E. B. (1903). *Souls of Black folk*. McClurg.

Garcia, B., & Van Soest, D. (2006). *Social work practice for social justice: Cultural competence in action*. Council on Social Work Education.
Greene, M. (1996). *The temple bombing*. Addison-Wesley.
hooks, B. (1984). *Feminist theory: From center to margin*. South End.
Hoops, J. G. (1982). Oppression based on color. *Social Work, 27*(1), 3–6.
Howe, I. (1982). *A margin of hope*. Harcourt Brace Jovanovich.
Hunter-Gault, C. (1992). *In my place*. Farrar.
Morrison, T. (1987). *Beloved*. Vintage Books.
Styron, W. (1976). *Sophie's choice*. Vintage Books.
West, C. (1993). *Race matters*. Vintage Books.
Wiesel, E. (1960). *Night*. Bantam Books.

Chapter 5
The Resilience-Enhancing Stress Model: A Practice Overview and Guide

Roberta Greene, Nancy Greene, and Connie Corley

Learning Objectives

This chapter provides an overview of the resilience-enhancing stress model's (RESM) methodology that can be used by practitioners to ameliorate stress and enhance resilience among diverse individuals, families, groups, and communities. On completing this chapter, you should better understand the practice steps taken during engagement, assessment, intervention, and evaluation. You should be prepared to answer the following questions:

- How is RESM narrative content organized?
- What person–environment (P-E) content is explored in a RESM narrative interview?
- How does narrative interview content lead to a client assessment profile?
- How does narrative interview content lead to a mutually developed (client-social worker) intervention plan?
- What steps are taken to evaluate the RESM social work process?

This chapter presents an outline of the methodological approach that supports the application of the RESM. It spells out steps social workers can take to assist clients and constituencies in ameliorating problems of daily living encountered during challenging person-environment encounters. The guide covers the four phases of the helping process used by social workers to gather data that individualizes a client's varying responses to stress or risks.

R. Greene (✉)
Steve Hicks School of Social Work, The University of Texas at Austin, Austin, TX, USA
e-mail: rgreene@utexas.edu

N. Greene
Ethelyn R. Strong School of Social Work, Norfolk State University, Norfolk, VA, USA
e-mail: nagreene@nsu.edu

C. Corley
Fielding Graduate University, Santa Barbara, CA, USA
e-mail: conniecorleyphd@gmail.com

R. Greene et al. (eds.), *Resilience Enhancement in Social Work Practice*,
https://doi.org/10.1007/978-3-031-38518-6_5

The purpose of the RESM's helping process is to help clients or constituencies reduce their risks, bolster their protective factors or strengths, and positively rewrite their narrative to maintain or regain resilient social functioning following a disruptive life event. The process results in an assessment profile and mutually developed intervention plan; while the goal is to set in motion a change process to help clients revise their negative meanings of events, find solutions, and develop a greater sense of agency (Greene, 2008).

The practice example in Box 5.1 illustrates how extreme environmental pressures such as the disruption to the ecosystem caused by the COVID-19 pandemic can interfere with people's social functioning and interrupt the fabric of societal institutions. Think about this practice example as you read through the guide.

Box 5.1: Practice Example: Transitioning Social Functioning from Pandemic to Recovery

As the World Health Organization declared the COVID-19 outbreak an international public health emergency on March 11, 2020, the pandemic became both a health crisis and a major global social and economic disruption. The United Nations Department of Economic and Social Affairs (2020) expressed alarm that, if not properly addressed, the COVID-19 pandemic would increase inequality, exclusion, discrimination, and global unemployment. The Department spokespersons went on to state that comprehensive, universal social protection systems were needed to safeguard people and to enhance their capacity to manage and overcome stress associated with such emergencies.

Repercussions of the virus have been severe and far-reaching, impacting all of society. Although all sections of society experienced negative effects, the pandemic had particularly detrimental to members of social groups who live in the most vulnerable, marginalized situations (Dubey et al., 2020).

For example, early data suggested that the health and economic impacts of the virus were experienced disproportionately by people living in poverty. In addition, because they were a large proportion of the workers in sectors of the economy severely affected by COVID-19, women faced severe negative economic outcomes. Older adults experienced increased social isolation, and African Americans and members of Tribal Nations faced additional health inequities.

In addition, people's concerns during the COVID-19 pandemic were compounded by the psychosocial burden of quarantine. Increases in mental health issues such as anxiety and depression were noted (Robinson et al., 2022). Social distancing and stay-at-home measures affected how people perceived and related to others, including families, friends, fellow students, and coworkers (Maryville University, 2022).

During the height of the pandemic, hospital staff around the country, including medical social workers, were overwhelmed. Lawrence, a social worker in the department of social services at a New York City hospital, was assigned to take calls from the Rosen family, whose mother and grandmother

(continued)

Box 5.1 (continued)

had been diagnosed with COVID-19 and was hospitalized in the intensive critical care unit. Grandma Rosen was on a ventilator and was not allowed visitors. Family members called many times a day to get an update on her situation and to complain about not being able to visit her.

When Grandma Rosen got off the ventilator, she learned that no visitors were allowed. She became depressed and cried about not seeing Ronald, her favorite grandchild. Lawrence was called in to intervene and got permission to arrange a Zoom meeting with Ronald and the family. Shortly thereafter Grandma Rosen improved enough to be moved to a lower level of care.

5.1 Preparing for RESM Practice

It may be argued that the "social worker's primary practice tool is the self—the social worker's capacity to communicate and interact with others in ways that facilitate change" (Sheafor & Horejsi, 2012, p. 49). The concept of the professional self has been defined as the ability to "manage the [practitioner's] influence of bias, power, privilege, and values in working with clients and constituencies" (Council on Social Work Education, 2022, p. 10). It is a process by which social workers monitor and become more aware of where they are situated in their community and in the world (Wexler, 2009). This sense of self requires that the social worker be reflective, put knowledge into action, and put actions into explicit wording to deal effectively with a client experiencing a specific critical event (Schon, 1983). In sum, the professional use of self is a form of self-observation that uses some of the skills defined in Box 5.2.

Box 5.2: Skill Box: Professional Use of Self

Skill	Social worker reflections
Ensuring readiness for practice	Reviewing one's knowledge, attitudes, and skills related to the practice context
Developing greater self-understanding	Considering one's experiences and values as relevant to the practice situation
Using self-reflection	Contemplating the choice of one's helping strategies, such as questions and prompts

5.1.1 Visualizing and Mapping Practice

RESM practice begins with social workers reflecting upon how they intend to carry out the helping process. That is, before they engage with a client or constituency, practitioners should create a mental picture of the content they expect to pursue. Mattingly (1991), who captured this intent, suggested that the professional's role in the social work narrative interview is to "facilitate yet-unformulated patient stories by entering [patients'] lives" (p. 1000). To gain this understanding, social workers collaborate with clients to map or trace the influences on their social functioning over time, singling out those factors that have led to distress (White, 2007).

5.2 Engagement: Forming a Third-Space Relationship

5.2.1 Central Focus

RESM engagement is a time for social workers to meet clients where they are. It is a transparent and collaborative process during which the practitioner joins forces with the client to create a third-space relationship, a form of communication exchange that gives clarity to different ideas and context encompassed in the narrative interview.

5.2.2 Terms

- *Transparency*. An open, mutually understood approach to practice.
- *Third space*. A safe zone in which all client voices are heard and respected.

5.2.3 Assumptions

- Social workers partner with clients to build symmetrical relationships characterized by trust, empathy, warmth, genuineness, and respect.
- A client–social worker relationship strives to be culturally sound.

As the engagement phase moves into the assessment phase, the social worker and client begin to gain an anchored (contextual) understanding of the client's situation and concerns. They start to talk about what can be done to resolve presenting difficulties or concerns.

5.3 Assessment: Cocreating a Narrative

5.3.1 Central Focus

The cocreation of a RESM client narrative is at the heart of the assessment process. The assessment is based on a P-E perspective that allows the social worker and client to evaluate the client's response to stress at a range of micro- to macrolevels (Gitterman & Germain, 2008; Greene, 2008). A response to a stressful critical event may be on a continuum from positive to negative. Namely, a P-E Dimensions may act as a risk or protective factor depending on the client's or constituencies' situational context and response to it. Box 5.3 summarizes some select P-E dimensions and indicates what research suggests how a dimension may influence the client's social functioning and resilience. The described content of the various dimension can be used to frame questions for the social worker to discuss during the cocreation of the narrative interview.

Box 5.3: P-E Dimensions: The Balance Between Risk and Protection

1. The consequences of time and place refer to the sociocultural and historical context (era and location) of the critical event that has distressed the client or constituency. Living in uncertain times is a risk that may diminish social functioning and client resilience.
2. A clients' response to the stress of past critical events is important to how they manage present concerns. Meeting past critical events successfully may act as a protective factor that can enhance current client's social functioning and resilience.
3. A clients' reaction to disruption of biopsychosocial and spiritual processes may be connected to a decline in functional status. When properly addressed, the risk of disruption may be decreased, and client's social functioning and resilience augmented.
4. A family's response to stress may propel the restructuring of its organizational and communication patterns, as well as belief systems. A family's positive capacity to restructure, when needed, is a protective factor that can enhance its social functioning and resiliency.
5. The consequences of social supports are related to people's interpersonal relationships and social connections. The availability of and participation in social supports can serve as a protective factor that may enhance client's social functioning and resilience.
6. The significance of favorable environments is related to the extent to which communities and neighborhoods provide clients and constituencies with nurturing and support. When clients perceive that they live in a nurturing environment, it acts as a protective factor that can enhance their social functioning and resilience.
7. The effects of strong cultural identity and ties are connected to clients' or constituencies' worldview and cultural resources. Relying on cultural resources and maintaining cultural ties can serve as a protective factor that enhances client's social functioning and resilience.
8. Human rights violations are oppressive and are linked to social and economic discrimination. When clients and constituencies take steps to resist or standup to human rights abuses and obtain entitlements, these responses can enhance their social functioning and resilience.
9. Having sufficient resources and services is critical to human well-being. The availability of and access to resources and services benefit client's functional capacity and resilience.
10. An ecosystem disruption (such as COVID-19) has a widespread disruptive ripple effect on all systems in the surrounding environs. Ameliorating the root sources of negative ecosystem disturbances can enhance people's resilient functioning and the social functioning of systems in which they interact.

5.3.2 Terms

- *Assessment.* A means of gathering client and constituency data contained in the client narrative.
- *Person–environment.* The parameters or guidepost to social work practice that distinguishes the client's life space and the ensuing scope of practice.
- *Narrative.* A story or account of events as told by a client or constituency.
- *Mapping.* Uncovering, interpreting, and outlining clients' P-E information as embedded in their narrative.
- *Risk factors.* P-E influences that increase the probability of a negative response to stress.
- *Protective factors.* P-E factors that shield people from risk.
- *Assessment profile.* The delineation of which P-E risk and protective factors are to be addressed during the intervention phase.
- *Resilience.* A response to stress or risk associated with positive social functioning.

5.3.3 Assumptions

- The narrative approach to story collection is considered relatively open ended.
- The practitioner may choose to use RESM tools to further individualize the helping process.
- Mapping the 10 P-E dimensions of the RESM listed above can allow clients to become more aware of the influences that impact their lives.
- Mapping can contribute to a positive response to stress and the maintenance of relatively resilient functioning.
- Tools to use to gather P-E dimensions include the following:
- A tool for clients to evaluate the saliency of their protective factors is in Table 5.1 (Greene's Risk-Protection and Resiliency Questionnaire).
- A tool for social workers to find questions and prompts to coconstruct a narrative appears in Table 5.2 (Greene's Chart of Person–Environment [P-E] Dimensions: Narrative Questions and Prompts).

As the assessment phase moves into the intervention phase, the social worker and client take the opportunity to compile an assessment profile (see Box 5.4).

Box 5.4: Assembling an Assessment Profile
In creating an assessment profile, the social worker compiles a summary of the efficacy of clients' or constituencies' P-E dimensions. Interventions are built on clients' perceptions of the saliency or strength of their protective factors. Tools available to the social worker to create an assessment profile include the following:

- A tool for social workers to write an assessment profile is in Table 5.3 (Person–Environment Blank Assessment Profile Chart).
- A tool for social workers to set goals and write an evaluation appears in Table 5.4 (Person–Environment Goal Setting and Evaluation Chart).

Table 5.1 Greene's risk-protection and resiliency questionnaire

Directions: On a scale from 1 to 5, please indicate the number that best describes your level of agreement with each item. 1 = strongly agree, 2 = agree, 3 = neither agree nor disagree, 4 = disagree, 5 = strongly disagree.	
1.	I am someone who pays close attention to current events.
	1 2 3 4 5
2.	I believe I can make difficult choices about events affecting my life.
	1 2 3 4 5
3.	I have had a positive experience with the stress of previous difficult/challenging times.
	1 2 3 4 5
4.	When times got difficult in the past, I believe I rose to the occasion.
	1 2 3 4 5
5.	A great deal of stress has interrupted my daily functioning.
	1 2 3 4 5
6.	When stress gets high, I can rearrange my priorities.
	1 2 3 4 5
7.	My family adapts to challenges by carrying out routines.
	1 2 3 4 5
8.	My family sometimes rearranges our daily schedule so we can keep going.
	1 2 3 4 5
9.	I have people around me that I can turn to when times get rough.
	1 2 3 4 5
10.	I get over life's difficulties through the help of positive relationships with friends and social support groups.
	1 2 3 4 5
11.	My neighborhood has helpful qualities.
	1 2 3 4 5
12.	I live in a community where people pitch in.
	1 2 3 4 5
13.	My cultural group and I celebrate traditions and holidays together.
	1 2 3 4 5
14.	When I experience a great deal of stress, I turn to my cultural community for support.
	1 2 3 4 5
15.	I think I live in an open society where everyone is welcome.
	1 2 3 4 5
16.	I find it more difficult to get over life's difficulties because I have been limited or excluded from equal participation in society.
	1 2 3 4 5
17.	I live in an area where government policies are supportive of our daily lives.
	1 2 3 4 5
18.	I live in an area where there is ample access to resources and services.
	1 2 3 4 5
19.	I am better able to handle life's difficulties when I have sufficient resources and services to meet my needs.
	1 2 3 4 5
20.	I notice that when the surrounding environment is more disrupted, it affects my daily functioning.
	1 2 3 4 5

Table 5.2 Greene's chart of person–environment (P-E) dimensions: narrative questions and prompts

P-E dimension 1. Consequences of time and place: Referring to the era and location of critical events Do you follow local or national events? If so, how do you think they affect your life?
P-E dimension 2. Response to the stress of past critical events: Managing past difficulties with relative success Have you been in similar circumstances before? What happened? What did you do?
P-E dimension 3. Reaction to disruption of biopsychosocial and spiritual processes: Determining clients' functional status Have there been any personal concerns lately that are causing difficulties? If so, what are they and what have you done?
P-E dimension 4. Family response to adversity or change: Restructuring family patterns when needed How does your family handle unexpected events? Do your family members like change? Try new things?
P-E dimension 5. Consequences of social supports: Seeking and accessing mutual aid Do you have friends with whom you talk? Do you have a certain person on whom you can depend?
P-E dimension 6. Significance of favorable environments: Receiving nurturance and support What is your neighborhood like? Is it friendly? Is there a nearby grocery you like?
P-E dimension 7. Effects of strong cultural identity: Relying on a worldview and cultural resources How would you describe your culture? Do you get together for celebrations?
P-E dimension 8. Effects of human rights violations: Experiencing social and economic discrimination Would you say you sometimes feel slighted by society? If so, in what ways are you let down?
P-E dimension 9. Concerns about insufficient resources and services: Experiencing barriers to resources Do you or your friends have trouble getting things like daily supplies? Are there doctors and a pharmacy within reach?
P-E dimension 10. Response to degradation of ecosystems: Undergoing ripple effect disturbances in human functioning Do you notice community-wide problems that negatively impact the lives around you? Are there problems connected to government resources, such as water supply and waste disposal?

Table 5.3 Person–environment blank assessment profile chart

	Person–environment dimension	Client indicators
1.	Consequences of time and place	________
2.	Response to the stress of past critical events	________
3.	Reaction to disruption of biopsychosocial and spiritual processes	________
4.	Family response to adversity or change	________
5.	Consequences of social supports	________
6.	Significance of favorable environments	________
7.	Effects of strong cultural identity	________
8.	Effects of human rights violations	________
9.	Concerns about insufficient resources and services	________
10.	Response to degradation of ecosystems	________

Table 5.4 Person–environment goal setting and evaluation chart

Person–environment dimension	Goal
1. Consequences of time and place Write goal(s) set Evaluation of action(s) taken	
2. Response to the stress of past critical events Write goal(s) set Evaluation of action(s) taken	
3. Reaction to disruption of biopsychosocial and spiritual processes Write goal(s) set Evaluation of action(s) taken	
4. Family response to adversity or change Write goal(s) set Evaluation of action(s) taken	
5. Consequences of social supports Write goal(s) set Evaluation of action(s) taken	
6. Significance of favorable environments Write goal(s) set Evaluation of action(s) taken	
7. Effects of strong cultural identity Write goal(s) set Evaluation of action(s) taken	
8. Effects of human rights violations Write goal(s) set Evaluation of action(s) taken	
9. Concerns about insufficient resources and services Write goal(s) set Evaluation of action(s) taken	
10. Response to degradation of ecosystems Write goal(s) set Evaluation of action(s) taken	

5.4 Intervention: Deconstructing and Reconstructing the Narrative

5.4.1 Central Focus

The mutually determined RESM intervention plan is derived from the client's assessment profile. The intervention plan gives an indication of what actions the client wants to take to reduce risk; bolster protective factors; and achieve enhanced, culturally sound resilient functioning. Interventions are intended to reconstruct a negative narrative to one that is more positive and goal-oriented and that reflects a client's goals for resilient functioning.

5.4.2 Terms

- *Narrative meaning-making*. A client's perception of whether a critical event is comprehensible, manageable, and meaningful (Antonovsky, 1987).
- *Externalization*. Placing the origin of the source of stress outside oneself or one's group (White & Epston, 1990).
- *Reconstructed narrative*. A negative client story that has been rewritten to express a positive, goal-oriented future.

5.4.3 Assumptions

- Culturally sound problem solving is a collaboration between the social worker and client.
- Attention to systemic discrimination is embedded in RESM practice.
- Goal setting is the social worker's opportunity to enhance client's resilient functioning.

A tool to use to mutually set client goals is available in Table 5.4 (Person–Environment Goal Setting and Evaluation Chart).

5.5 Evaluation: Engaging in Evaluation

5.5.1 Central Focus

During the evaluation phase, social workers and clients reflect on whether clients perceive themselves as functional, resilient, and causal agents. In addition, practitioners may want to critique how effectively they have carried out their social work practice.

5.5.2 Terms

- *Causal agent*. A person who has confidence in their ability to make choices and to act on their environment.
- *Functionality*. The capacity to meet life tasks and make social connections.

Table 5.5 An evaluation of client resilient outcomes

The client was able to do the following:	
Identify personal and environmental risks	☐
Recognize their protective factors	☐
Better balance their response to stress	☐
Make meaning of events	☐
Rewrite a negative narrative	☐
Build on their strengths	☐
Make choices	☐
Seek further connections with others	☐
Celebrate their cultural differences	☐
Understand the process of change	☐
Identify institutional sources of limited opportunities	☐
Realize that they can take part in resistance	☐
Distinguish how a privileged status impacts access to health, education, and welfare	☐

5.5.3 Assumptions

- Social workers explain the purpose(s) of the evaluation process.
- Social workers and clients reflect on what they have learned during the helping process.

As the evaluation phase comes to an end, social workers and clients have identified what resilient behaviors clients have increasingly demonstrated. They reflect on what clients think about the progress they have made in meeting identified goals, their plans for the future, and their belief in their eventual success. Practitioners may also want to examine their professional use of self.

Tools the social worker can use in the evaluation include the following:

- A tool the social worker and client can use to reflect on the progress made during the helping process appears in Table 5.5 (An Evaluation of Client Resilient Outcomes).
- Social workers who want to monitor their practice can use Table 5.6 (A Self-Inventory).

5.6 A RESM Practice Guide for Work With Family, Group, and Community Systems

Although many of the guiding principles above are suitable for resilience-enhancing practice with families, groups, and communities, some specific practice assumptions for working with these social systems are described here.

Table 5.6 A self-inventory

I am a social worker who focuses on client strength and resilience. I	
Engaged in self-monitoring	☐
Gave preeminence to the client's understanding of the facts	☐
Believed the client's account of events	☐
Discovered what the client wants to change	☐
Made assessment a joint activity between myself and the client	☐
Moved the assessment toward personal/environmental strengths and resilience	☐
Realized that my own ethnic and class background may influence my effectiveness	☐
Considered it an obligation to familiarize myself with the client's culture, history, and other ethnically related responses to the problem(s)	☐
Became aware of systemic sources of client problems (racism, poverty, prejudice)	☐
Collaborated with the client to set and achieve their self-defined choices and goals	☐

Note. Summarized from Greene (2006). See also Cowger (1994) and Ho (1990)

5.6.1 Family-Centered Social Work Practice

5.6.1.1 Central Focus

The exploration of family resilience focuses on the "adaptive qualities of families as they encounter stress" (Hawley & DeHaan, 1996, p. 284). Family-centered RESM social work practice requires that practitioners and the family discern the pattern of relationships members have developed as they have interacted with one another over time. Social workers and the family also collaborate to learn how the family has been disrupted by an adverse event. The purpose of family practice is to coach the family on how to enhance organizational, communication, and belief patterns that contribute to an effective life transition and enhanced resilient social functioning.

5.6.1.2 Terms

- *Family*. A social system of interdependent persons with its own unique structure and cultural form.
- *Adaptiveness*. A person or group's capacity to discriminate well and act effectively on the environment.

5.6.1.3 Assumptions

- Social workers acknowledge that there are diverse family forms.
- Social workers become conversant with a family's cultural belief system.

5.6.1.4 Engagement

- Social workers and the family determine who will participate in the helping process.
- Practitioners collaborate with family members to establish a third-space relationship.
- Social workers observe family patterns in the here and now to help family members become aware of their influence on social functioning.

5.6.1.5 Assessment

- Social workers and the family cocreate a family narrative during which assessment data are revealed.
- The narrative interview is used to learn how members of the family system work together.
- Narrative questions and prompts can help practitioners uncover the family's hierarchy, or the ranking of members by power and control.
- The family group and social worker determine patterns that are disruptive to resilient functioning and reflect on what can be done to resolve them.
- The social worker and family examine whether there is congruence between the family's environmental quality and its internal functions and needs.

Table 5.7 (Family Resilience Template) provides a tool the social worker can use to help the family assess its social functioning.

5.6.1.6 Intervention

- The social worker and family explore the meaning of the family's ongoing life transition.
- The social worker and family explore what negative meanings stem from external environmental challenges. They then may decide to deconstruct and reconstruct the family narrative accordingly.
- The social worker fosters correspondence between the family's environmental quality and its internal functions and needs.

5.6.1.7 Evaluation

- The social worker and family reflect on and review the family's new patterns of organization or role definitions.
- The social worker and family appraise the progress of the family as a unit.

Table 5.7 Family resilience template

How effectively does your family function? Have you					
1.	Developed positive interrelationships				
	Strongly disagree 1	2	3	4	5 strongly agree
2.	Formed an effective structure				
	Strongly disagree 1	2	3	4	5 strongly agree
3.	Joined in problem solving				
	Strongly disagree 1	2	3	4	5 strongly agree
4.	Taken part in successful decision making				
	Strongly disagree 1	2	3	4	5 strongly agree
5.	Developed effective patterns of communication				
	Strongly disagree 1	2	3	4	5 strongly agree
6.	Effectively accomplished your caregiving tasks				
	Strongly disagree 1	2	3	4	5 strongly agree
Do you think you have rebounded from disruptive events? Do you					
1.	Take on positive challenges				
	Strongly disagree 1	2	3	4	5 strongly agree
2.	Identify many risk factors or demands				
	Strongly disagree 1	2	3	4	5 strongly agree
3.	Know and use protective factors (resources and strengths)				
	Strongly disagree 1	2	3	4	5 strongly agree
4.	Feel you have a sense of cohesion/togetherness				
	Strongly disagree 1	2	3	4	5 strongly agree
5.	Take steps to connect to extended family and friends				
	Strongly disagree 1	2	3	4	5 strongly agree
6.	Make affiliations in your community				
	Strongly disagree 1	2	3	4	5 strongly agree
7.	Feel you are in control of your life situation				
	Strongly disagree 1	2	3	4	5 strongly agree
8.	Envision new possibilities				
	Strongly disagree 1	2	3	4	5 strongly agree
9.	Celebrate holidays				
	Strongly disagree 1	2	3	4	5 strongly agree
10.	Want more services				
	Strongly disagree 1	2	3	4	5 strongly agree
11.	Have enough help from family and friends				
	Strongly disagree 1	2	3	4	5 strongly agree
12.	Consider your family resilient				
	Strongly disagree 1	2	3	4	5 strongly agree

Note. See Greene (2012) and Isserman et al. (2014)
Directions: How would you rate your family on these functions? Have a family meeting and choose the rating that best fits your family. 1 = strongly disagree, 5 = strongly agree

5.6.2 *Group Social Work Practice*

5.6.2.1 Central Focus

The intent of RESM group practice is to create a working group whose members learn strategies to promote resilient functioning. Working groups can be subgroups within a workplace or community-based project that is designed to explore and support resilience. The social worker acts as a coach who enables members to connect with one another and to form a problem-solving unit.

5.6.2.2 Terms

- *Group.* Two or more people who come together with a common purpose or interest.
- *Working group.* People who collaborate on achieving a common goal or agenda.

5.6.2.3 Assumptions

- Social workers facilitate respect for diversity within the group.
- Group members learn to acknowledge members' different positionalities and worldviews.

5.6.2.4 Engagement

- Engagement begins when social workers conduct outreach to enlist stakeholders or bring people together for a common purpose.
- Social group work can foster trust among group members and build human connections.
- The social worker acts as a facilitator who strives to create a give-and-take dynamic or group atmosphere.
- The social worker helps group members hear different voices and "leave space" to find common ground.

5.6.2.5 Assessment

- Social workers and group members reflect on the various responses group members have to the stressor(s) in question. That is, social workers assure group members that concerns are being explored from different points of view.
- The information shared in the group may be synthesized to reflect a grand group narrative of members' perceptions of difficulties and possible solutions.

5.6.2.6 Intervention

- The social worker and group members decide what resilience-enhancing intervention strategies and goals the working group members want to adopt to arrive at a common solution.

5.6.2.7 Evaluation

- Evaluation of the group initiative is often delegated to group members or may be done by an outside organization.

Social workers can use Table 5.8 (Group Facilitator Checklist) to evaluate their roles as group facilitators.

5.6.3 Community-Based Social Work Practice

5.6.3.1 Central Focus

RESM community-based practice occurs in a set locality and emphasizes the resilient functioning of the community as a social system. The promotion of resilience in communities depends in part on the policies and availability of community-based resources and services and the social organizations that provide them (Benard, 2004). Therefore, practitioners bring together diverse stakeholders to explore the efficacy of necessary service systems to determine whether they are perceived as satisfying residents' daily living needs and functions.

Table 5.8 Group facilitator checklist

Did the group facilitator	
Make clear who would be recruited as members	☐
Clarify the purpose of the group	☐
Promote respect for group members' contrasting views	☐
Assist members in developing trust and reaching a common agenda	☐
Learn how group members function under personal or environmental demands	☐
Cocreate a group grand narrative	☐
Mutually discover what further support group members need	☐
Reframe group narrative content to reflect a more positive future	☐
Help group members gauge whether they are ready to act on identified concerns	☐

5.6.3.2 Terms

- *Community*. A physical location composed of social units and systems that carry out policies and perform major social functions that have local relevance. A group of people with a common interest.
- *Stakeholders*. People with an interest in the goals and priorities in question.

5.6.3.3 Assumptions

- Communities should function to aid members with the daily needs and services they require in times of difficulty.
- Social workers are concerned with how accountable a community is to its members.

5.6.3.4 Engagement

- Social workers and stakeholders establish the community's boundaries or the relevant locale or place.
- The outreach conducted by the social worker needs to be culturally sound and enlist diverse subcommunities in resilience-enhancing activities.
- To accomplish community development projects, social workers establish mutual relationships with both leaders and grassroots community members.

5.6.3.5 Assessment

- Social workers and stakeholders explore the needs of the community system from multiple points of view.
- An important focus is learning how community members relate and function together.
- Social workers and constituencies describe community risks and protective factors that affect common needs.
- Social workers and community members collaborate on discovering what systemic injustices need to be redressed.
- Social workers and community members ascertain whether community resources, services, and assets are available and accessible.

5.6.3.6 Intervention

- Social workers and community members outline plans for making community resources and services more available and accessible.

Table 5.9 Community practice

Social workers engaged in community practice
Establish the community's local resources and demographics
Recruit diverse leaders, stakeholders, and networks
Establish a common agenda
Determine the need for working groups
Obtain information on perceived needs
Identify community risks
Distinguish community protective factors
Build a development plan based on community human capital or assets
Increase development by using and increasing tangible physical assets
Establish a starting point for a community vision
Reflect on what would make for a more resilient community

Note. See Community and Regional Resilience Institute (2011)

- Community-wide interventions function best when social workers and stakeholders articulate a community vision that reflects the needs of its members.

5.6.3.7 Evaluation

- Steps taken by the community to improve its resilient social functioning should be evaluated by members and the results of the evaluation disseminated for feedback.

  Table 5.9 (Community Practice) can be used to reflect on community functions.

5.7 Summary and Conclusion

This chapter has described the RESM anti-oppressive methodology and its application with clients and constituencies who are facing stressful transitions or adverse events. See Chaps. 6, 7, 8, 9, 10, and 11 for examples of the use of the toolkit and further suggestions for helping individuals, families, groups, and communities maintain or regain resilient functioning.

Summary of Learning Outcomes
Keep in mind the following:

- Social workers can use the P-E perspective as a guidepost for social work practice.
- Social workers collaborate with clients and constituencies to set the helping agenda and goals.

Discussion Questions

1. How would you apply the 10 P-E dimensions with a client transitioning to recovery from COVID-19?
2. Why would the resolution of past difficulties during a life transition impact present client functioning?

Chapter Exercise

Write a one-page reflection paper on how COVID-19 influenced you and your neighborhood.

RESM Toolkit

Table 5.1 Greene's Risk-Protection and Resiliency Questionnaire is a 20-item questionnaire social workers can use to ascertain clients' perceptions of the saliency of their P-E dimensions. Does each dimension primarily act as a risk factor or serve as a protective factor? The questionnaire may be self-administered, or it may be reviewed in collaboration with the social worker.

Table 5.2 Greene's Chart of Person–Environment (P-E) Dimensions: Narrative Questions and Prompts present probes the social worker can use to improve the flow of the narrative interview.

Table 5.3 Person–Environment Blank Assessment Profile Chart can be used to link P-E dimensions with client assessment indicators. These indicators are then synthesized into an assessment profile and a mutually developed intervention plan.

Table 5.4 Person–Environment Goal Setting and Evaluation Chart can be used to reflect on and establish client goals.

Table 5.5 An Evaluation of Client Resilient Outcomes can be used to examine clients' resilient behaviors.

Table 5.6 A Self-Inventory can be used by social workers to explore their professional use of self.

Table 5.7 Family Resilience Template provides a checklist for families to assess their functioning.

Table 5.8 Group Facilitator Checklist offers a means of evaluating a group facilitator.

Table 5.9 Community Practice can be used to reflect on community functions.

References

Antonovsky, A. (1987). *Unraveling the mystery of health: How people manage stress and stay well.* Jossey-Bass.

Benard, B. (2004). *Resiliency: What we have learned.* WestEd.

Community & Regional Resilience Institute. (2011, August). *Community Resilience System Initiative (CRSI) Steering Committee final report—A roadmap to increased community resilience*.

Council on Social Work Education. (2022). *Educational policy and accreditation standards*. Retrieved September 22, 2022, from https://www.cswe.org/getmedia/94471c42-13b8-493b-9041-b30f48533d64/2022-EPAS.pdf

Cowger, C. (1994). Assessing client strengths: Clinical assessment for client empowerment. *Social Work, 39*(3), 202–208.

Dubey, S., Biswas, P., Ghosh, R., Chatterjee, S., Dubey, M. J., Chatterjee, S., Lahiri, D., & Lavie, C. J. (2020). Psychosocial impact of COVID-19. *Diabetes & Metabolic Syndrome, 14*(5), 779–788.

Gitterman, A., & Germain, C. (2008). *The life model of social work practice: Advances in knowledge and practice* (3rd ed.). Columbia University Press.

Greene, R. R. (2006). The assessment and intervention planning workbook. In R. Greene (Ed.), *Contemporary issues in life care* (pp. 341–370). Haworth Press.

Greene, R. R. (2008). *Human behavior theory and social work practice* (3rd ed.). Aldine Transaction Press.

Greene, R. R. (2012). *Resiliency theory: An integrated framework for practice, research, and policy* (2nd ed.). NASW Press.

Hawley, D. R., & DeHaan, L. (1996). Toward a definition of family resilience: Integrating lifespan and family perspectives. *Family Process, 35*(3), 283–298.

Ho, M. K. (1990). Use of Ethnic-Sensitive Inventory (ESI) to enhance practitioner skills with minorities. *Journal of Multicultural Social Work, 1*(1), 57–68.

Isserman, N., Greene, R. R., Bowen, S., Hollander-Goldfein, B., & Cohen, H. (2014). Intergenerational families of Holocaust survivors: Designing and piloting a family resilience template. *Evidence-Based Social Work Practice, 30*(1), 62–67.

Maryville University. (2022). *Social analysis of a pandemic: How COVID-19 impacted society*. Retrieved November 14, 2022, from https://online.maryville.edu/blog/social-analysis/

Mattingly, C. (1991). The narrative nature of clinical reasoning. *American Journal of Occupational Therapy, 45*(11), 998–1005.

Robinson, E., Sutin, A. R., Daly, M., & Jones, A. (2022). A systematic review and meta-analysis of longitudinal cohort studies comparing mental health before versus during the COVID-19 pandemic in 2020. *Journal of Affective Disorders, 296*, 567–576. https://doi.org/10.1016/j.jad.2021.09.098

Schon, D. A. (1983). *The reflective practitioner: How professionals think in action*. Basic Books.

Sheafor, B. W., & Horejsi, C. J. (2012). *Techniques and guidelines for social work practice* (9th ed.). Allyn & Bacon.

United Nations Department of Economic and Social Affairs. (2020). *Everyone included: Social impact of COVID-19*. Retrieved November 14, 2022, from https://www.un.org/development/desa/dspd/everyone-included-covid-19.html

Wexler, L. (2009). The importance of identity, history, and culture in the wellbeing of in Indigenous youth. *Journal of the History of Childhood and Youth, 2*(2), 267–276.

White, M. (2007). *Mapping of narrative practice*. Norton.

White, M., & Epston, D. (1990). *Narrative means to therapeutic ends*. Norton.

Chapter 6
Transitioning from Hospital to Home: Resilience-Enhancing Skills for Health Care Social Workers

Roberta Greene and Elizabeth Cummings

Learning Objectives

This chapter proposes skills a social worker can use when assisting patients and their families in making a health care transition from hospital to home. This chapter describes how social workers can integrate clinical social work skills from the resilience-enhancing stress model (RESM) with the Bridge Model to ensure that clients have sufficient health care resources and services to support their social functioning and resiliency. On completing this chapter, you should better understand how social workers serve in the health care arena. You should be prepared to answer the following questions:

- What major risks or harms may be faced by patients who are transitioning from hospital care to home care?
- What RESM social work skills support a patient's positive transition from hospital to home?
- What case management skills support a patient's effective transition from hospital to home?
- How does the cocreated client or family narrative provide assessment data, reveal psychosocial health care needs, and suggest intervention strategies?

R. Greene
Steve Hicks School of Social Work, The University of Texas at Austin, Austin, TX, USA
e-mail: rgreene@utexas.edu

E. Cummings (✉)
Rush University Medical Center, Chicago, IL, USA

Center for Health and Social Care Integration, Chicago, IL, USA
e-mail: Elizabeth_Cummings@rush.edu

R. Greene et al. (eds.), *Resilience Enhancement in Social Work Practice*,
https://doi.org/10.1007/978-3-031-38518-6_6

According to the 2019 American Community Survey, the health care industry is one of the largest and fastest growing economic sectors in the United States (U.S. Census Bureau, 2019). Furthermore, the demand for social workers in outpatient health care services is relatively high across all indicators (George Washington University Health Workforce Institute, 2021). In the past decade, social work programs nationwide have enhanced their preparation of master's in social work students for employment in integrated health care settings (Jones et al., 2020). To further meet this end, the Council on Social Work Education (2023) has released the *Specialized Practice Curricular Guide for Health Social Work*, which sees health through a person–environment (P-E) lens and discusses the pursuit of well-being for individuals, families, communities, and populations. This holistic view of health encompasses an array of factors, including cultural, environmental, economic, historical, communal, psychological, relational, social, and biological factors.

At the same time, social workers currently entering practice in the health care arena may find the industry in "a perpetual state of flux" (Grazier, 2008, p. 141) and in need of change and innovation (Chin et al., 2007). Yet careers in health care can enable social workers to apply resilience-enhancing social work practice skills on behalf of clients experiencing health care risks. The move from hospital to home is a critical juncture when patients with complex needs are at high risk for poor health outcomes and hospital readmissions. Research suggests that in addition to medical concerns, nonmedical issues rooted in psychosocial determinants of health are frequently involved in readmission events (Altfeld et al., 2013; Davis et al., 2012).

This chapter highlights the knowledge and skills social workers need to support patients and their families making such transitions and to ensure they have sufficient resources and services to maintain their optimal level of social functioning. The practice example of Marcia and her social worker Joan continued from Chap. 1 illustrates the transition process and why a blend of RESM social work skills and case management skills is well suited to meeting patients' needs during the transition from hospital to home (see Box 6.1).

Box 6.1: Practice Example: Transitioning from Hospital to Home

Marcia, a 33-year-old African American patient, was referred to the hospital-at-home program at Rush University Medical Center for help recovering from surgery to install a heart monitor. Joan, her social worker, brought her skills in traditional resource coordination and management together with a narrative approach to learn how Marcia might fare during her transition home. The primary goal was to speed up her recovery from surgery and reduce her risk of being readmitted to the hospital.

During her first meeting with Marcia, Joan asked her to describe herself. Joan learned that Marcia perceived herself as a type A personality—"a very well-organized person." Joan encouraged Marcia to be an ally in her recovery by collaborating in the coordination of her care.

6.1 Combining the RESM and the Bridge Model

One of the areas of health care practice that is being redefined involves programs that reposition health care from the hospital to the home. Hospital-to-home interprofessional programs are designed to attend to post-hospital medical challenges and better identify and address psychosocial needs to reduce readmissions after hospital discharge (Boutwell et al., 2016). Many model hospital-to-home programs are based on the medical model of care. However, a growing body of evidence and experience suggests that to reduce avoidable readmissions, hospital-to-home programs such as the Bridge Model described in this chapter can benefit from social workers attending to patients' social and behavioral health needs (Carlisle et al., 2014).

Since the inception of the profession and the work of pioneers like Mary Richmond and Jane Addams, social workers have included a blend of clinical diagnostic assessment skills and case management strategies in their practice armamentarium (Weil & Karls, 1985; see Table 6.1). The social work interviews presented in this chapter are hypothetical examples of how social workers may combine these skills to assist hospitalized patients in making an effective transition to care in their home.

6.2 Social Workers on Health Care Teams

The increasing complexity of health care provision and medical interventions requires collaboration among large numbers of professionals who often work on interprofessional health care teams. Health care teams may be multi-, inter-, or transdisciplinary in nature depending on their interactions and pattern of work (Singh et al., 2018).

Table 6.1 Resilience-enhancing stress model and case management practice principles

Develop therapeutic relationships with clients that provide safe environments for them to share their stories, problems, and feelings (National Association of Social Workers, 2013).
Ensure that clients feel heard so they continue to share information.
Be empathetic so clients may have a higher probability of positive clinical outcomes.
Use reflection to clarify what clients are saying.
Apply evidence-based practice skills to identify and determine what works, for whom, and in which situations (NASW Foundation, n.d.).
Encourage partnership in the helping process.
Support client self-determination.
Provide services or resources that are managed to help people reach their goals (Rapp & Goscha, 2004).
Adopt client management software that complies with industry data standards, facilitates streamlined intake and assessment, allows for seamless generation of reports, and meets professional ethical standards (Reamer, 2018).

- Multidisciplinary team members tend to stay within their professional boundaries, but all members communicate with the others and draw on their disciplinary knowledge.
- Interdisciplinary team members analyze, synthesize, and make links among disciplines to coordinate care into a coherent activity.
- A transdisciplinary team approach involves team members from different disciplines collaborating on a common purpose, setting goals, making decisions, and sharing resources and responsibilities. On some occasions, one member may assume another team member's role (Choi & Pak, 2006).

This chapter draws on Rush University Medical Center's Bridge Model, described in Box 6.2, to illustrate how social workers contribute to an interdisciplinary team as they deliver best practices and services in transitional care.

Box 6.2: Practice Example: An Exemplary Case Management Program
Rush University Medical Center's Bridge Model is a person-centered transitional care program that helps patients make a seamless transition during the stressful time of moving from hospital to home. This interdisciplinary health care program combines three key components—patient engagement, care management, and care coordination.

Ideally, a clinical social worker from the Bridge program meets with patients right before they are discharged from the hospital to explain the program's purpose and to engage them in a telephone-based patient contact program that may continue for up to 4 weeks or more.

A Bridge social worker specifically addresses psychosocial barriers to care to ensure that each patient's immediate medical and psychosocial needs are being met. In addition to coordinating care, care coordinators provide case management, which includes planning, seeking out, advocating for, and monitoring services from different social service providers or health care organizations on behalf of the client (Barker, 2003). Calls to service providers are made to monitor resources and services that are provided.

Bridge social workers receive training on the program as well as clinical supervision. As licensed clinical social workers, members of the Bridge program link patients to community resources. They also utilize clinical skills rooted in social work professional competencies to provide direct psychotherapeutic support (Boutwell et al., 2016).

The Bridge Model has been replicated in approximately 200 hospitals, health systems, or community-based organizations and can be adapted for different client populations with various health care needs.

6.3 Blending the RESM with the Bridge Model

According to Boutwell et al. (2016), a social work transitional care model such as the Bridge Model can reap great results because it is designed to assess the needs of the whole person and anticipates that the individual's needs may change over time. These researchers concluded that "a major strength of social work models of care management is their repeated assessments, customized interventions, and the ability to link individuals to existing community providers and services" (p. 1107).

As can be seen in Table 6.2, both the RESM and the Bridge Model embody traditional social work practice elements and share theoretical frameworks. The models

- Center on patients' values and preferences
- Are rooted in social work professional competencies
- Are based on a person-in-environment perspective
- Draw on ecological theory and systems theory

Practitioners who use these models

- Gather assessment information by listening to client narratives
- Reflect on the assessment information with the patient
- Endeavor to reduce harm and bolster protective factors or strengths

Table 6.2 Phases of social work practice

Resilience-enhancing stress model	Bridge Model
	Referral: Preintervention planning
	Identify patients in need of resources and services
Engagement: Establish a third-space relationship	Engagement: Describe role, develop rapport, and set expectations
Set a mutual agenda with the patient	Discover the patient's needs and preferences
Assessment: Cocreate a narrative	Assessment: Complete assessment forms with the patient
Consider person–environment dimensions	Discuss assessment with the patient
Intervention: Reconstruct the narrative	Care planning: Explicitly discuss care with the patient derived from the narrative
Enhance client resilient functioning	
	Care management: Assess progress on the care plan
	Troubleshoot
Evaluation: Appraise progress	Goal attainment: Summarize progress
Explore resilient outcomes	Ensure long-time supports

6.4 The Four Phases of the RESM Augmented by the Bridge Model

6.4.1 *Engagement*

When patients are referred to hospital-to-home programs, they may experience stress and confusion. Engagement is a phase of treatment during which the social worker learns “what is important to the patient, what matters most, and what goals they hope to achieve” (Center for Health and Social Care Integration, 2022, p. 10).

6.4.1.1 Forging a Relationship

The RESM is a person-centered approach similar to the Bridge program that requires social workers to forge authentic relationships with their clients and leverage those relationships to affect behavioral change (Alvarez et al., 2016). The mutual relationships that are built with patients allow practitioners to act as the “glue … that oils the wheels” in this relational approach to care (Boutwell et al., 2016, p. 1105).

6.4.1.2 Respecting Client Values

Social workers in health care need to be aware of the cultural values that play a role in care decisions. This may involve asking what keeps the patient going during difficult times or learning about a patient’s faith or spiritual traditions (Center for Health and Social Care Integration, 2022).

6.4.1.3 Navigating Health Care Systems

Social workers in health care are guides who help patients navigate the health care system (see Box 6.3). This purpose is made transparent during engagement. The Bridge social worker may say something along the lines of “This is a team. I am here to help connect the dots with you and to be sure your medical-social needs are met. You should never wonder where we are or what we are doing. As any questions come up along the way related to your care and needs, I am here to support in the time we have together.”

Box 6.3: Skill Box: RESM Case Management Engagement Skills

Skill	Practitioner statement
Displaying open curiosity	“I hope to learn about the stresses in your daily living situation.”
Developing rapport	“Can you share with me how you feel about being home?”
Sharing the purpose	“We can work on the challenges of getting the right services together.”

6.4.2 Assessment

6.4.2.1 Features Common to Both Models

This chapter describes how social workers can address the distress caused by a disruption in a client's biopsychosocial functioning as well as pinpoint the resources and services needed to ameliorate the situation. Both the RESM and the Bridge Model are used to ensure that patients in recovery have sufficient resources and services. Assessment is a framework for understanding patients' current situations and the nature of their presenting concerns. The data obtained during assessment serve as a basis for setting goals and planning interventions (Bisman, 2004; Hepworth et al., 2017).

Assessment requires the social worker to gather, analyze, and synthesize client data to produce a concise picture of clients and their needs and strengths (Hepworth et al., 2017). The aim is to understand individuals in relation to their environment to improve, maintain, or bring about changes in the person and/or environment so the patient can achieve the optimal level of social functioning (Coulshed & Orme, 2013).

The practice example in Box 6.4 illustrates how practice moves from the engagement phase to assessment. The assessment phase was the point in time when Joan, the social worker, wanted to learn about Marcia's past successes and what she hoped to accomplish in the not-so-distant future.

Box 6.4: Practice Example: Getting to Know Marcia

Joan: I am glad I met you in person at the hospital. I hope it makes it easier for you to talk with me today by phone.

Marcia: Yes. I'm beginning to get an idea of how this all works.

Joan: To better understand how we can work together, it would help me to know what challenges you feel you've overcome in the past. Is that okay with you?

Marcia: Yes it is. I can't believe this has happened to me at my age. I am the only child of a pretty poor family, but I was determined to get a college degree. I did, and I am now on the upswing of my career in human resources.

Joan: Would I be right if I guessed you want to return to the office—maybe virtually?

Marcia: You bet! It was hard growing up, but I was able to overcome many social constraints. I love helping others at work do the same.

Joan: Do you want to say what stands out to you about that time?

Marcia: All I can say is that Dad worked two jobs to keep the family together.

Joan: I understand what that has meant. Let's partner to get your current goals met. By our next phone call, we may know what the next steps are. Would you be ready to set some goals?

Marcia: Of course.

6.4.2.2 Practice Example Analysis: Steps Taken

Because Joan had built a relationship with Marcia based on trust and transparency, Marcia felt free to mention the poverty she had experienced as a child. In a holistic assessment, it is important to take into account the fact that some patients may have faced environmental (P-E) disparities.

6.4.3 Intervention

6.4.3.1 Social Determinants of Health

RESM social work interventions address inequities in health care. Health care inequities are difficulties associated with the unfair distribution of health care resources to different populations. In contrast, social determinants of health are environmental disparities due to wealth or income, education, criminal justice, the physical environment, health care, housing, employment, stress, and racism or discrimination that affect a wide range of health, functioning, and quality-of-life outcomes and risks. According to Zerden et al. (2020),

> expanding health care beyond traditional medical settings will require health system administrators, practitioners, researchers, and policy makers to expand their emphasis on health care delivery to include social care (i.e., the services that address social risks) as an essential component of a program for optimizing clients' health. (p. 310)

Among other things, attending to social care involves identifying the social risks and assets of defined patients and populations (Zerden et al., 2020) and modifying care provision to combine medical and psychosocial care to provide a more comprehensive and effective experience (Greene & Kropf, 2014). Attending to social needs may improve health outcomes and decrease health disparities among people who have been marginalized by social risk factors such as race or ethnicity, socioeconomic status, or geographic location (CareWorks, n.d.). Table 6.3 delineates terms pertinent to social risks.

6.4.3.2 Key Features of Assessment in the Bridge Model

Follow-up care coordination and care management assessments in the Bridge Model are comprehensive and strength based. They include statements about the care plan, finances, housing, insurance, functional status, support systems, mental health, personal safety, cognition, caregiver burden, substance use, and advance directives.

Effective patient assessments consider the entire spectrum of patients' psychosocial needs after discharge (Alvarez et al., 2016). Social workers must ensure that patients know what life will be like after they transition from hospital to home. They explore whether patients are aware of their medications. They determine whether home modifications are needed, obtain medical equipment, secure home-based

Table 6.3 Delineating social inequities, determinants of health, and environmental justice

Health care inequities are difficulties associated with the unfair distribution of health care resources to different populations. These inequities cause *health disparities*, or differences in health outcomes across subgroups of the population.
Health disparities adversely affect groups of people who have systematically experienced greater obstacles to health care based on race or ethnicity; religion; socioeconomic status; gender; age; mental health; cognitive, sensory, or physical disability; sexual orientation or gender identity; geographic location; or other characteristics historically linked to discrimination or exclusion (Office of the Surgeon General, 2017).
Social determinants of health reflect the conditions in which people are born, grow up, live, work, and age. Social determinants of health are environmental disparities due to wealth or income, education, criminal justice, the physical environment, health care, housing, employment, stress, or racism or discrimination (Ferraro & Farmer, 1996).
Environmental justice is concerned with people receiving fair treatment as they interact with their environments. In other words, are people's rights obstructed by "oppressive structural barriers that interfere and obstruct with social goods, rights, and responsibilities being distributed equitably" (Council on Social Work Education, 2015, p. 5)? For example, does a client have safe and affordable housing? Sufficient and nutritious food? Health insurance? Transportation?

medical services, and determine whether the patient is eligible to receive services covered by their insurance.

The questions in Box 6.5 are key Bridge assessment questions that can supplement those provided in Table 5.2, Greene's Chart of Person–Environment (P-E) Dimensions: Narrative Questions and Prompts, in Chap. 5.

6.4.3.3 Practice Example Analysis: Steps Taken

The social worker is responsible for monitoring the implementation of the individual care plan to ensure that the client is seen for medical, psychiatric, dental, and other therapeutic appointments. The delivery of care coordination and management interventions is based on three questions that explore the degree to which patients are engaged in their own care:

1. What can patients do to navigate resources and services for themselves?
2. What can patients do with the help of the social worker?
3. What must the social worker address (Center for Health and Social Care Integration, 2022)?

Box 6.5: Bridge Assessment Questions

- What were your instructions for home? Do they make sense to you?
- What are your medical conditions, and how do you manage them?
- What do you hope to get back to doing as you recover?
- What are your challenges?
- From whom do you receive social supports?
- What do you want to accomplish?

Based on Marcia's narrative and the steps she took to follow up on referrals, Joan concluded that Marcia had demonstrated significant self-efficacy.

6.4.4 *Assessment*

As emphasized throughout the text, the RESM focuses on clients who are experiencing environmental challenges or threats that can interrupt their social functioning. The RESM suggests that social workers and clients explore 10 P-E dimensions to evaluate the client's response to stress at a range of micro- to macrolevels (see Chap. 5). Box 6.6 emphasizes two of these P-E dimensions and their respective questions or prompts.

Box 6.6: RESM Assessment Questions

- A client's reaction to disruption of biopsychosocial and spiritual processes may be connected to a decline in functional status.
  - "Have you had any personal concerns lately that are causing difficulties in day-to-day functioning?"
  - "If so, what are they and what have you done?"
- Resilience is associated with the availability of and access to resources and services that support the client's functional capacity.
  - "Do you or your friends have difficulty getting things like daily supplies?"
  - "Are there doctors and a pharmacy within reach?"

6.4.4.1 Creating an Assessment Profile

The purpose of the RESM assessment profile is to gain a picture of a patient's risks and protective factors following a disruptive life event. One result of the mutual patient–social worker activity of narrative cocreation is the rewriting of the patient narrative. In short, the cocreation of a narrative set in motion a change process that helps patients achieve their optimal level of social functioning.

6.4.4.2 Risk and Protective Factors

The decline in Marcia's heart function may be considered a risk. She had a heart monitoring device implanted to monitor disruptions in her heart function so she would know when to seek further medical intervention. A device like Marcia's records the patient's heart rhythm and allows the doctor to monitor changes from his or her office.

The resources and services Marcia was receiving from the Bridge program may be viewed as protective factors. One protective service involved Joan arranging a care continuity telephone appointment with Marcia's primary care physician, her cardiologist, and her surgeon. This preventive strategy closed the loop among care providers.

As can be seen in Table 6.4, a review of Marcia's P-E Assessment Profile Chart revealed that the resources and services provided by the Bridge program acted as protective factors as well as served as sources of social support for Marcia.

6.4.4.3 Interviewing to Set Functional Goals

Treatment goals set by patients and their social workers may encompass personal psychosocial and medical aims. Social workers who use the RESM or a case management approach ascertain what barriers the patient perceives to performing enjoyable activities. They also learn what might stand in the way of clients reaching short-term and long-term goals. However, an emphasis is placed on identified strengths or patient assets.

Table 6.4 Person–environment (P-E) assessment chart: Marcia

P-E dimension	Indicator
Consequences of time and place	The hospital experience can be taxing and confusing for patients and their families, in particular those with limited economic and social resources (Alvarez et al., 2016). Marcia was relieved to know she was going to receive guidance in obtaining care.
Response to the stress of past critical events	Marcia expressed pride in overcoming past childhood disparities related to social determinants of health.
Reaction to disruption of biopsychosocial and spiritual processes	Marcia was distressed to learn that she had a disruption in biological functioning. However, she used her telephone interviews with Joan to confront her situation.
Family response to adversity or change	Marcia's father acted as a role model, as he had held two jobs to help the family escape poverty.
Consequences of social supports	The Bridge program served as a source of social support for Marcia.
Significance of favorable environments	Marcia's experience of overcoming childhood poverty inspired her to want to help others in her workplace.
Effects of human rights violations	Research suggests that social inequities can be stressors that negatively influence health. Marcia was able to reflect on her progress in combating such abuses.
Concerns about insufficient resources and services	The provision of sufficient resources and services is positively linked to resilience. This was the situation in Marcia's personal life and workplace.

6.4.4.4 Practice Example Analysis: Steps Taken

As shown in Box 6.7, Joan was aware that patient resilience is enhanced when clients maintain strong social supports. Consequently, Joan built on Marcia's ability to be well organized to keep her connected with colleagues in the workplace.

6.4.5 *Evaluation*

6.4.5.1 Documenting the Use of Technology

The increased move toward technologically driven practice has been dramatic. According to Reamer (2018), "The advent of technology—including Internet, text (SMS), email, video, social media and networking, cloud storage, and other forms of digital communication and software—has introduced novel and unprecedented ethical challenges" in health care delivery (p. 71). Therefore, appropriate social work practice in the digital age requires knowing what technology is available and learning about its documented effectiveness and limitations.

In 2015, the National Association of Social Workers and the Association of Social Work Boards collaborated to develop standards for social workers to ethically integrate technology into their practice (Association of Social Work Boards,

Box 6.7: Practice Example: A Conversation About Marcia's Functional Goals

Joan:	Did you get a chance to think about your health care goals? Remember, I said we would work together on getting things done.
Marcia:	Absolutely! Let's write the goals down so I can put them on my refrigerator.
Joan:	Where do you want to start? What is important to you, and what kind of things do you like to do?
Marcia:	I'm not really thinking about when I can go out and have fun again; I'm just worried about getting back to work. I wonder if my colleagues have forgotten about me.
Joan:	Has anyone been in touch with you? It sounds like you want to stay connected.
Marcia:	Yes, I got a lot of get well cards.
Joan:	Would you want to get back to any of them?
Marcia:	That sounds like an idea to follow up on! I will list it as goal number one.
Joan:	Any others?
Marcia:	A speedy recovery of my scar and losing 5 pounds!
Joan:	Sounds like a plan. All your services seem to have fallen into place and are moving along as they should be.

2015). These standards address ethical issues such as technical competence, client privacy and confidentiality, and case documentation.

6.4.5.2 Bridge Medicare Program Evaluation

Program evaluations examine the effectiveness and outcomes of agency or hospital initiatives. Findings from a 2012–2014 Community-Based Care Transitions Program—a Medicare demonstration project for Medicare beneficiaries with multiple chronic conditions at six Chicago-area sites ($n = 5753$)—indicated that Bridge participants had 30.7% fewer 30-day readmissions, 9.4% fewer 60-day readmissions, and 13.9% fewer 90-day readmissions than the other programs. These findings also showed Bridge participants also had increased attendance at post-discharge physician appointments (Alvarez et al., 2016).

6.4.5.3 Bridge Clinical Social Work Supervision

Clinical supervision is another mechanism used in the Bridge program to ensure patients receive quality care as well as to prevent practitioner burnout. Bridge social workers take a "fidelity check" to review the quality of patients' care.

6.4.5.4 RESM Professional Self-Monitoring

The RESM also has methods social workers can use to monitor their professional use of self. *Professional use of self* has been defined as the ability to "manage the [practitioner's] influence of bias, power, privilege, and values in working with clients and constituencies" (Council on Social Work Education, 2022, p. 10). It is a process by which social workers become more aware of where they are situated in their community and in the world (Wexler, 2009). This process required that Joan put knowledge into action and be reflective (Schon, 1983). Joan also contemplated whether her choice of helping skills and strategies reduced Marcia's risks and promoted her protective factors. In sum, professional use of self is a form of self-observation that fosters effective practice.

6.4.5.5 Evaluating Patient Goals and Outcomes

As in the RESM, social workers in the Bridge program recommend that goals to improve health outcomes be explicitly set with the patient. Joan took the opportunity to reflect on progress during the helping encounter by collaborating with Marcia to assess how she perceived she had reached her goals. Did she understand her personal and environmental risks? Did she recognize her protective factors? Had she attained a more balanced response to stress? A tool for mutually setting and evaluating client goals, the Person–Environment Goal Setting and Evaluation Chart, is available as Table 5.4 in Chap. 5.

6.5 Summary and Conclusion

Both the RESM and the Bridge Model use a narrative style of communication to obtain an expanded view of clients (Davis et al., 2012). In both models, information gathered during the social worker–client cocreation of the narrative reveals previously unidentified issues to resolve and helps patients and their caregivers respond to stress.

Summary of Learning Outcomes
Keep in mind the following:

- Social workers can help patients who are transitioning from hospital to home create narratives about past successes.
- Social workers can help patients make informed decisions about their care.

Discussion Questions

1. Why would ensuring sufficient availability of resources and services serve as a protective factor for a patient?
2. Why is encouraging a patient to make informed choices an act of empowerment?

Chapter Exercise
Write a one-page reflection paper about what would be important to you if you were being discharged from hospital care to home care.

Glossary

Care coordination The deliberate organization of patient care activities and sharing of information among all participants concerned with a patient's care to achieve safer and more effective care.

Care transitions The movements patients make between health care practitioners and settings as their condition and care needs change during the course of a chronic or acute illness.

Ecological systems theory A theoretical that describes the interaction and interdependence of individuals with their surrounding systems; this theory encourages social workers to assess how individuals affect and are affected by such physical, social, political, and cultural systems.

Holistic care Care that considers all factors in a person's life—including the environment, family dynamics, culture, and more—when determining a path to care and examining client behavior.

Person-centered care Care that integrates health care services delivered in a setting and manner that is responsive to individuals and their goals, values, and preferences in a system that empowers patients and providers to make effective care plans together.

Person-in-environment An individual in the context of his or her environment (e.g., physical, familial, spiritual, social, political, or societal environment).

Resilience The ability to adapt to difficult or challenging life experiences, especially through mental, emotional, and behavioral flexibility, and to adjust to external and internal demands.

Social determinants of health Nonmedical factors that influence health outcomes; the "conditions in which people are born, grow, work, live, and age, and the wider set of forces and systems shaping the conditions of daily life" (World Health Organization, 2023, para. 1).

Social needs "A patient-centered concept that incorporates a person's perception of his or her own health-related needs" (National Academies of Sciences, Engineering, and Medicine, 2019, p. 28).

Supervision A relationship between a supervisor and a supervisee in which responsibility and accountability for the development of competence, demeanor, and ethical practice take place.

Transitional care "A set of actions designed to coordinate continuity of health care as patients transfer between different locations or different levels of care within the same location" (Coleman & Berenson, 2004, p. 533).

References

Altfeld, S. J., Shier, G. E., Rooney, M., Johnson, T. J., Golden, R. L., Karavolos, K., Avery, E., Nandi, V., & Perry, A. J. (2013). Effects of an enhanced discharge planning intervention for hospitalized older adults: A randomized trial. *The Gerontologist, 53*(3), 430–440.

Alvarez, R., Ginsburg, J., Grabowski, J., Post, S., & Rosenberg, W. (2016). The social work role in reducing 30-day readmissions: The effectiveness of the Bridge Model of transitional care. *Journal of Gerontological Social Work, 59*(3), 222–227.

Association of Social Work Boards. (2015). *Model regulatory standards for technology and social work practice*. Retrieved July 28, 2017, from https://www.aswb.org/wp-content/uploads/2015/03/ASWB-Model-Regulatory-Standards-for-Technology-and-Social-Work-Practice.pdf

Barker, R. L. (2003). *The social work dictionary* (5th ed.). NASW Press.

Bisman, C. (2004). Social work values: The moral code of the profession. *The British Journal of Social Work, 34*(1), 109–123.

Boutwell, A. E., Johnson, M. B., & Watkins, R. (2016). Analysis of a social work–based model of transitional care to reduce hospital readmissions: Preliminary data. *Journal of the American Geriatrics Society, 64*(5), 1104–1107.
CareWorks. (n.d.). *Solutions*. Retrieved March 8, 2023, from https://www.careworks.co.uk/solutions/
Carlisle, A. J., Tibrewala, A., Novak, E., Singh, J., & Amin, A. P. (2014). The 'frequent flyer' hypothesis and increased risk of thirty day readmission after percutaneous coronary intervention [Abstract]. *Circulation: Cardiovascular Quality and Outcomes, 7*(Suppl. 1).
Center for Health and Social Care Integration. (2022). *CHaSCI Care Model Toolkit* [Training materials]. Retrieved February 26, 2023, from https://www.chasci.org/s/CHaSCI-toolkit-2022.pdf
Chin, D., Rosenblatt, A., Simon, G., & Lauer, C. (2007). Straighttalk. Creating a climate of innovation: The healthcare industry's biggest challenge. Panel discussion. *Modern Healthcare, 37*(43), 39–42.
Choi, B. C. K., & Pak, A. W. P. (2006). Multidisciplinarity, interdisciplinarity and transdisciplinarity in health research, services, education and policy: 1. Definitions, objectives, and evidence of effectiveness. *Clinical and Investigative Medicine, 29*(6), 351–364.
Coleman, E. A., & Berenson, R. A. (2004). Lost in transition: Challenges and opportunities for improving the quality of transitional care. *Annals of Internal Medicine, 141*(7), 533–536. https://doi.org/10.7326/0003-4819-141-7-200410050-00009
Coulshed, V., & Orme, J. (2013). *Social work practice*. Bloomsbury Academic.
Council on Social Work Education. (2015). *Educational policy and accreditation standards for baccalaureate and master's social work programs*. Council on Social Work Education.
Council on Social Work Education. (2022). *Educational policy and accreditation standards*. Retrieved March 8, 2023, from https://www.cswe.org/getmedia/94471c42-13b8-493b-9041-b30f48533d64/2022-EPAS.pdf
Council on Social Work Education. (2023). *Specialized practice curricular guide for health social work*. Council on Social Work Education.
Davis, M. M., Devoe, M., Kansagara, D., Nicolaidis, C., & Englander, H. (2012). "Did I do as best as the system would let me?" Healthcare professional views on hospital to home care transitions. *Journal of General Internal Medicine, 27*(12), 1649–1656.
Ferraro, K. F., & Farmer, M. M. (1996). Double jeopardy to health hypothesis for African Americans: Analysis and critique. *Journal of Health and Social Behavior, 37*(1), 27–43.
George Washington University Health Workforce Institute. (2021). *Indicators of demand for recent master's of social work graduates: Findings from the 2018 Survey of Social Work Graduates*. George Washington University Health Workforce Institute.
Grazier, K. L. (2008). Healthcare industry in a perpetual state of flux. *Journal of Healthcare Management, 53*(3), 141.
Greene, R. R., & Kropf, N. P. (2014). *Caregiving: A caresharing perspective*. NASW Press.
Hepworth, D. H., Rooney, R., Rooney, G. D., & Strom, K. (2017). *Direct social work practice: Theory and skills* (10th ed.). Cengage.
Jones, B., Currin-McCulloch, J., Petruzzi, L., Phillips, F., & Smith, B. (2020). Transformative teams in health care: Enhancing social work student identity, voice and leadership in a longitudinal interprofessional education (IPE) course. *Advances in Social Work, 20*(2), 424–439.
NASW Foundation. (n.d.). *Social Work Policy Institute*. Retrieved May 1, 2023, from https://www.naswfoundation.org/Our-Work/Social-Work-Policy-Institute
National Academies of Sciences, Engineering, and Medicine. (2019). *Integrating social care into the delivery of health care: Moving upstream to improve the nation's health*. National Academies Press.
National Association of Social Workers. (2013). *NASW standards for social work case management*. National Association of Social Workers.
Office of the Surgeon General. (2017). *Social determinants of health*. Office of the Surgeon General.

Rapp, C. A., & Goscha, R. J. (2004). The principles of effective case management of mental health services. *Psychiatric Rehabilitation Journal, 27*(4), 319–333.
Reamer, F. G. (2018). Ethical standards for social workers' use of technology: Emerging consensus. *Journal of Social Work Values and Ethics, 15*(2), 71–80.
Schon, D. A. (1983). *The reflective practitioner: How professionals think in action*. Basic Books.
Singh, R., Küçükdeveci, A. A., Grabljevec, K., & Gray, A. (2018). The role of interdisciplinary teams in physical and rehabilitation medicine. *Journal of Rehabilitation Medicine, 50*(8), 673–678.
U.S. Census Bureau. (2019). *American Community Survey 3-year public use microdata samples* [SAS Data file]. Retrieved from https://factfinder.census.gov/faces/nav/jsf/pages/searchresults.xhtml?refresh=t
Weil, M., & Karls, J. (1985). *Case management in human service practice: A systematic approach to mobilizing resources for clients*. Jossey-Bass.
Wexler, L. (2009). The importance of identity, history, and culture in the wellbeing of indigenous youth. *Journal of the History of Childhood and Youth, 2*(2), 267–276.
World Health Organization. (2023). *Social determinants of health*. Retrieved May 11, 2023, from https://www.who.int/health-topics/social-determinants-of-health#tab=tab_1
Zerden, L. D. S., Cadet, T. J., Galambos, C., & Jones, B. (2020). Social work's commitment and leadership to address social determinants of health and integrate social care into health care. *Journal of Health and Human Services Administration, 43*(3), 309–323.

Supplemental References

Blaschke, C. M., Freddolino, P. P., & Mullen, E. E. (2009). Ageing and technology: A review of the research literature. *British Journal of Social Work, 39*(4), 641–656. https://doi.org/10.1093/bjsw/bcp025
Block, S. R., Wheeland, L., & Rosenberg, S. A. (2014). Improving human service effectiveness through the deconstruction of case management: A case study on the emergence of a team-based model of service coordination. *Human Service Organizations Management, Leadership & Governance, 38*(1), 16–28.
Calvillo-King, L., Arnold, D., Eubank, K. J., Lo, M., Yunyongying, P., Stieglitz, H., & Halm, E. A. (2013). Impact of social factors on risk of readmission or mortality in pneumonia and heart failure: Systematic review. *Journal of General Internal Medicine, 28*(2), 269–282.
Fabbre, V. D., Buffington, A. S., Altfeld, S. J., Shier, G. E., & Golden, R. L. (2011). Social work and transitions of care: Observations from an intervention for older adults. *Journal of Gerontological Social Work, 54*(6), 615–626.
Healthy People 2030. (n.d.). *Social determinants of health*. Retrieved May 8, 2023, from https://health.gov/healthypeople/objectives-and-data/social-determinants-health
National Association of Social Workers. (2020). *The social work profession: Findings from three years of surveys of new social workers*. National Association of Social Workers.

Chapter 7
Envisioning Functions and Skills for Resilience-Enhancing Nursing Home Social Workers

Roberta Greene, Nancy Greene, and Connie Corley

Learning Objectives

This chapter discusses the use of the anti-oppressive resilience-enhancing stress model (RESM) with people who are transitioning to life in a nursing home. A practice example illustrates the use of the RESM and how it may contribute to a more wide-ranging view of a nursing home social worker's role, functions, and skills. The hope is to support the maintenance of residents' positive social functioning and identity.

On completing this chapter, you will better envision what you might do as a nursing home social worker to contribute to the promotion of resilient social functioning among nursing home residents and their families by reducing risk and bolstering protective factors. RESM functions and skills to redress the stressors that disrupt care are presented. You should be prepared to answer the following questions:

- Why should the resilience of nursing home residents be viewed from a person–environment (P-E) systems perspective?
- How can the RESM be used to provide more far-reaching psychosocial care to enhance the resilient social functioning of nursing home residents, their families, and the volunteer community?

This chapter discusses practice ideas from the anti-oppressive resilience-enhancing social work model of practice that may contribute to the delivery of psychosocial

R. Greene
Steve Hicks School of Social Work, The University of Texas at Austin, Austin, TX, USA
e-mail: rgreene@utexas.edu

N. Greene
Ethelyn R. Strong School of Social Work, Norfolk State University, Norfolk, VA, USA
e-mail: nagreene@nsu.edu

C. Corley (✉)
Fielding Graduate University, Santa Barbara, CA, USA
e-mail: conniecorleyphd@gmail.com

R. Greene et al. (eds.), *Resilience Enhancement in Social Work Practice*,
https://doi.org/10.1007/978-3-031-38518-6_7

care in a nursing home environment. It specifically explores the use of resilience-enhancing social work methods and how these methods may add to the quality of care in nursing homes as well as improve nursing home life.

Despite critical milestones and decades of efforts to improve the quality of care in nursing homes, significant challenges remain. The enormous toll wrought by the COVID-19 pandemic on nursing home residents, their families, and staff brought renewed attention to the long-standing shortfalls that continue to plague nursing homes.

As the COVID-19 crisis grew more intense, the National Academies of Sciences, Engineering, and Medicine established a committee to update a previous study on the status of care in US nursing homes (Institute of Medicine, 1985). A 2022 report by the National Academies of Sciences, Engineering, and Medicine titled *The National Imperative to Improve Nursing Home Quality: Honoring Our Commitment to Residents, Families, and Staff* sounded the alarm about the poor status of care in many of the nation's nursing homes. The report called for "each and every resident in every nursing home" to receive "high-quality physical care, behavioral health, safety, and psychological support" (p. xviii). In addition, the report concluded that "the way in which the United States finances, delivers, and regulates care in nursing home settings is ineffective, inefficient, fragmented, and unsustainable" (p. 495) and argued for immediate action to initiate fundamental change. The remainder of this chapter describes how nursing home social workers can play a more active role in contributing to efforts to enhance psychosocial care.

7.1 Setting the Boundaries of Psychosocial Care

7.1.1 Mandating Psychosocial Care

According to the U.S. Centers for Medicare and Medicaid Services (2021), psychosocial care is associated with quality of care, resident assessment, and quality of life. Regulations mandate that nursing homes provide the necessary care and services for residents to attain or maintain the highest practicable physical, mental, and psychosocial well-being based on a comprehensive assessment and plan of care. The prevention of avoidable declines in social interaction, resident choice, and family involvement in care are also seen as necessary.

7.1.2 Professionalizing Psychosocial Care

The National Association of Social Workers (NASW, 2003) specifically addressed the professional parameters of social workers' role in nursing homes in *NASW Standards for Social Work Services in Long-Term Care Facilities* (Table 7.1). The

Table 7.1 NASW standards for social work services in long-term care facilities (2003)

Standard 1. Ethics and Values
Social workers in long-term care facilities shall demonstrate a commitment to the values and ethics of the social work profession, emphasizing resident empowerment and self-determination, and shall use NASW's *Code of Ethics* (2000) as a guide to ethical decision making.
Standard 2. Service Plan
The long-term care facility shall maintain a written plan for defining social work services designed to ensure their availability to all residents and their families. The plan for social work services shall be guided by a written statement of philosophy, objectives, and policies.
Standard 3. Responsibilities of Social Work Department
The social work director shall carry primary responsibility for social work services, including the development of organizational plans and administrative policies and procedures and coordination of services.
Standard 4. Program Functions
The functions of the social work program shall include, but not be limited to, direct services to residents, families, and other individuals involved with residents' care; advocacy; care planning, discharge planning and documentation; participation in policy and program planning; quality improvement; staff education pertaining to social services; liaison to the community; and consultation to other staff members.
Standard 5. Staffing
A sufficient number of appropriately trained licensed or credentialed and experienced social work and supportive personnel shall be available to plan, provide, evaluate, and modify all social work services.
Standard 6. Professional Development
Social workers in long-term care settings shall assume personal responsibility for their continued professional development in accordance with the *NASW Standards for Continuing Professional Education* (NASW, 2002) and state requirements.
Standard 7. Personnel Policies and Procedures
A written statement of the personnel policies and procedures of the facility for the social work department, the NASW *Code of Ethics*, and all other relevant NASW practice standards shall be available to each staff member.
Standard 8. Documentation
Documentation of social work services provided to residents, family members, and other individuals involved with the resident's care must be recorded in the medical record.
Standard 9. Work Environment
There should be adequate budget, space, facilities, and equipment to fulfill the professional and administrative needs of the social work program.
Standard 10. Cultural Competence
Social workers shall provide residents and their families with social services in the context of multicultural understanding and competence.
Standard 11. Interdisciplinary Collaboration
Social workers should be part of an interdisciplinary effort for the comprehensive delivery of long-term care services and should strive to enhance interdisciplinary and interorganizational cooperation. Social workers shall work in partnerships that include mutual respect, shared information, and effective communication.

Note. From National Association of Social Workers (2003). Used with permission

standards suggest procedures for social workers in social services departments to follow and suggest how social workers can work as members of the health care team. Standards were also put forth for high-quality ethical practice, professional development, work environment, and family engagement.

7.1.3 Advocating for Psychosocial Care

Social workers are members of nursing home professional health care teams who collaborate with other staff to deliver psychosocial care. In an editorial in the *Journal of the American Medical Directors Association*, social workers Kusmaul et al. (2022) responded to the report of the National Academies of Sciences, Engineering, and Medicine on the nursing home crisis as follows:

> The problem is simple: in nursing homes, psychosocial care and well-being have been, and in some cases remain, neglected, or regarded as secondary. Until we prioritize residents' quality of life and psychosocial care such that their importance is at least equal to that of their physical care, people will never want to live in a nursing home. (p. 1439)

7.1.4 Researching Social Workers' Delivery of Psychosocial Care

Past research on nursing home social work functions has shed some light on how social workers can participate in actualizing the requirement that nursing home residents receive high-quality psychosocial care by delineating the functions that should be performed by these workers (Vourlekis et al., 1992a, b). For example, NASW surveyed homes across the country and found that the following psychosocial needs were perceived as most important to nursing home residents:

- Support during the transition to the nursing home
- Help dealing with grief and loss
- Assistance with relatedness and intimacy issues (Vourlekis et al., 1992a)

A similar study documented that the following social work functions were the functions most often performed by departments of social work across the country:

- Talking with staff about the family's emotional needs
- Training staff on how to identify abuse
- Arranging transportation for residents to receive health care
- Recruiting and coordinating volunteers
- Helping feed residents at mealtime (Bern-Klug & Kramer, 2013)

7.2 Proposing RESM Social Worker Psychosocial Care Functions

The remainder of the chapter delineates psychosocial care needs and social work functions associated with the four phases of the RESM approach to nursing home practice. Functions in the four RESM practice phases include the following:

1. Engaging the resident at the time of the care transition
2. Assessing the resident from a risk and protection perspective
3. Intervening to cocreate new meaning for an event and helping the resident achieve the best possible resilient social functioning
4. Obtaining resident feedback

The complete list of functions appears in Table 7.2 and can be used to follow the chapter practice example in Box 7.1.

Box 7.1: Practice Example: A Transition from Living at Home to Residing in a Nursing Home

Rose was 64 years old and a new resident of Garden Springs Nursing Home. She had been admitted to the home because her multiple sclerosis (MS) had progressed to the stage that she and her family could no longer manage care at home. MS occurs when the immune system attacks the protective sheath (myelin) that covers nerve fibers, causing communication problems between the brain and the rest of the body (Mayo Clinic, 2023).

Nursing home admissions staff helped Rose and her daughter Rochelle complete the Minimum Data Set (MDS) admissions questionnaire required of all residents of long-term care nursing facilities certified to participate in Medicare or Medicaid. The MDS is a standardized federally mandated health status screening and assessment tool used to evaluate a resident's functional capabilities and health needs, including psychosocial, cognitive, and mobility status. It is a major source of care planning data used by nursing home care teams.

Following the completion of the MDS, Tanya, the nursing home social worker, met with Rose to cocreate a narrative that would further reveal an understanding of Rose as a whole person. This would provide additional vital psychosocial information for care planning.

Tanya learned that Rose was a retired tour director in a US company with more than 20 years of work experience. During that time, Rose had made many relationships with company employees and amassed hundreds of photographs. Upon her admission to the home, Rose and Rochelle spoke sadly about Rose's growing withdrawal and sense of isolation from her former life.

Table 7.2 Envisioning functions and skills for resilience-enhancing nursing home social workers

RESM nursing home social workers
Acknowledge residents' and families' feelings during their care transition
Get to know residents as whole people
Become aware of residents' past role performance
Enable residents to continue performing preferred activities and behaviors
Facilitate residents' expression of and continuity of self
Encourage resident opportunities and choice
Ameliorate risk and strengthen the saliency of multilevel protective factors
Learn about the significant people in residents' lives and work to maintain those relationships
Seek innovative means of linking residents with others
Mutually reflect on residents' narratives
Support and promote residents' environmental competence within their cultural context
Collaborate with residents to create new meanings of life events
Mutually deconstruct and reconstruct resident narratives
Support the highest level of residents' social functioning
Act as part of a team with nursing home staff
Strive to effect a home-like, person-centered nursing home environment
Participate in state oversight and accreditation processes for the nursing home
Monitor, report, and try to ameliorate abuses of nursing home practices, regulations, and rules

Note. RESM resilience-enhancing stress model

7.3 Engagement

Social workers need to recognize that being admitted to a nursing home is often a difficult, stressful care transition at best. New residents may be leery of what lies ahead and even fearful of how they can manage in their new environment. Although a social worker's engagement of a nursing home resident builds on information from the MDS questionnaire, it goes well beyond this.

New residents may perceive the transition as timely, untimely, or both. For example, Rose's physical condition made it difficult to maintain care in the home. However, her readiness to move into a nursing home had the potential to exacerbate her feelings of social isolation and withdrawal. RESM engagement is critical for helping social workers gain residents' trust and help them (and their families) deal with the stressors involved in the transition to nursing home life.

The prospect that Rose might experience a sense of loss during her transition to Garden Springs tested Tanya's ability to be empathetic. How could Tanya truly imagine how Rose was feeling? Tanya used the skill of genuineness to acknowledge that Rose's admission to the home must have been a double-edged sword—an unwelcome symbol of the progression of her MS but a welcome break in the overwhelming struggle to manage care at home. These concerns were pursued further during Rose's psychosocial social work assessment.

7.4 Assessment

7.4.1 Providing Health Care Based on Clients' Narratives

During a RESM assessment, the social worker collaborates with the resident to coconstruct a narrative. The purpose is to identify risks that are to be ameliorated and reveal protective factors that may be bolstered. These data then lead to mutually agreed-on interventions that may be incorporated into the resident's care plan. Box 7.2 provides a brief list of social work functions that can be carried out with individual residents as they transition to life in a nursing home environment.

Box 7.2: Practice Steps: Nursing Home Social Worker and Individual Resilience Checklist

When I meet with residents, I will

- Learn about their life story
- Help raise their consciousness about their capacity to function as members of the nursing home system
- Identify and encourage activities that promote residents' social participation
- Promote residents' capacity to reach out to others
- Help residents connect with people in their social environment
- Discover and try to ameliorate the discriminatory institutionalized policies that impact residents' lives

7.4.2 Mapping Risks

A resilience-enhancing P-E assessment perspective allows the social worker and resident to evaluate responses to risks at a range of levels, from micro- to macrolevel. The major goal is to learn about the resident's balance between risk and protective factors so that risks may be reduced, and protective factors strengthened. Major risks for nursing home residents are loneliness and lack of social connections. To map risk and protective factors, social workers may ask some of the questions in Box 7.3.

Box 7.3: Questions for Nursing Home Residents: Mapping Risks at Admission

- Is the resident feeling a sense of grief or loss?
- Will the resident be able to maintain a positive sense of personal identity?
- How can the resident experience the best quality of life or P-E fit in his or her new home?
- Does the resident experience any problems that are perceived as oppressive in nature?

7.4.3 Uncovering Protective Factors

As stated in Chap. 5, the social worker and client begin to understand the client's situation and concerns as they have a conversation about what can be done to resolve present difficulties or concerns. To uncover a resident's protective factors, it is important to remember the adage that "the person is not the disease." According to Clark (2001), a patient's narrative or story can have two major life plots: (a) Victims portray their lives as passive and outside of their control. Their stories are problem oriented. (b) Agents are ready to make choices and start something new. Their stories can be rewritten to become goal oriented. In making this distinction, Tanya wanted to avoid depersonalizing Rose. As the narrative was cocreated, Tanya explored some of the questions in Box 7.4.

Box 7.4: Questions for Nursing Home Residents: Mapping Protective Factors at Admission

- How did the resident experience or appraise the meaning of her diagnosis of MS?
- What activities and roles had been important to the resident before the disease emerged?
- What valued activities and roles could the resident continue to perform?
- Did the resident envision a future that she cared about?
- Could the resident prioritize her goals for life at Garden Springs? (Clark, 2001)

7.4.4 Interviewing for a RESM Assessment

The outcome of a RESM assessment is an assessment profile that maps the indicators of a client's P-E dimensions or the balance between risk and protection. In nursing home care, the data are reviewed as part of care planning with other staff members. An excerpt from an early assessment interview during which Tanya began to cocreate Rose's narrative is presented in Box 7.5.

Box 7.5: Practice Example: Acknowledging Loss

Tanya:	I know you are just trying to settle in to life at Garden Springs. When I first met you and your daughter at admission, you mentioned there were times when you felt alone. Can you tell me more about that?
Rose:	It is so hard to even think about it.
Tanya:	Yes, it is. Maybe we can begin by talking about what you miss. Life can seem more different from what we can ever imagine. I see you worked for many years as a tour director. Can we start out by talking about why you chose that line of work?
Rose:	That was so many years ago. I was so young and loved to travel. Every city was on my bucket list or wish list. I wanted to go everywhere!
Tanya:	What were your top two cities?
Rose:	New York and San Francisco.
Tanya:	What did you like about them?
Rose:	These are cities you must see by taking walking tours. Oh, I remember how wonderful it was to walk the hills of San Francisco or the paths of New York City's Central Park. Now I can barely make it to the dining room.
Tanya:	I think that change would be very hard. Is it too soon to consider how these important memories can be revisited?
Rose:	I have a box of slides in my daughter's garage—so many slides.
Tanya:	Maybe your daughter can bring those slides here so we can see some of them together.
Rose:	There are too many to sort through.
Tanya:	Maybe among the three of us we can come up with an idea.
Rose:	You think so? I am not so sure. I must warn you—it could take forever to sort through those slides.
Tanya:	Is it okay to ask your daughter to bring them?
Rose:	Yes, I guess so. You're awfully optimistic!

7.4.4.1 Practice Example Analysis: Steps Taken

This example from Rose's assessment interview illustrates how narratives can begin to uncover important behaviors and events in a client's life. Tanya's purpose was to use the interview to further reveal ways to enhance Rose's resiliency in her nursing home life. A later interview explored how Rose's daughter Rochelle and a community volunteer could sort the slides. Tanya wondered to herself whether the activity director could later arrange for Rose to lead a Friday night virtual city tour. If Rose agreed, she could be on a path to combatting her sense of social isolation.

7.4.5 Determining the Balance Between Risk and Protection

The cocreation of the narrative set-in motion Rose's capacity to reduce risks and strengthen protective factors. Tanya's main goal was to learn what Rose thought would help her achieve the most optimal or practicable level of functioning in the nursing home. Tanya obtained Rose's assessment data using the P-E assessment chart and the questions in Box 7.6. These data were summarized in the assessment profile, as shown in Table 7.3.

Box 7.6: Questions: P-E Assessment Profile Questions for Rose

- What were Rose's responses to past critical events?
- What were Rose's reactions to the disruption of biopsychosocial processes?
- What was Rose's daughter's capacity to restructure family care under stress?
- What were envisioned as the consequences of bolstering Rose's social supports?
- How could the nursing home be perceived as a more favorable environment?

7.5 Multisystemic Intervention

The deconstruction and reconstruction of client narratives is central to RESM interventions. The purpose is to reduce risks/stress, support protective factors, and enhance resilience by rewriting a client's story. This was accomplished when Tanya collaborated with Rose to challenge the meaning of negative life events.

Table 7.3 Person–environment (P-E) assessment chart: Rose and her daughter Rochelle

P-E dimension	Indicator
Consequences of time and place	Rose experienced the need to live in a nursing home as a loss but eventually came to terms with it.
Response to the stress of past critical events	Rose had been a successful and well-organized tour director. She was better able to adjust to living at Garden Springs Nursing Home when she reviewed these successes.
Reaction to disruption of biopsychosocial and spiritual processes	Rose perceived that her diagnosis of muscular sclerosis omit dystrophy led to social isolation and withdrawal. However, she gradually reengaged with others.
Family response to adversity or change	Rose's daughter Rochelle transitioned caregiving activities from the home to the nursing home. Rochelle joined with a community volunteer to sort Rose's tour slides with the goal of creating a virtual travel tour.
Consequences of social supports	Rochelle and a community volunteer collaborated to help Rose maintain a sense of positive self and resiliency.
Significance of favorable environments	The nursing home staff incorporated social support activities into Rose's care plan, making the environment more nurturing.

7.5.1 *Externalizing the Problem*

The question for Tanya and Rose was how Rose could separate from or externalize the problem of MS—or, as stated best by O'Hanlon (1994), how they could avoid the "hazard of being captured by [the] client's despair" (p. 24). Osis and Stout (2001) contended that by giving prompts during the narrative that move the narrator's storyline back and forth between past, present, and future, clinicians can help the client develop meaning or a framework for purpose in his or her life. The outcome can be a new preferred story and identity based on the ability to reengage with a positive sense of self as well as connect with others. The skills in Box 7.7 may assist social workers in this process.

Box 7.7: Skill Box: Externalizing the Problem

Skill	Definition	Practitioner statement
Not knowing	Acknowledging the practitioner's need to learn	"I don't know as much as I would like. Can you tell me more?"
Individualizing client identity	Addressing the client's life (course) and influential experiences	"Are any past events more important to you now than others?"
Appraisal	Reflecting on the client's life events	"I am wondering what you think that means."
Meaning-making	Using reflection to generate new ideas that reconstruct a narrative	"Can we begin to make any sense of that?"
Interpretation	Hypothesizing about meaning	"I think X could be the case, but I'm not sure."

7.5.2 *Connecting to Family*

Supporting the family's participation in the life of a nursing home resident is a critical role of the nursing home social worker (Greene, 1982). This is particularly true at the time of admission when new residents and their families are facing the crisis of institutionalized care (see Box 7.8). When a family such as Rose's has a resident's permission to take part in planning care, it adds an important dimension to understanding the resident's psychosocial care needs. Because Tanya effectively engaged Rose's daughter Rochelle at the time of admission, Rochelle was later available to enrich Rose's life and the lives of other residents.

Box 7.8: Practice Steps: Nursing Home Social Worker and Family Checklist
When I meet with residents' families, I will

- Learn about the family's narrative
- Help raise family members' consciousness about their capacity to function within the nursing home system
- Help families remain connected with their family member by promoting their capacity to reach out to one another
- Identify and encourage activities that promote family members' social participation in nursing home activities

7.5.3 Training Staff

Staff turnover and adequate training are important to nursing quality and resiliency. Nursing home data reported to the Centers for Medicare and Medicaid Services suggest that roughly 50% of nursing homes have annual turnover rates between 40% and 60%. This means that half the nursing homes in the United States must replace half their staff each year (Bern-Klug & Kramer, 2013). Social workers may play a role in ensuring that the training new staff receive is designed to meet the unique demographic, cultural, linguistic, and transportation needs of the community in which the nursing home is situated.

Staff may also be trained on how to have better conversations with the residents they serve. These trainings may address *ageism*, or anti-ageist societal attitudes that may lead to resident neglect. Staff-centered social work practice skills are listed in Box 7.9.

Box 7.9: Practice Steps: Nursing Home Social Worker and Staff Resilience Checklist
When I meet and interact with nursing home staff, I will

- Understand and respect how they perceive the climate or culture of the nursing home
- Help staff connect positively with residents and family members
- Help raise staff members' consciousness about ways in which they can function as protective factors for nursing home residents
- Promote staff members' capacity to work as a team on behalf of residents and families

7.5.4 Recruiting Community Volunteers

Most nursing home residents are frail people who can benefit from social support and a strengthening of connections to their community. In a study by social work researchers Greene et al. (2005), nursing home residents indicated that intergenerational visits from local children and youth were a favored best practice. This underscores residents' psychosocial need to live lives within a community of others within the context of a specific institution (Osis & Stout, 2001, p. 273). Box 7.10 suggests further community-related functions that social workers can initiate.

Box 7.10: Practice Steps: Nursing Home Social Worker and Community Checklist

When I meet and interact with community members, I will

- Help raise community members' consciousness about their capacity to act as volunteers with nursing home residents
- Identify and encourage activities that promote volunteers' social participation in the lives of residents and the home
- Bolster community members' capacity to work as part of the nursing home team on behalf of residents, families, and staff

7.5.5 Advocating for Sound Regulations and Policy

Nursing home social workers have first-hand knowledge of the psychosocial care needs of nursing home residents and therefore are highly suited to sharing ideas about nursing home regulations. For example, groups such as the National Nursing Home Social Work Network give opinions to the Centers for Medicare and Medicaid Services about their views on changes to regulations posted in the *Federal Register*. (The *Federal Register* is a publication of the US federal government that disseminates possible rule changes for comment; see U.S. Centers for Medicare and Medicaid Services, 2021.) Social work policy practice skills are listed in Box 7.11.

Box 7.11: Practice Steps: Nursing Home Social Worker, Home Regulator, and Social Policy Checklist

When I interact with regulators and policy makers, I will

- Help raise surveyors' consciousness about the effects of rules and regulations on nursing home residents
- Identify and advocate for activities that enhance the resilient social functioning of nursing home residents

7.6 Evaluation

7.6.1 Certifying a Nursing Facility

Each state is responsible for sending a specially trained team to conduct on-site surveys to evaluate a nursing home's compliance or noncompliance with standards of care, subject to approval by the Centers for Medicare and Medicaid Services. During the survey, surveyors select patients at random and use their medical records to evaluate compliance with standards. In addition, they trace a patient's experience in the health care organization by talking to the doctors, nurses, and other staff who have interacted with the patient. They also observe doctors and nurses providing care and often speak to the patients themselves.

7.6.2 Evaluating Nursing Home Social Work Function

As with all social work practice, social workers should monitor their professional use of self as they deliver person-centered psychosocial care. Feedback on whether they are meeting resident personal goals is also important. Table 5.4, the Person–Environment Goal Setting and Evaluation Chart, in Chap. 5 may be used to map this process. For example, how successful did Rose think she was in enhancing her ties to social supports?

7.7 Summary and Conclusion

As can be seen from the practice example in this chapter, Tanya aimed to help Rose achieve the best possible social functioning as she transitioned to life at Garden Springs. However, nursing home social workers attend to more than just an individual resident's psychosocial well-being. The overarching or core psychosocial care function of RESM social workers is to connect nursing home residents with people in their multifaceted environments and to interact with the nursing home team to establish a resilient culture for all residents.

Summary of Learning Outcomes
Keep in mind the following:

- Nursing home social workers can advocate for nursing home residents' psychosocial needs.
- Nursing home social workers can engage residents in narratives that promote a P-E fit and lead to resilient social functioning.

Discussion Questions

1. Why is continuity in self-identity important to resiliency in nursing home life?
2. Why is systems thinking important to social work nursing home practice?

Chapter Exercise

Write a one-page reflection paper on how you think you would feel if you were in Rose's shoes and being admitted to Garden Springs Nursing Home.

Glossary

Advocating Promoting policy based on facts and client evidence.

Ageism A form of discrimination that devalues people based on their age.

Balancing risk and protection Exploring harmful and beneficial environmental factors.

Certified nursing facility A skilled nursing home that complies with standards of health and psychosocial health care.

Minimum Data Set A tool used to delineate and assess the health status, needs, and functional capacity of nursing home residents.

Multisystemic intervention The use of helping strategies across micro- and macrolevels.

Psychosocial care Care for individual needs that keeps social factors in mind.

Quality of care The level of care and services necessary to attain or maintain the highest practicable physical, mental, and psychosocial well-being based on a comprehensive assessment and plan of care.

Staff-centered training Training that focuses on the educational needs and culture(s) of staff.

Systems thinking A way of thinking that examines the functioning of a group or system as a whole.

References

Bern-Klug, M., & Kramer, K. W. O. (2013). Core functions of nursing home social services departments in the United States. *Journal of the American Medical Directors Association, 14*(1), 75.e1–75.e7.

Clark, P. (2001). Narrative gerontology in clinical practice: Current applications and future prospects. In G. Kenyon, P. Clark, & B. de Vries (Eds.), *Narrative gerontology: Theory, research, and practice* (pp. 193–214). Springer.

Greene, R. R. (1982). Families and the nursing home social worker. *Social Work in Health Care, 7*(3), 57–67.
Greene, R., Graham, S., Haulotte, S., & Gleason-Wynn, P. (2005). The nursing home crisis: A consumer study of Texas nursing home care. *Journal of Gerontological Social Work, 45*(4), 101–123.
Institute of Medicine. (1985). *Improving the quality of care in nursing homes*. Institute of Medicine.
Kusmaul, N., Galambos, C., & Zimmerman, S. (2022). The key to wanting to live in a nursing home. *Journal of the American Medical Directors Association, 23*(9), 1439–1441.
Mayo Clinic (2023). *Multiple Sclerosis*. Retrieved July 30, 2023 from https://www.mayoclinic.org/diseases-conditions/multiple-sclerosis/symptoms-causes/syc-20350269
National Academies of Sciences, Engineering, and Medicine. (2022). *The national imperative to improve nursing home quality: Honoring our commitment to residents, families, and staff*. National Academies of Sciences, Engineering, and Medicine.
National Association of Social Workers. (2000). *Code of ethics of the National Association of Social Workers*. National Association of Social Workers.
National Association of Social Workers. (2002). *NASW standards for continuing professional education*. National Association of Social Workers.
National Association of Social Workers. (2003). *NASW standards for social work services in long-term care facilities*. Retrieved January 6, 2023, from https://www.socialworkers.org/LinkClick.aspx?fileticket=cwW7lzBfYxg%3d&portalid=0; https://naswpress.org/product/53604/nasw-standards-for-social-work-services-in-long-term-care-facilities
O'Hanlon, B. (1994). The third wave. *Networker, 18*(6), 19–29.
Osis, M., & Stout, L. (2001). Using narrative therapy with older adults. In G. Kenyon, P. Clark, & B. de Vries (Eds.), *Narrative gerontology: Theory, research, and practice* (pp. 273–290). Springer.
U.S. Centers for Medicare and Medicaid Services. (2021). *About CMS*. Retrieved May 5, 2023, from https://www.cms.gov/About-CMS/About-CMS
Vourlekis, B. S., Gelfand, D. E., & Greene, R. R. (1992a). Psychosocial needs and care in nursing homes: Comparison of views of social workers and home administrators. *The Gerontologist, 32*(1), 113–119. https://doi.org/10.1093/geront/32.1.113
Vourlekis, B. S., Greene, R. R., Gelfand, D. E., & Zlotnik, J. L. (1992b). Searching for the doable in nursing home social work practice. *Social Work in Health Care, 17*(3), 45–70.

Supplemental References

Davis, M. M., Devoe, M., Kansagara, D., Nicolaidis, C., & Englander, H. (2012). "Did I do as best as the system would let me?" Healthcare professional views on hospital to home care transitions. *Journal of General Internal Medicine, 27*(12), 1649–1656.
Greene, R., Graham, S., Haulotte, S., & Gleason-Wynn, P. (2005). The nursing home crisis: A consumer study of Texas nursing home care. *Journal of Gerontological Social Work, 45*(4), 101–123.
Greene, R. R., Vourlekis, B. S., Gelfand, D. E., & Lewis, J. S. (1992). Current realities: Practice and education needs of social workers in nursing homes. *Journal of Gerontological Social Work, 18*(3/4), 39–54.
Lyng, H. B., Ree, E., Wibe, T., & Wiig, S. (2021). Healthcare leaders' use of innovative solutions to ensure resilience in healthcare during the Covid-19 pandemic: A qualitative study in Norwegian nursing homes and home care services. *BMC Health Services Research, 21*(1), 878.

Simons, K. V. (2006). Organizational characteristics influencing nursing home social service directors' qualifications: A national study. *Health & Social Work, 31*(4), 266–274.

Vourlekis, B., Zlotnik, J. L., Simons, K., & Yoni, R. (2005). *Blueprint for measuring social work's contribution to psychosocial care in nursing homes: Results of a national conference*. Retrieved May 8, 2023, from https://www.bu.edu/cader/files/2010/03/FinalIGSW-IASWRBriefWinter2005.pdf

Chapter 8
Resilience-Enhancing Skills for Developmental Transitions: Children with Autism Spectrum Disorder

Roberta Greene and Jackie Bartell

Learning Objectives

This chapter describes the role of a social worker who served on an interdisciplinary therapeutic team that combined skills from the resilience-enhancing stress model (RESM) with techniques from child and family therapy to assist a family with a child who had autism spectrum disorder (ASD). Practice examples illustrate the use of these skills as the respective members of the interdisciplinary school-based educational team collaborated to ameliorate the symptoms of the child's ASD and to enhance the relationships and communication patterns of the child–family unit. On completing this chapter, you should be better able to act on a team as a school social worker who endeavors to improve the social functioning of child–family units experiencing difficulties in social functioning. You should be prepared to answer the following questions:

- What risks and protective factors associated with ASD are revealed during the cocreation of the child–family narrative?
- Why do strengthening child–family connections act as a protective factor for a child–family unit?
- How can a child–family narrative be coconstructed, deconstructed, and reconstructed to improve social functioning and reflect an optimistic future?
- What are the major features of an interdisciplinary team?

R. Greene
Steve Hicks School of Social Work, The University of Texas at Austin, Austin, TX, USA
e-mail: rgreene@utexas.edu

J. Bartell (✉)
ICDL Expert Training Leader/Special Education Teacher, Rochester, NY, USA
e-mail: jackiebartell626@gmail.com

R. Greene et al. (eds.), *Resilience Enhancement in Social Work Practice*,
https://doi.org/10.1007/978-3-031-38518-6_8

Box 8.1: Practice Example: Charlie Barton Enters School

The Barton family–child unit was receiving at-home services from an early interventionist to ameliorate difficulties in social functioning associated with their son Charlie's diagnosis of ASD. Mr. and Mrs. Barton and their 12-year-old daughter, Stephanie, had been trained to use a Developmental, Individual-differences, and Relationship-based (DIR) model called DIRFloortime to foster Charlie's use of communication and thinking skills necessary for optimal social participation. The family was experiencing anticipatory stress as they awaited a change from at-home treatment to school-based interventions at Lincoln Elementary School, where Charlie would be attending kindergarten. They were aware that Charlie faced sensorimotor and developmental risks that needed to be addressed in his treatment plan.

The educational/therapeutic team at Lincoln Elementary School met to prepare for a new school year by getting to know their incoming students. The team included the early interventionist, Ralph, the current teacher/developmental specialist, Arlene; the social worker, Harris; and the receiving teacher, Maria.

School social workers provide services related to the social and emotional lives of students and their families as well as their adjustment to school and/or society. Most important, they support students' academic and social success and are important links between the home, school, and community (School Social Work Association of America, n.d.). Rather than working in a social service agency, school social workers are employed in what is known as a host setting, often as members of a professional educational team.

This chapter describes the Barton family and the ongoing developmental challenges associated with their child Charlie's diagnosis of ASD. It explores the cutting-edge role a team social worker might take to support the resilience of such a family during a difficult life transition. The practice example in Box 8.1 introduces the child–family unit as they were preparing to transition from receiving services from an at-home early interventionist to receiving them from a school-based interdisciplinary team that included a developmental specialist/special education teacher and a school social worker. The team members implemented selected aspects of the RESM augmented with therapeutic play and family therapy skills and techniques to meet the goal of ameliorating issues of social functioning related to ASD.

8.1 A Perspective on ASD

The first step in creating a cohesive school-based team was for its members to gain a common perspective on the nature of Charlie's ASD. They turned to a statement from the National Institute of Mental Health (2022) that defines ASD as a neurological and developmental disorder that affects how people interact with others, communicate, learn, and behave. The statement goes on to say that ASD can be diagnosed at any age and that its manifestations are highly variable, ranging from a nonspeaking student to a language-capable student all with a wide range of academic capabilities. Despite this variation in symptoms, the team members agreed that their efforts would focus on treating ASD as a process that is linked to the learned capacity to communicate and interact positively with the environment (Muhle et al., 2004).

8.2 Defining Developmental Ecological Systems

Another point of consensus for the school-based treatment team was their adoption of Bronfenbrenner's (1979) well-known bioecological theory of human development as their theoretical lens for understanding child development. Bronfenbrenner's approach was in accordance with the team's person–environment (P-E) approach, which underscored development as the "scientific study of the progressive, mutual accommodation, throughout the life course between an active, growing human being and his or her environment" (Bronfenbrenner, 1979, p. 188). Bronfenbrenner's theory expanded on this view, suggesting that a child's unique temperament and physiology is shaped by the multiple nested systems—family, community, and society—in which development occurs. These common theoretical lenses were used to assist the Barton family.

8.3 Tracing Developmental Resilient Pathways

Bronfenbrenner's ecological theory of human development is akin to the RESM concept of developmental resilient pathways. The idea of tracing a client's developmental resilient pathway is a RESM assessment tool members of Charlie's treatment team used to explore how to combat the Barton family's stress and risks and support their protective factors and resilience. The goal was for all team members to purposefully interrupt the negative trajectory of the Bartons' developmental path and to enhance those factors that affirm healthy development. These interventions were also intended to increase Charlie's sense of competence.

8.4 Learning About DIRFloortime®

The members of the school-based team agreed that they would become knowledgeable about the general concepts and skills that made up DIRFloortime, a person-centered relationship-based developmental model. The early interventionist explained that the knowledge he provided could serve as a general guide for better understanding a child with ASD in terms of the child's feelings, relationships with caregivers, functional emotional developmental capacity, and individual differences in his or her ability to process and respond to sensory information (Mercer, 2017). The team subscribed to the model's primary construct, which suggests that a child must first begin to attain healthy relationships that foster emotional development to move forward and feel comfortable interacting with and connecting to others in the environment.

When utilizing DIRFloortime, a child increases their capacity to form relationships that foster development. DIRFloortime uses relationships to support children around their sensory processing challenges. Children start to acquire skills that serve as a foundation for communication and other higher level thinking capacities so they are able to engage and interact with caregivers, parents, and instructional experiences in the learning arena. As seen in Table 8.1, the major premises of DIRFloortime are congruent with the RESM, as both models share a number of terms and assumptions, especially the assumption that progress in treatment is founded on building relationships.

Table 8.1 The resilience-enhancing stress model and DIRFloortime: joint terms and assumptions

Connections. Connections between and among people come about as they interact and communicate with others
Developmental turning points. Developmental turning points are naturally occurring. This is especially true when developmental processes converge to provide an opportunity for people to make changes in their social functioning (Masten, 2014)
Emotional development. Emotional development is a necessary correlate of social development. It occurs when a person is more able to regulate their sensory and motor systems, communicate, and act within a social system
Individualizing assessment. The assessment of child development is tailored to each child–family unit and is based on unique responses to person–environment dimensions
Life course approach. The developmental resilient path is a life course perspective that is nonlinear and not on a prescribed timeline. Rather, it is a depiction of people's journey as they interact with and respond to others in their environment
Person centeredness. A helping process is person-centered when the professional follows the client's lead and interests as well as the client's unique developmental capacity
Reciprocal relationships. Reciprocal relationships form when individuals connect with others in a social system through the roles they occupy in it. The roles that a person with autism spectrum disorder plays can be fostered and affirmed
Resilience. Resiling starts when someone perceives an environmental challenge or threat. Children with autism spectrum disorder have underlying processing differences in how they manage to meet a threat
Therapeutic relationship. A therapeutic client–social worker relationship is a nonhierarchical partnership that enhances a resilient response

8.5 Organizing the Treatment Team

Each member of the Lincoln Elementary school-based team had a different profession, yet they all needed to work together to achieve the same goals and provide a cohesive treatment plan. The practice example in Box 8.2 describes a meeting of the family and school personnel during which they began to plan how to support Charlie in his transition from home-based treatment to school.

The conversation included Charlie's family, the Bartons, and the treatment team. Draft treatment goals were formulated by the school team and were reviewed at the family transition meeting. The goals included the following:

1. Beginning a risk and protective factor assessment of the Barton family–child unit
2. Developing an individualized transition plan for Charlie and his family based on the assessment

Box 8.2: Practice Example: A Team Conversation as Charlie Enters Kindergarten

Harris:	Thank you all for coming together to talk about Charlie's transition to kindergarten. We know the Bartons gave permission to the early interventionist to send a formal report to school personnel. Based on that report, our team sent you an email about possible treatment goals that our group has for Charlie. Feedback during this meeting will be much appreciated. Can we each take a turn giving our opinion? Let's start by hearing from the family.
Mrs. Barton:	I want to go first and thank Ralph, our interventionist, who helped bring us to this point. Charlie is so much more responsive and is paying a lot more attention to things going on around the house.
Mr. Barton:	I agree. I am only hoping to see him get even further ahead in school.
Harris:	What do you think that would look like? What would you wish to see?
Arlene:	Yes, it would be helpful for me to know your goals.
Maria:	I would like to know them too.
Mrs. Barton:	In the past, Charlie has been so reactive, especially to loud noises. But now he is more engaged with me. We can share a series of short back-and-forth conversations. But I too would like to see him get even more involved with people.

Arlene:	Those interactions can sometimes happen in a classroom. We try to support students playing in groups and talking with one another.
Ralph:	I know that our team will build on the ways the Bartons have engaged Charlie. You have been successful so far in encouraging Charlie to experience the world around him.
Mr. Barton:	Charlie has started to actively participate in family activities. He loves to dance. Just yesterday he participated in a dance party with his sister, Stephanie! My wish is for him to learn school things, like math and reading. And be able to make friends.
Stephanie:	Yeah, but could he try to talk to me more?
Arlene:	How do you feel he will experience his first days at school?
Mrs. Barton:	I hope he is not too afraid.
Harris:	You will be getting feedback as we move along. Would you like to keep this conversation going? I wonder if the family would be willing to have a meeting with me and our developmental specialist once or twice a month.

Box 8.3: Skill Box: RESM Team Skills

Skill	Practitioner statement
Establishing a transparent agenda	"The team has reviewed Charlie's progress to date. We need your feedback"
Listening to multiple voices	"We would like to get all your opinions"
Reflecting on expressed needs	"It sounds like you have more goals you want Charlie to achieve. We are going to take them into consideration"

3. Continuing to support Charlie and his family on their developmental resilient path
4. Identifying and initiating steps to support Charlie's further development as a causal agent better able to make choices and initiate action

8.5.1 Practice Example Analysis

The conversation between the family and professional team revealed that Charlie's DIRFloortime therapy with the early interventionist had improved his communication and increased his attention span. Charlie had also developed an interest in family activities, such as dancing. The conversation also clarified that the family had additional developmental goals, such as seeing Charlie talk more and learn math and reading (see Box 8.3).

8.6 Family Resilience Theory and Family-Focused Social Work Practice

The primary goal of the school social worker was to assist the Barton family–child unit in enhancing their resilience and attaining increased social functioning. To accomplish this task, he relied on seven practice principles:

1. Understanding the family as a system
2. Enlisting the family as a member of the therapeutic team
3. Comprehending family communication styles
4. Exploring family role development
5. Respecting family belief systems and narratives
6. Mapping family developmental resilient pathways
7. Helping reconstruct the family narrative (Greene et al., 2019)

8.6.1 Supporting Family Resilience

According to Walsh (1997), family resilience involves a family struggling with, effectively working through, understanding, and making meaning of adversity. Harris, the school social worker, turned to general systems theory (as embedded in the RESM) to guide his understanding of the resiliency of the family as a unit. This required that he gain an understanding of the Barton family as a system with unique communication, organizational, and developmental patterns as well as its own belief system.

8.6.2 Enlisting the Family as a Member of the Team

A major protective factor for families with children who have ASD is being able to secure appropriate educational and therapeutic services as well as establish and maintain relationships with service providers. At the same time, service providers form a partnership with the family (Bayat & Schuntermann, 2013). As can be seen by the example of the Barton family's participation, this can be better accomplished when the family is considered a member of the treatment team.

8.6.3 Understanding Family Communication

Communication is the flow of information within a system or a way of transmitting information between two or more family members. A continuous interchange of this kind is also the basis for forming positive ongoing family relationships (Walsh, 2006). The most pertinent aspect of communication in families with members with

ASD is that there is always some form of communication, whether it be silence, a verbal tirade, a pout, a shrug, formal speech, a smile, or a tear. That is, communication may be verbal or nonverbal (Greene & Dubus, 2017).

8.6.4 Exploring Family Role Development

Family development needs to be appreciated from a systemic point of view. Translating the concept of reciprocal roles into systems terms means that no one family member develops in isolation. Rather, as family members respond to stressors, and to one another, they shift and alter their mutual role relationships. In other words, at each stage of life, people perform new roles, adjust to changing roles, and relinquish old ones (Greene, 2008). Over time, family members come to expect certain behaviors of one another depending on their respective definition of a particular situation (Goffman, 1963).

A social worker's understanding of how DIRFloortime influences role transformation contributes to the restructuring of the family with a member who has ASD. In this context, DIRFloortime activities become a modified form of communication that fosters child's ability to interact with his or her parents. These interactions, which may involve increasing levels of communication, may eventually lead to the child performing new roles.

8.6.5 Comprehending Belief Systems and Family Narratives

In addition to family role formation, family interaction creates a set of culturally specific attitudes, beliefs, and values. This *family belief system* can be understood when social workers listen for and interpret narrative themes. In short, the therapeutic skills of listening to and reflecting on a family narrative became central to school team members' ability to assess and intervene in a family's developmental resilient path.

8.6.6 Mapping a Client's Developmental Resilient Pathway

As stated before, mapping a developmental resilient pathway is a major technique used in the RESM. Social workers apply the concept to trace people's interpersonal interactions or social connections across time. They then partner with the client to reflect on whether the critical event is perceived as a risk or protective factor. As shown in Box 8.4, children who experience the risks associated with ASD may need family support.

Box 8.4: Practice Example: A Team Conversation With Charlie's Family

Arlene:	Thank you for coming in for an update. My colleagues and I would like to know if Charlie brought any new behaviors home.
Harris:	Have you seen any changes since school began?
Mrs. Barton:	Yes, there have already been several. Charlie seems to get into more conversations. We've noticed him engaging more with his sister. He also talks about the boy who sits next to him in class. He wanted to know if he could play ball with him. Maybe he can ask him?
Arlene:	That is great! We also like to hear that he is getting together with his sister.
Mr. Barton:	Still another achievement! Charlie was able to stay with me while I watched a basketball game. I can't begin to say how great it was to share a game! He used to run away from the TV noise, but he seems to handle it more easily now.
Arlene:	I also noticed something similar. When Charlie first came to school, he had a hard time with my joyful loud efforts to welcome him to class. I then learned to welcome him by using less loud language and fewer gestures.

8.6.6.1 Practice Example Analysis

The school-based team met to take progress notes on how the family and therapeutic team were experiencing Charlie's development. This set the stage for including the family on the school-based team (see Box 8.5).

Box 8.5: Skill Box: RESM Family-Centered Skills

Skill	Practitioner statement
Acknowledging coproduced stories	"Can we hear about Charlie's new behaviors at home?"
Affirming the family's lived experience	"Can you tell us about what you see at home on a daily basis?"
Encouraging reconstructing the family story	"I too can say I see changes in Charlie's behavior"

8.7 Four Phases of RESM Social Work Practice

8.7.1 Early Engagement

To truly engage in treatment for ASD, Charlie needed to increase his capacity to self-regulate and expand his attention span. These behaviors were fostered when the early interventionist taught Mr. and Mrs. Barton to observe, understand, and respond to the micro moments of their intersubjective experiences with Charlie during play. These DIRFloortime techniques became a catalyst for change.

DIRFloortime is a therapeutic technique that centers around caregivers or professionals finding a shared world with a child in a wide range of environments, even sometimes by playing on the floor. The pair engage in one-on-one interactions as they explore the child's interests and join together in using sensorimotor toys or experiences, objects, or toys that are of interest to the child. The adult observes the child's responses and then imitates, labels, or names the child's play through the use of words, gestures, and/or positive affect. Families with various social and play traditions may modify their activities accordingly. For example, a child may have a favorite holiday toy or activity, such as spinning a dreidel or lighting a Christmas tree.

Early engagement DIRFloortime activities are practiced with a parent to facilitate the rhythm of the interaction between parent and child, leaving spaces for the two to better communicate with each other. The intent is to "achieve a 'closed circle of communication' [between professionals, family, and child] that increases the child's social competence" (Mercer, 2017, p. 627).

DIRFloortime therapeutic play techniques may eventually lead to developmental outcomes that enable the child–family unit to develop new thoughts, feelings, and intentions. They also can lay a foundation for the creation of a new family narrative composed of parents' different views of their child and new ideas of their own evolving parenting skills (Kennedy et al., 2010, p. 63).

8.7.2 RESM Engagement

RESM engagement is a time for professionals to build relationships based on trust. Relationships are nonhierarchical and transparent and can be fostered among family members using such skills as those illustrated in Box 8.6.

Box 8.6: Skill Box: RESM Engagement Skills

Skill	Practitioner statement
Observing interactions	"We will be using therapeutic play techniques to identify and name Charlie's behaviors"
Interpreting behaviors	"What do you think Charlie was expressing?"
Affirming progress	"Can you see the difference in Charlie since the last time we met?"

8.7.2.1 Narrative Themes

As Harris continued to engage Mr. and Mrs. Barton in achieving the therapeutic goals reviewed at the initial team meeting, he collaborated with them on the cocreation of the family narrative. Early reflection on the Bartons' narrative revealed their concern about Charlie's transition to school-based education. The Bartons wondered whether the school program would support the positive changes Charlie had already made during his preschool years. The practice example in Box 8.7 illustrates how the school social worker acknowledged the Bartons' concerns about maintaining weekly contact with school personnel.

8.7.2.2 Practice Example Analysis

The Bartons and the social worker, Harris, held a meeting and addressed concerns about communication between school and home. Harris also encouraged the Bartons to act as a team member by asking them to clarify what helping strategies were the most successful with Charlie.

Box 8.7: Practice Example: The Social Worker's Conversation with Charlie's Family

Harris:	It looks like you anticipated Charlie's move into school. You have organized all of Charlie's transitional material, reports, and information. I'm impressed with how on top of this you are. This can definitely support his transition.
Mrs. Barton:	Yes, I have worked hard to keep it all organized.
Harris:	I know it will be very helpful in making the transition go as smoothly as possible. Do you think it would beneficial if we explore the materials together and create a chart that indicates what techniques you think worked best with Charlie?
Mrs. Barton:	Yes, that would be helpful. I am quite concerned that I will lose contact with his program. I now understand what strategies we have used that have been successful. I was wondering if we could create a communication system between home and school. I am thinking that we could share what is happening at home, and the school could send information home. It would be hard for me to just send him to school without knowing what is happening. I don't mean to offend you, but this is a surprisingly scary time for me.
Harris:	You didn't offend me. Communicating about Charlie is important for all of us. It is great that you can tell me what you are thinking.
Mr. Barton:	Thank you for recognizing this.
Harris:	Should we see what Charlie's educational team is proposing for communication? I believe we do something like you suggested with all our families.

8.7.3 RESM Assessment

8.7.3.1 Creating an Assessment Profile

Assessment profiles are created to reach hypotheses or tentative conclusions about a client's use of the helping process and point to the need for possible interventions. The P-E dimensions suggest possible stressors associated with the client's environment that may be perceived as interfering with optimal social functioning.

As discussed in Chap. 5, the practitioner listens to a client narrative, focuses on the balance between P-E risk and protective factors, and discerns what responses the client has made to 10 P-E dimensions (for the 10 P-E dimensions, see Chap. 5, Box 5.3).

In short, data on the Bartons' responses to the P-E dimensions were synthesized to create an assessment profile that reflected the family's capacity to balance their risk and protective factors. The profile then offered insights into what interventions might be needed to enhance the family's optimal social functioning.

8.7.3.2 Balancing Risk and Protection

The educational team highlighted two interconnected P-E dimensions in the Barton family assessment profile:

1. Charlie's reaction to the disruption of biopsychosocial and spiritual processes
2. The Barton family's response to adversity or change

Reaction to Biopsychosocial Disruption The use of the DIRFloortime techniques was considered a protective factor that supported much of Charlie's considerable developmental progress. Charlie's effective response to past DIRFloortime therapy sessions also enhanced the child–family unit's resiliency, which made each session more advanced and doable.

However, Charlie's ability to make a smooth transition to school was made more difficult by his ongoing biopsychosocial risks. A risk assessment by the developmental specialist showed that Charlie continued to face difficulties in the following areas:

- Sensory processing and auditory processing were straining his self-regulation capacities, especially in environments with too many visual stimuli and excessive noise.
- Visuospatial processing put excessive pressure on self-regulation capacities when physical environments were changed or modified.
- Motor control issues brought about a diminished capacity to organize motions that supported communication or the exchange of ideas.

Family Response to ASD The Bartons demonstrated an ability to respond to the stressors associated with ASD by gradually reconstructing their family's organizational and communication patterns. At the same time, Mr. and Mrs. Barton said they sometimes felt isolated because Charlie's challenges with sensory processing made him less likely to participate with the family on social occasions. Charlie's parents were also leery about being in public places where Charlie might face discrimination.

Plans for Intervention and Change Charlie's intervention plan stated that school personnel needed to continue to affirm his past successes but at the same time be aware of and address his ongoing delays in motor control and sensory processing. Mr. and Mrs. Barton said they planned to expand their circle of relationships as treatment progressed and Charlie became more socially attuned. Table 8.2 presents a more detailed assessment profile.

Table 8.2 Person–environment (P-E) assessment chart: Charlie and the Barton family

P-E dimension	Indicator
Consequences of time and place	The Americans with Disabilities Act of 1990 banned discrimination based on physical or mental disability in all parts of public life. People with disabilities could no longer be denied access to jobs, schools, or transportation. However, far too often people with disabilities continue to face discrimination
Response to the stress of past critical events	The Barton family responded well to past critical events involving Charlie's experiences with autism spectrum disorder. They continued to persevere with DIRFloortime interventions and the school-based program
Reaction to disruption of biopsychosocial and spiritual processes	The Barton family began treatment with disruptions in Charlie's overall development. Although Charlie had progressed along his developmental path, challenges remained
Family response to adversity or change	The Barton family demonstrated the capacity to change or reconstruct their organizational and communication patterns and behavior
Consequences of social supports	Charlie's family garnered support by hiring an early intervention specialist who came to the home. They then transitioned to a public school–based educational team
Significance of favorable environments	The Barton family lived in a favorable environment with access to schools, pharmacies, groceries, and parks
Effects of strong cultural identity	The Bartons incorporated favorite toys into their DIRFloortime practice
Effects of human rights violations	The Disability Rights Education and Defense Fund, "located in Berkeley, California, and Washington, DC, USA is a national cross-disability civil rights law and policy center directed by individuals with disabilities and parents who have children with disabilities" (Wikipedia, 2022, para. 1). Mr. Barton was a member
Concerns about insufficient resources and services	The Bartons responded to the risks associated with autism spectrum disorder by researching and obtaining services that provide DIRFloortime, a strengths-based model to support child development

8.7.4 RESM Intervention

Coconstructing and reconstructing the Barton family narrative was the central intervention used to help them attain their optimal social functioning. To achieve this, the social worker helped the family counter negative societal attitudes by externalizing negative stereotypes.

8.7.4.1 Countering Negative Societal Attitudes

Unfortunately, some families may feel limited by the behaviors associated with a member's ASD and may be less likely to create a positive family narrative. Professionals need to acknowledge that such families live in American society, which is characterized by widespread negative images of people with disabilities. *Ableism* is a pervasive societal attitude that stereotypes, discriminates, and devalues a person with disabilities. These prejudices are based on the mistaken premise that it is better to be able bodied.

8.7.4.2 Externalizing Negative Stereotypes

When discriminatory attitudes are internalized, a family with a child who has a disability may accept these labels and misconceptions as correct. This negative stereotyping may lead to self-blame. Externalizing such negative messaging or recognizing the influences of systemic prejudice is a major anti-oppressive intervention that can enhance a family's sense of resilience (see Box 8.8).

8.7.4.3 Bolstering Developmental Protective Factors

Pioneering research on resilience revealed that children who have different developmental responses to stressors or risk also have protective P-E factors that can increase their effective social functioning as well as bolster their resiliency (Rutter, 1987, 1989; Werner & Smith, 1982). The research findings suggest that positive connections within one's family and strong relationships with others, such as

Box 8.8: Skill Box: RESM Externalizing Skills

Skill	Practitioner statement
Prompting information about sensitive topics	"I know that was hard to deal with. I wouldn't want my child to face that discrimination"
Clarifying a client's literal statement	"I would like to understand. Can you say that another way?"
Exploring a silence	"That must be difficult to talk about. Would you like to take a few minutes to think?"

teachers and mentors, are protective factors that serve as the bedrock for resilient social functioning.

8.7.5 *RESM/DIRFloortime Evaluation*

Research findings support the idea that DIRFloortime is a means of effectively treating young children with ASD (Mercer, 2017). Reported resilient outcomes include the development of a sense of self-identity and competence (Maurya, 2016). Not only did Charlie's therapeutic team notice a change in his self-confidence, but they also saw a shift in the family narrative from an emphasis on negative behaviors and feelings to opportunity for growth and transformation. The family and school-based treatment team met and concluded that it had been worthwhile to "develop various capacities related to social communication in a pragmatically appropriate social context rather than target behaviors themselves" (Mercer, 2017, p. 626). This was evidenced when Charlie came to dance, play ball, and watch basketball games when his emotional development converged with his social development to take advantage of developmental turning points.

8.8 Summary and Conclusion

The Lincoln Elementary School professional team treated the Barton family–child unit as a dynamic social system capable of growth. The team was successful in helping Charlie strengthen his sensorimotor skills. This, combined with the family's reconstructed organizational and communication patterns and a newly configured understanding of Charlie's actions, resulted in a transformation in social functioning.

Summary of Learning Outcomes

Keep in mind the following:

- Social workers contribute to professional teams by emphasizing family collaboration in their practice.
- Social workers often recruit families to be members of the treatment team.
- Social workers may adopt skills from allied disciplines to assist their clients.

Discussion Questions

1. How did Barton family restructuring act as a protective factor for **the family**?
2. In what ways did the Barton family's participation on the school-based team illustrate their capacity to transform?

Chapter Exercise
Write a one-page research paper on how the family therapy movement influenced social work practice. Use two to four references.

Glossary

Auditory processing The process of an individual's brain understanding and making sense of what is being heard.
Circle of communication A communication exchange that includes an opening initiation of communication, a response from another, and a closing by the initiator.
DIRFloortime A Developmental, Individual-differences, and Relationship-based model that provides a foundational framework for understanding human development and learning and how each person individually perceives and interacts with the world by outlining the critical role socioemotional development has on overall human development.
Host setting A social work practice setting that is defined and dominated by people who are not social workers.
Interdisciplinary team A group of different professionals working together with a common purpose, making decisions, and sharing resources.
Nonspeaking Describing a person who does not speak or can only say a few words.
Self-regulation The ability to adapt neurological arousal, emotional state, motor activity, attention, and behavior to meet one's needs and the demands of a situation.
Sensory processing The effective registration and interpretation of sensory stimuli or input in the environment; the way the brain receives, organizes, and responds to sensory stimuli or input to behave in a meaningful and consistent manner.
Therapeutic play framework The utilization of play to support and enhance a child's emotional development.
Visuospatial processing The processing of visual information to inform where objects are in space and how far away objects are from oneself (including one's own body parts) and each other.

References

Bayat, M., & Schuntermann, P. (2013). Enhancing resilience in families of children with autism spectrum disorder. In D. Becvar (Ed.), *Handbook of family resilience* (pp. 409–424). Springer.
Bronfenbrenner, U. (1979). *The ecology of human development*. Harvard University Press.
Goffman, E. (1963). Stigma: Notes on the management of spoiled identity. Prentice Hall.
Greene, R. R. (2008). *Social work with the aged and their families* (3rd ed.). Aldine Transaction Press.
Greene, R. R., & Dubus, N. (2017). *Resilience in action*. NASW Press.

Greene, R. R., Wright, M., Herring, M., Wright, T., & Dubus, N. (2019). *Human behavior theory and social work practice with marginalized oppressed populations*. Routledge.
Kennedy, H., Landor, M., & Todd, L. (2010). Video interaction guidance as a method to promote secure attachment. *Educational and Child Psychology, 27*(3), 59–72.
Masten A. S. (2014). Global perspectives on resilience in children and youth. Child Dev. Jan-Feb;85(1):6–20. https://doi.org/10.1111/cdev.12205. Epub 2013 Dec 16. PMID: 24341286.
Maurya, R. K. (2016). Use of family narratives as a tool of effective parenting. *International Journal of Indian Psychology, 3*(2) Retrieved February 14, 2023, from https://ijip.in/pdf-viewer/?id=12093
Mercer, J. (2017). Examining DIR/Floortime™ as a treatment for children with autism spectrum disorders: A review of research and theory. *Research on Social Work Practice, 27*(5), 625–635.
Muhle, R., Trentacoste, S. V., & Rapin, I. (2004). The genetics of autism. *Pediatrics, 113*(5), 472–486.
National Institute of Mental Health. (2022). *Transforming the understanding and treatment of mental illnesses*. National Institute of Mental Health.
Rutter, M. (1987). Psychological resilience and protective mechanisms. *American Journal of Orthopsychiatry, 57*(3), 316–331.
Rutter, M. (1989). Pathways from childhood to adult life. *Journal of Psychology and Psychiatry, 30*(3), 23–51.
School Social Work Association of America. (n.d.). *Role of school social worker*. Retrieved February 15, 2023, from https://www.sswaa.org/school-social-work
Walsh, F. (1997). Families in later life: Challenges and opportunities. In B. Carter & M. McGoldrick (Eds.), *The expanded life cycle: Individual, family, and social perspectives* (pp. 307–324). Allyn & Bacon.
Walsh, F. (2006). *Strengthening family resilience*. Guilford Press.
Werner, E., & Smith, R. (1982). *Vulnerable but invincible: A longitudinal study of resilient children and youth*. McGraw-Hill.
Wikipedia. (2022, December 10). *Disability rights education and defense fund*. Retrieved February 15, 2023, from https://en.wikipedia.org/wiki/Disability_Rights_Education_and_Defense_Fund

Supplemental References

Besame for KosAbility. (2021). *KosAbility: Internalized ableism is a consequence of an ableist society. Let's dismantle both*. Besame for KosAbility.
Butler, S., Guterman, J. T., & Rudes, J. (2009). Using puppets with children in narrative therapy to externalize the problem. *Journal of Mental Health Counseling, 31*(3), 225–233.
Delahooke, M. (2019). *Beyond behaviors: Using brain science and compassion to solve children's behavioral challenges*. PESI Publishing & Media.
Greene, R., & Schriver, J. (2017). *Human behavior and the social environment: An ecological base*. Routledge.
Greenspan, S. I. (1992). *Infancy and early childhood: The practice of clinical assessment and intervention with emotional and developmental challenges*. International Universities Press.
Greenspan, S. I., & Greenspan, N. T. (2010). *The learning tree: Overcoming learning disabilities from the ground up*. Da Capo Press.
Greenspan, S. I., & Wieder, S. (2006). *Engaging autism: Using the Floortime approach to help children relate, communicate, and think*. Da Capo Press.
Sealy, J., & Glovinsky, I. P. (2016). Strengthening the reflective functioning capacities of parents who have a child with a neurodevelopmental disability through a brief, relationship-focused intervention. *Infant Mental Health Journal, 37*(2), 115–124. https://doi.org/10.1002/imhj.21557

Shanker, S. (2013). Calm, alert, and learning: Classroom strategies for self-regulation. .
Solomon, R., Van Egeren, L., Mahoney, G., Quon Huber, M., & Zimmerman, P. (2014). PLAY Project Home Consultation intervention program for young children with autism spectrum disorders: A randomized controlled trial. *Journal of Developmental and Behavioral Pediatrics, 35*(8), 475–485.
Zand, D. H., Braddock, B., Baig, W., Deasy, J., & Maxim, R. (2013). Role of pediatricians in fostering resilience in parents of children with autism spectrum disorders. *Journal of Pediatrics, 163*(6), 1769–1771.

Chapter 9
Transmitting Resilience Through Family Communication and Organization

Roberta Greene, Nancy Greene, and Connie Corley

Learning Objectives

This chapter highlights skills and techniques social workers need to provide resilience-enhancing, family-focused coaching to military personnel. The emphasis is on helping a family learn to modify its communication and organizational patterns, as well as its belief systems, as it sets goals to effectively reunite when a family member has returned home from combat. Narrative interviews and homework assignments provide a foundation for the family to understand its compositional patterns, risks, and protective factors and how these various influences impact its functional capacity. On completing this chapter, you should be better able to assist families who are experiencing disruptions associated with military deployment. You should be prepared to answer the following questions:

- What are some of the barriers soldiers and their families face when seeking counseling services?
- What risks do soldiers and their families face due to operational stress?
- What protective factors can ameliorate these stressors?
- What coaching skills can social workers use to help support positive family adaptation and functioning?

A family waiting to reunite with a member returning from combat is usually highly emotional and happy to know that the separation is almost over. Yet ironically, when a member of a military family is deployed and then reunites with family members,

R. Greene (✉)
Steve Hicks School of Social Work, The University of Texas at Austin, Austin, TX, USA
e-mail: rgreene@utexas.edu

N. Greene
Ethelyn R. Strong School of Social Work, Norfolk State University, Norfolk, VA, USA
e-mail: nagreene@nsu.edu

C. Corley
Fielding Graduate University, Santa Barbara, CA, USA
e-mail: conniecorleyphd@gmail.com

R. Greene et al. (eds.), *Resilience Enhancement in Social Work Practice*,
https://doi.org/10.1007/978-3-031-38518-6_9

multiple stressors may occur. However, most families are poised to reintegrate and remain relatively resilient (Park, 2011).

The focus of this chapter is the use of social work coaching skills that foster a family's capacity to reflect on how it has experienced deployment and its current capacity to make the changes necessary to maintain its resiliency (Beardslee et al., 2013). Skills often involve helping a family to ameliorate post-deployment stress, reorganize its biopsychosocial balance, and readjust family members' role assignments (Wooten, 2013; see Box 9.1).

Box 9.1: Practice Example: The Templeton Family Gets Back Together
The Templeton family consisted of Lt. and Mrs. Templeton and their sons Adam, age 9, and Proctor, age 11. The family met with a social worker, Bernard, to learn how to enhance its current level of resilience. Lt. Templeton, who came from a long line of military personnel, had just returned from Yemen, where a civil war was underway. He had been participating in a US Navy and multicountry naval blockade of Yemen's ports that had begun in 2021. Since the inception of the blockade, the United States and partner maritime forces had seized 15,000 illegal arms unlawfully shipped to Yemen. The Templeton family met with social worker Bernard to explore issues related to the reunion, including how the family was taking on new role patterns for managing daily affairs.

9.1 Exploring Family Well-Being and Military Readiness

The ultimate goal in military social work is to support military personnel and their families to maintain resilience and their ongoing capacity to contribute to overall military readiness. Understanding military readiness requires that social workers comprehend the complex intersection of military culture, chain of command and responsibility, as well as the behaviors soldiers adopt to survive. This process is illustrated here as social worker Bernard helped Lt. Templeton and his family reunite following the lieutenant's return from naval duty.

9.2 Understanding Workplace Fit

As already mentioned, the role of the military social worker is to focus on both family well-being and military readiness. Resilience in the military requires that families achieve a multisystemic balance between the requirements members place on themselves and those placed on them by the military system's larger social context (National Academies of Sciences, Engineering, and Medicine, 2019). Together the social connections between the workplace and the military family may be thought of as *workplace fit*.

Like person–environment (P-E) fit, work–family fit suggests that people vary in their abilities and needs, just as the workplace varies in its demands and supports. This point of view leads to an understanding that both the workplace and families contribute to the perception of fitness. In essence, the entire family needs to be prepared to cope with home and work demands, and at the same time the workplace needs to be perceived as rewarding and supportive (McFadyen et al., 2005). In this way, the Templeton family's resiliency may be viewed as part of a larger military enterprise.

9.3 Coping with Multiple Deployments and Relocations

When a military family is required to frequently relocate or face a member's deployment, it can face several major challenges. This chapter explores the fundamental question of what helps military families confront significant risk, resist this risk, and successfully navigate or recover from the challenges associated with multiple military deployments and/or geographic relocations.

Like a civilian move, a military personnel's permanent change of station can be expensive and can involve, among other things, finding new housing, schools, and a job for a nonmilitary family member. The greatest difference between a civilian move and a permanent change of station is frequency, with military personnel moving an average of every 2.5 years (Military OneSource, n.d.).

9.4 Consequences of Stress

A soldier reuniting with a family may demonstrate stress and exhibit behaviors that are effective in combat but not so effective in the home zone. This way of thinking and behaving is called Battlemind (Ruff & Kern, 2014; Wilson et al., 2014). Social workers should familiarize themselves and their client families with the tenets of Battlemind compiled by the U.S. Walter Reed Army Institute of Research so they can help identify and, when necessary, react to a soldier's behavioral health warning signs. Battlemind training tenets suggest successful combat zone behaviors that might be unnecessary or hazardous once a soldier transitions from a combat zone to home.

Although the treatment of posttraumatic stress disorder is beyond the scope of this chapter, social workers should keep in mind select premises of Battlemind psychoeducational training when coaching military families. The literature on Battlemind suggests that professionals and families should be aware of the following:

- Although military missions should not be talked about, soldiers can be encouraged to share their general war stories with families and friends the way they want to.
- Although a military weapon is necessary in combat, a weapon is not needed at home. If a weapon is retained, the soldier should adhere to strict laws and rules regarding its maintenance.
- Although combat skills necessitate hypervigilance or alertness, this practice is neither necessary nor effective at home.
- Whereas survival in combat depends on being given commands, home behaviors are negotiated.
- Finally, but most important, family and friends of returning military personnel need to be on alert for high levels of depression and suicidal thoughts and reach out to mental health resources and hotlines as necessary.

9.5 Delineating Family Resilience

One of the social worker's major roles when working with military personnel is to foster deployment resilience. *Deployment resilience* is a soldier's capacity to resist the stress of transitioning to and from combat (Wooten, 2013). This is congruent with *family resilience*, which is defined as "the adaptive qualities of families as they encounter stress" (Hawley & DeHaan, 1996, p. 284). Therefore, family-focused coaching with military personnel highlights the "common and unique life transitions and events that confront a family over time that may set family transformations in motion" (Germain, 1994, p. 89).

9.5.1 Resilience: Common Characteristics

The resilience approach to social work involves several common characteristics that "fit within the broader rubric of resiliency" (Greene, 2012, p. 12). Family resilience enables the family to strengthen its own healing resources, marshaling community resources to foster healing and growth (Walsh, 1998, 2003), and to build on family assets and survival skills to avert negative stressors and confront adversity (Germain, 1994).

9.6 Defining Family P-E Fit

Hawley and DeHaan (1996) underscored the premise that family resilience is based on the fit between the family's strengths and its specific P-E circumstances. They went on to say that

> family resilience describes the path a family follows as it adapts and prospers in the face of stress, both in the present and over time. Resilient families respond positively to these conditions in unique ways, depending on the context, developmental level, the interactive combination of risk and protective factors, and the family's shared outlook. (p. 293)

9.7 Coaching a Family in Transition

Stressful transitional change can be tackled when practitioners act as consultants or family coaches. Coaching skills were used in interviews with the Templeton family to develop family self-awareness, identify life choices, and find solutions. Homework assignments were given to assist the family and social worker in creating an action or intervention plan based on the goal of enhancing resilient social functioning.

Coaching may be thought of as different from therapy. Although family therapy and coaching may both focus on the here and now of client behaviors, therapy has a greater focus on emotional or behavioral issues and mental health disorders. In contrast, coaching is more focused on the attainment of personal, family, and professional goals (Burroughs et al., 2017). In the case of the Templeton family, coaching was a form of "partnering with [them] in a thought-provoking and creative process that inspire[d] them to maximize their personal and professional potential" (International Coaching Federation, 2023).

The practice example in this chapter illustrates how social work coaching skills can be used to assist family members in reconfiguring their roles as they go about a family self-assessment to identify sources of stress. Early intervention and prevention initiatives that consider the interpersonal and educational constructs that form resilience may act as protective factors to mitigate against adverse deployment stress.

9.8 Resilience-Enhancing Stress Model (RESM) Engagement: Stigma and Mental Health Services

The military culture celebrates the traditional warrior ethos and qualities of courage and fortitude. When soldiers seek mental health services, they can be perceived as weak and not service ready. This in turn may result in their being stigmatized (Nash et al., 2011). According to a seminal work by Goffman (1959), a stigmatized person is socially undesirable and has lost his or her status or reputation.

Stigma can complicate the engagement of military families in social work services. However, research underscores the need to combat stigma (Ben-Zeev et al., 2012; Hoge et al., 2008). For example, Hoge et al. (2008) investigated help-seeking and barriers to care among US soldiers and marines after their deployments to Iraq and Afghanistan. Study findings emphasized the importance of reducing stigma and barriers to care in the military through education, outreach programs, and changes in health care delivery.

Box 9.2: Practice Example: Resilience and Getting Reacquainted

Bernard:	Welcome to our first get-reacquainted interview. I wonder if you think it is strange to get reacquainted.
Proctor:	I do. I will be 11 years old next week.
Adam:	I am not that young either.
Mrs. Templeton:	You think we are all the same since Dad was deployed?
Lt. Templeton:	I turned 40 aboard my ship.
Proctor:	We didn't get to blow out your candles.
Adam:	And you didn't get to blow out mine.
Bernard:	Maybe we have some catching up to do. Who will go first answering the question "Who am I?"?
Proctor:	I better get right to it, or Dad will take charge. I am beginning middle school and know how to go about things. I have been the oldest man in the house until now, and I can mow the grass.
Lt. Templeton:	So we may have to learn about each other's duties?
Mrs. Templeton:	You can have my turn washing the car.
Lt. Templeton:	No one can mess with my gear.
Adam:	Mom will give you a place to put it.
Bernard:	It sounds like we've made a good start in achieving the goal of talking about the way the family may want to reorganize now that Dad has come home.

Although Lt. Templeton was leery about going for counseling, he accepted his next-door neighbor and friend's referral to Bernard. Bernard was transparent with the family, explaining that he had a set of homework assignments the family could work on at home and then follow up on with a discussion in his office. As shown in Box 9.2, coaching provided the members of the Templeton family with an opportunity to learn that they were happy to reunite and reintroduce themselves to one another.

9.8.1 Practice Analysis: Steps Taken

Research suggests that early intervention and prevention can foster resilience in children. As seen in Box 9.2, using a narrative as a tool provides children with a positive behavioral intervention. In addition, early intervention and prevention initiatives that consider the interpersonal and educational constructs that form resilience may act as protective factors to mitigate adverse stress among military families.

9.9 RESM Assessment

RESM assessment helps clients reduce their risks, bolster their protective factors or strengths, and positively rewrite their narratives to maintain or regain resilient social functioning following a disruptive life event or stressful change. The process results in an assessment profile and mutually developed intervention plan. The Templeton family assessment consisted of three parts:

1. The Family Coaching Checklist offered a family self-checklist for members to rate daily family functionality (see Table 9.1).
2. The Family Resilience Template provided an additional, more formal means of professionally assessing the family's resilient functioning (see Table 9.2).
3. The P-E assessment chart was used to further map the family's environmental functioning (see Table 9.3).

Bernard used these three forms to record his assessment of the Templeton family.

Table 9.1 Family coaching checklist: functionality

1. Our family has positive relationships, feels connected, and provides support				
Low 1	2	3	4✓	5 high
2. Family members take on jobs that let us get through the day				
Low 1	2	3	4	5 high
3. Our family shares ideas and values that contribute to our being able to get things done				
Low 1	2	3	4	5 high
4. Problem solving is based on talking things through and communicating effectively				
Low 1	2	3	4	5 high
5. Our family identifies and responds to risks or things that get in our way				
Low 1	2	3	4	5 high
6. Our family can reconstruct or change as needed, rebounding from difficult challenges				
Low 1	2	3	4	5 high
7. Our family uses its resources to effectively plan for life transitions				
Low 1	2	3	4	5 high
8. Our family reaches out to others to establish relationships with neighbors and community members				
Low 1	2	3	4	5 high

Directions: Rate your impression of your family on a scale from 1 to 5. 1 = low, 5 = high

Table 9.2 Family resilience template

How effectively does your family function? Have you				
1. Developed positive interrelationships				
Strongly disagree 1	2	3	4	5 strongly agree
2. Formed an effective structure				
Strongly disagree 1	2	3	4	5 strongly agree
3. Joined in problem solving				
Strongly disagree 1	2	3	4	5 strongly agree
4. Taken part in successful decision making				
Strongly disagree 1	2	3	4	5 strongly agree
5. Developed effective patterns of communication				
Strongly disagree 1	2	3	4	5 strongly agree
6. Effectively accomplished your caregiving tasks				
Strongly disagree 1	2	3	4	5 strongly agree
Do you think you have rebounded from disruptive events? Do you				
1. Take on positive challenges				
Strongly disagree 1	2	3	4	5 strongly agree
2. Identify many risk factors or demands				
Strongly disagree 1	2	3	4	5 strongly agree
3. Know and use protective factors (resources and strengths)				
Strongly disagree 1	2	3	4	5 strongly agree
4. Feel you have a sense of cohesion/togetherness				
Strongly disagree 1	2	3	4	5 strongly agree
5. Take steps to connect to extended family and friends				
Strongly disagree 1	2	3	4	5 strongly agree
6. Make affiliations in your community				
Strongly disagree 1	2	3	4	5 strongly agree
7. Feel you are in control of your life situation				
Strongly disagree 1	2	3	4	5 strongly agree
8. Envision new possibilities				
Strongly disagree 1	2	3	4	5 strongly agree
9. Celebrate holidays				
Strongly disagree 1	2	3	4	5 strongly agree
10. Want more services				
Strongly disagree 1	2	3	4	5 strongly agree
11. Have enough help from family and friends				
Strongly disagree 1	2	3	4	5 strongly agree
12. Consider your family resilient				
Strongly disagree 1	2	3	4	5 strongly agree

Note. See Greene (2012) and Isserman et al. (2014)

Directions: How would you rate your family on these functions? Have a family meeting and choose the rating that best fits your family. 1 = strongly disagree, 5 = strongly agree

Table 9.3 Person–environment (P-E) assessment chart: the Templeton family

P-E dimension	Indicator
Consequences of time and place	Lt. Templeton was serving in the military at a time when a Gallup Poll found that the withdrawal from Afghanistan lowered approval ratings of the US military
Response to the stress of past critical events	The Templeton family had met past deployments well
Reaction to disruption of biopsychosocial and spiritual processes	The Templeton family was responsive to emotional and physical changes in its members
Family response to adversity or change	The family responded well to stress
Consequences of social supports	Neighbors of the Templetons supported them during their reunion
Significance of favorable environments	Although the military workplace environment provided needed resources and services, the family may evaluate the need for more in the future
Effects of strong cultural identity	Lt. Templeton came from a line of military service personnel. He and his family built on this culture
Effects of human rights violations	It was not clear how human rights abuses in Yemen may have affected its civil war
Concerns about insufficient resources and services	The Templeton family was using military resources to adjust to the reintegration
Response to degradation of ecosystems	The strait linking the Red Sea and the Gulf of Aden, one of world's most active shipping lanes, was being degraded during the civil war in Yemen

9.9.1 Initial Family Assessment

Bernard started the Templeton family on reflecting on its family functionality using the checklist in Table 9.1. His goal was to obtain an initial picture of the Templeton family dynamics. Bernard drew on the multitheoretical base of the RESM, with its emphasis on systems theory as a means of assessing the life of the family group. The Templetons were asked to complete the checklist at home and bring their answers to their next meeting with Bernard (see Box 9.3).

9.9.2 Social Worker Assessment

9.9.2.1 Delineating Organizational, Communication, and Belief Patterns

Bernard conducted his professional social work assessment based on the well-known theoretical family resilience framework developed by Froma Walsh (1997, 1998). She suggested that practitioners assess three key family features associated with resiliency that can be modified through coaching:

Box 9.3: Practice Example: The Templeton Family Reflects on the Checklist

Bernard:	I see you all took a look at your homework. The questions were designed to see what you think about how your family gets things done. I am interested in what you think you do well and what you want to improve. What item(s) got the highest marks?
Lt. Templeton:	Too soon to know.
Mrs. Templeton:	I vote for number 8. I like the way we get along with our neighbors. That was so important, especially when my husband was away.
Adam:	I go with number 5! My brother always helps me get around my problems.
Bernard:	Any others?
Proctor:	No, I go with those.
Bernard:	What questions do you think could get higher marks and be worked on here? They may help us set goals.
Proctor:	Oh, I think it has to be number 6. We just keep the same old schedule all the time. Maybe it's time for a new one?
Adam:	I think so too. Same old, same old. I am old enough now to go places alone.
Mrs. Templeton:	I agree. I have kept the rules pretty much the same while Dad was away. Maybe we can begin to take a look?
Lt. Templeton:	After being shipboard for so long, I will have to work on being more flexible.
Adam:	We love you Dad, but you get upset too quick.
Lt. Templeton:	I'm sure you won't hesitate to tell me not to get revved up.
Mrs. Templeton:	No, we won't. We want to see your good side! Let's hug!

1. The family belief system, which reflects a family's shared view of social reality (Koerner & Fitzpatrick, 1996) and establishes the family's ideas about how members should act
2. Family organizational patterns, which involve the family's structure and how members carry out tasks
3. Communication patterns, which encompass the exchange of information and agreement between family members

Table 9.2 provides a means of recording these assessment features.

9.9.2.2 Charting a P-E Assessment

The RESM P-E assessment chart was used to review the broad environmental context that impacted the Templeton family's functionality (see Table 9.3). This included the global footprint of the military, societal perceptions of the military, and the Templeton family's support system. As assessment information was compiled and reflected on, the Templeton family assessment profile was established. The profile concluded that although the family members were making a positive response to deployment stress, they should meet with Bernard periodically to support continued success.

9.10 RESM Intervention

9.10.1 Meaning-Making

Traditional definitions of meaning-making emphasize that the process involves people's appraisal of their existence and adjustment to life stress. That is, meaning is created as people interact and reflect on their P-E situation (Park & Folkman, 1997). Making sense of a situation (Antonovsky, 1987) was at the core of the Templeton family's deconstruction and reconstruction of its family narrative.

9.10.2 Reconstructing a Family Narrative

Although many families spontaneously transform themselves during a crisis, grave life stressors may require major changes in family structure and meaning, necessitating outside intervention (Germain, 1994). Perhaps the most telling way the Templeton family reconstructed its narrative was in using a conversation orientation to family communication. According to Wilson et al. (2014), a conversation orientation to family communication are families that share age-appropriate information about struggles, parent safety, and financial difficulties and have more reported prosocial behaviors and more effective social functioning.

9.11 RESM Evaluation

A RESM evaluation explores what clients have learned and how they have grown from adversity. The question is whether the family assigns meaning to adversity, shows transcendence, shows posttraumatic growth, and is able to go on with a sense of meaning and purpose (Janoff-Bulman & Berger, 2000). This is explained below as resilient reintegration, and it encompasses client insight or growth.

9.12 Military-Level Intervention

9.12.1 Forming the Theoretical Basis of Military Resilience

A major reason the concept of resilience was adopted by the US military was to evaluate a soldier's readiness to remain engaged in battle despite combat distress. Using this method of care required that treatment be provided in or as near as possible to the battle zone, as soon as possible after the injury was sustained, and that whenever possible soldiers needed to return to their unit and resume their former duties (Langston et al., 2007).

This approach to dealing with combat zone stress necessitated a means of classifying a soldier's readiness (attributes) to return to combat, which reflected that soldier's resilience. To accomplish this task, the military adopted a schema based on Richardson's (2002) resiliency model. Richardson hypothesized that after people experience disruptions in resilient functioning, they may reach one of four levels of reintegration of resilient functioning along a continuum:

1. *Resilient reintegration*, which encompasses client insight or growth
2. *Reintegration back to biopsychospiritual homeostasis*, which refers to people healing or getting beyond the disruption
3. *Recovering with loss*, which indicates that there is some permanent physical or emotional loss
4. *Dysfunctional reintegration*, which occurs when people resort to substance abuse or destructive behaviors to deal with stress

This typology acted as a metric for the U.S. Defense Department's Readiness Stress Deployment Continuum.

9.12.2 Outlining the Military Resilience Continuum

The U.S. Defense Department's Readiness Stress Deployment Continuum mirrors Richardson's theoretical framework and is composed of different levels of positive and negative combat stress outcomes. As described in Box 9.4, this multiphase continuum outlines a soldier's functional readiness for service, ranging from optimal readiness (the green zone) to ill prepared (the red zone):

The green zone is associated with attributes related to optimal or high levels of physical and cognitive functioning.

The yellow zone is associated with attributes associated with mild and temporary distress.

The orange zone is linked to attributes that indicate persistent and severe distress.

The red zone is related to attributes that indicate a need for the soldier to obtain mental and behavioral health services (Nash et al., 2011; see Table 9.4).

Table 9.4 A resilience continuum: a range of functioning during transition

	Green zone	Yellow zone	Orange zone	Red zone
	(Optimal)	(Reacting)	(Injured)	(Ill)
Attributes	Effective mastery of stress High levels of performance Accepts challenges and sense of purpose	Mild and temporary distress May be irritable or overwhelmed Reactions to stress are temporary	More persistent and severe distress May be anxious and fatigued Preclinical symptoms may be long-lasting	Severe mental disorders May be angry or a danger to oneself Clinical symptoms require professional diagnosis and treatment
Readiness	Mission ready	Temporary removal from combat stress	Disruption requires combat stress intervention	Referral for treatment as soon as possible

Box 9.4: Practice Example: Templeton Family Reconstruction
Biopsychospiritual homeostasis or balance is a point in time when a family achieves stability, adapting physically, mentally, and spiritually to a set of circumstances known as its comfort zone (Richardson, 2002). When the family is in a state of balance, it effectively meets the challenges of life transitions. For example, following Lt. Templeton's deployment to Yemen, each member of the family met the disruption by accepting new or modified definitions of their roles or family tasks. However, the Templeton family's biopsychospiritual balance was once again disrupted when Lt. Templeton returned home. The family's conversations with Bernard facilitated a return to its comfort zone. As the Templeton family meetings progressed, Bernard thought about where Lt. Templeton fell along the U.S. Defense Department's Readiness Stress Deployment Continuum, evaluating whether there was a need for Lt. Templeton to receive additional resources and services.

9.13 Summary and Conclusion

Social workers who practice with members of the military population can benefit from understanding that military readiness and the resilience of soldiers and their families go hand in hand. Reducing the stigma associated with seeking services can go a long way toward seeing that this population takes advantage of the many services offered to it (Health.mil, 2023).

Summary of Learning Outcomes
Keep in mind the following:

- Social workers can act as coaches or facilitators to enhance the resilience of military families.
- Social workers enable family conversations to set the change process in action.

Discussion Questions

1. Why did the Templeton family need to get reacquainted following its reunion?
2. How can homework assignments facilitate family reconstruction?

Chapter Exercise

Select one of the family therapy theorists in Table 9.5 and write a paper on one of their interventions that you would use as a homework assignment.

Table 9.5 Family therapy models

Family therapists focus on the interaction between family members, analyzing the role each member plays in maintaining the system. Family therapy can be especially helpful for dealing with problems that develop in response to a particular event or situation, such as divorce, remarriage, or the birth of a new sibling
Minuchin, S. (2013). *The craft of family therapy: Challenging certainties.* Routledge *Structural family therapy, developed by Salvador Minuchin, looks at family relationships, behaviors, and patterns as they are exhibited within the therapy session to evaluate the structure of the family. Using activities such as roleplay in session, therapists also examine subsystems within the family structure, such as parental or sibling subsystems. The therapy views a family's behavior patterns and rituals as central to the problems of its individual members. Poor communication skills play a key role in perpetuating destructive interactions within families, such as the formation of alliances among some family members against others. The goals of structural family therapy include strengthening parental leadership, clarifying boundaries, enhancing coping skills, and freeing family members from their entrenched positions within the family structure*
Haley, J., & Hoffman, L. (1994). *Techniques of family therapy.* Basic Books *Strategic family therapy, developed by Jay Haley, Milton Erickson, and Cloé Madanes, among others, examines family processes and functions, such as communication or problem-solving patterns, by evaluating family behavior outside the therapy session. Therapeutic techniques may include reframing or redefining a problem scenario or using paradoxical interventions (e.g., suggesting that the family act seemingly in opposition to its therapeutic goals) to create the desired change. Strategic family therapists believe change can occur rapidly, without intensive analysis of the source of the problem*
Satir, V., & Baldwin, M. (1994). *Satir step by step: A guide to creating change in families.* Science and Behavior Books *Satir transformational systemic therapy is primarily concerned with communication. Satir's system combines the teaching of family communication skills, the promotion of self-esteem, and the removal of obstacles to emotional growth so family members can have full access to their innate resources. Some of her basic beliefs include the following:*
• All people all have the internal resources they need to cope successfully with whatever situations life provides and to grow through them. All necessary internal resources reside within, even those that people may have learned to judge in a negative way or those that are yet undiscovered • The problem is not the problem; how people cope with the problem is the problem. How seriously people experience the problem through the meanings they make, their worries, and their coping impacts on how great of a problem it becomes for them • People cannot change past events; they can only change the impact that past events have on them. It is possible to resolve impacts from the past to live with more positive energy and be free of old hurts, angers, fears, and negative messages in the present

Glossary

Battlemind The experience of thinking and feeling like one is in combat when actually one is at home.

Deployment resilience The ability to resist the stress of transitioning to and from combat.

Deployment-related stress Stress associated with being assigned to military action.

Developmental resilient path The trajectory of a person's response to stress, both in the present and over time.

Family role assignments Family tasks or obligations.

Homework assignment A therapeutic exercise to carry out at home.

Military culture The organizational structure and command of the military as well as soldiers' values and obligations.

Military readiness A state that depends on equipment and the training and resilience of personnel.

Permanent change of station The experience of a soldier (and his or her family) relocating to a new geographic place.

Readiness Stress Deployment Continuum A tool used to evaluate a soldier's readiness to remain engaged in battle.

References

Antonovsky, A. (1987). *Unraveling the mystery of health: How people manage stress and stay well*. Jossey-Bass.

Beardslee, W. R., Klosinski, L. E., Saltzman, W., Mogil, C., Pangelinan, S., McKnight, C. P., & Lester, P. (2013). Dissemination of family-centered prevention for military and veteran families: Adaptations and adoption within community and military systems of care. *Clinical Child and Family Psychology Review, 16*(4), 394–409.

Ben-Zeev, D., Corrigan, P. W., Britt, T. W., & Langford, L. (2012). Stigma of mental illness and service use in the military. *Journal of Mental Health, 21*(3), 264–273.

Burroughs, M., Allen, K., & Huff, N. (2017). The use of coaching strategies within the field of social work. *Coaching, 10*(1), 4–17.

Germain, C. B. (1994). Human behavior in the social environment. In F. G. Reamer (Ed.), *The foundation of social work knowledge* (pp. 88–121). Columbia University Press.

Goffman, E. (1959). *The presentation of self in everyday life*. Anchor.

Greene, R. R. (2012). *Resiliency theory: An integrated framework for practice, research, and policy* (2nd ed.). NASW Press.

Hawley, D. R., & DeHaan, L. (1996). Toward a definition of family resilience: Integrating lifespan and family perspectives. *Family Process, 35*(3), 283–298.

Health.mil. (2023, March 8). *About the military health system*. Retrieved April 29, 2023, from https://www.health.mil/About-MHS

Hoge, C. W., Castro, C. A., Messer, S. C., McGurk, D., Cotting, D. I., & Koffman, R. L. (2008). Combat duty in Iraq and Afghanistan, mental health problems and barriers to care. *U.S. Army Medical Department Journal*, 7–17. https://doi.org/10.1056/NEJMoa040603

International Coaching Federation. (2023). *All things coaching: What is coaching?* Retrieved April 28, 2023, from https://coachingfederation.org/about

Isserman, N., Greene, R. R., Bowen, S., Hollander-Goldfein, B., & Cohen, H. (2014). Intergenerational families of Holocaust survivors: Designing and piloting a family resilience template. *Evidence-Based Social Work Practice, 30*(1), 62–67.

Janoff-Bulman, R., & Berger, A. R. (2000). The other side of trauma: Towards a psychology of appreciation. In J. H. Harvey & E. D. Miller (Eds.), *Loss and trauma: General and close relationship perspectives* (pp. 29–44). Brunner-Routledge.

Koerner, A. F., & Fitzpatrick, M. A. (1996). Family type and conflict: The impact of conversation orientation and conformity orientation on conflict in the family. *Communication Studies, 48*(1), 59–75.

Langston, V., Gould, M., & Greenberg, N. (2007). Culture: What is its effect on stress in the military? *Military Medicine, 172*(9), 931–935.

McFadyen, J. M., Kerpelman, J. L., & Adler-Baeder, F. (2005). Examining the impact of workplace supports: Work-family fit and satisfaction in the U.S. military. *Family Relations, 54*(1), 131–144.

Military OneSource. (n.d.). *Moving and PCS*. Retrieved April 28, 2023, from https://www.militaryonesource.mil/moving-pcs/

Nash, W. P., Steenkamp, M., Conoscenti, L., & Litz, B. T. (2011). *The stress continuum model: A military organizational approach to resilience and recovery*. Available at https://www.cambridge.org/core/books/abs/resilience-and-mental-health/stress-continuum-model-a-military-organizational-approach-to-resilience-and-recovery/68447CAF0030032EBA99683CF1D5A809

National Academies of Sciences, Engineering, and Medicine. (2019). *Strengthening the military family readiness system for a changing American society*. National Academies Press. https://doi.org/10.17226/25380

Park, N. (2011). Military children and families: Strengths and challenges during peace and war. *American Psychologist, 66*(1), 65–72.

Park, C. L., & Folkman, S. (1997). Meaning in the context of stress and coping. *Review of General Psychology, 1*(2), 115–144. https://doi.org/10.1037/1089-2680.1.2.115

Richardson, G. E. (2002). Metatheory of resilience and resiliency. *Journal of Clinical Psychology, 58*(3), 307–321.

Ruff, S. B., & Kern, M. A. (2014). Revolving doors: The impact of multiple school transitions on military children. *The Professional Counselor, 4*(2), 103–113.

Walsh, F. (1997). Families in later life: Challenges and opportunities. In B. Carter & M. McGoldrick (Eds.), *The expanded life cycle: Individual, family, and social perspectives* (pp. 307–324). Allyn & Bacon.

Walsh, F. (1998). *Strengthening family resilience*. Guilford Press.

Walsh, F. (2003). Family resilience: A framework for clinical practice. *Family Process, 42*(1), 1–18.

Wilson, S. R., Chernichky, S. M., Wilkum, K., & Owlett, J. S. (2014). Do family communication patterns buffer children from difficulties associated with a parent's military deployment? Examining deployed and at-home parents' perspective. *Journal of Family Communication, 14*(1), 32–52.

Wooten, N. R. (2013). A bioecological model of deployment: Risk and resilience. *Journal of Human Behavior in the Social Environment, 23*(6), 699–717.

Supplemental References

Beadle, S., Farrelly, A., Forster, R., & Smith, K. (2015). *Building resilience in children and young people: A literature review for the Department of Education and Early Childhood Development (DEECD)*. Melbourne Graduate School of Education Youth Research Centre.

Bowen, G. L., & Martin, J. A. (2011). The resiliency model of role performance for service members, veterans, and their families: A focus on social connections and individual assets. *Journal of Human Behavior in the Social Environment, 21*(2), 162–178.

Greene, R. R. (2010). Family dynamics, the Nazi Holocaust, and mental health treatment. *Journal of Human Behavior in the Social Environment, 20*(4), 469–488.

Greene, R. R. (2011, July 17). *Holocaust research: Implications for returning veterans*. Presentation to the physical readiness test/significant military equipment Department of Psychological Health, Army Medical Department Soldier and Family Support Branch, .

Greene, R. R., & Schriver, J. (2016). *A handbook of HBSE*. Aldine Transaction Press.

Henry, C. S., Morris, A. S., & Harrist, A. W. (2015). Family resilience: Moving into the third wave. *Family Relations, 64*(1), 22–43.

Tillott, S., Weatherby Fell, N., Pearson, P., & Neumann, M. (2022). Using storytelling to unpack resilience theory in accordance with an internationally recognised resilience framework with primary school children. *Journal of Psychologists and Counsellors in Schools, 32*(1), 134–145.

Chapter 10
Maintaining Resilience Following Loss or Illness

Roberta Greene, Nancy Greene, and Connie Corley

Learning Objectives
This chapter presents a postmodern approach to grief and bereavement, emphasizing experiences that disrupt people's worlds of meaning, which then propels them to search for a sense of significance in their lives. Meaning is associated with the construction of one's life narrative and the retention of important relationships (Neimeyer et al., 2010). When social workers realize that a resilient trajectory can be maintained following loss through storytelling and connections to others, they are better able to help clients in the aftermath of loss. On completing this chapter, you should be able to use therapeutic strategies for helping clients integrate loss and demonstrate resilient social functioning.

You should be prepared to answer the following questions:

- What is a narrative approach to bereavement?
- How does constructing a narrative help clients redefine their lives?
- Why does sharing one's story help affirm life's meaning?
- What is collective loss?

Clinical social work practice with people experiencing loss and grief has evolved over time, shifting from an emphasis on stage theory to "a process of reconstructing a world of meaning that has been challenged by loss" (Neimeyer et al., 2009, p. 455). In 1969, the well-known psychiatrist Elisabeth Kübler-Ross identified grief as an emotional and psychological reaction to the loss of a significant other that may

R. Greene
Steve Hicks School of Social Work, The University of Texas at Austin, Austin, TX, USA
e-mail: rgreene@utexas.edu

N. Greene (✉)
Ethelyn R. Strong School of Social Work, Norfolk State University, Norfolk, VA, USA
e-mail: nagreene@nsu.edu

C. Corley
Fielding Graduate University, Santa Barbara, CA, USA
e-mail: conniecorleyphd@gmail.com

R. Greene et al. (eds.), *Resilience Enhancement in Social Work Practice*,
https://doi.org/10.1007/978-3-031-38518-6_10

engender psychological distress, necessitating a progression through therapy stages to reach a resolution (Maciejewski et al., 2007). However, since that time, the field of grief therapy appears to be shifting from the use of stage theories to a view of recovery from loss that embodies a pattern of resilience (Bonanno et al., 2006; Rasouli et al., 2022).

Although between 5% and 25% of people may experience long-lasting distress following great adversity, most people successfully navigate bereavement, with the majority demonstrating a resilient trajectory (Bonanno & Diminich, 2013; Bonanno et al., 2002, 2006). The death of a loved one is a universal experience, and bereavement is a natural process people engage in to understand and make sense of loss. However, each person explores grief and makes sense of loss differently (Flesner, 2013), which has larger implications for the collective.

One contemporary approach in such therapeutic endeavors "emphasizes how individuals construct meanings about the self and about the world through relationships and narratives" (Flesner, 2013, p. 2). This process of reconstructing a new narrative that integrates loss is illustrated here through the practice example of Janet, who lost her single mother to the opioid epidemic.

10.1 The Opioid Epidemic and Child Welfare

The decrease in life expectancy in the United States between 2000 and 2015 was due to drug poisoning largely attributable to opioids (Dowell et al., 2017). Recent data show a small decline in opioid-related mortality following a decade during which it more than doubled to nearly 53,000 in 2018. Dependency on opioids remains one of the most urgent challenges confronting public health officials in the United States.

The unprecedented rates of drug misuse and overdose deaths, in particular opioid-related incidents, in the United States have had very harmful effects on child health and safety. Among the difficulties are impaired parenting and attachment, inadequate child supervision and care, and diminished financial resources (Feder et al., 2019). Another damaging effect has been the placement in foster care of children whose parents are addicted to opioids or died of an overdose (Ghertner et al., 2018; Quast et al., 2018).

The opioid crisis is placing even more demands on the already overburdened child welfare system. For example, West Virginia, the state with the highest rate of opioid overdose death, also has the highest rate of foster care placements at 41 per 1000 births compared to 5 per 1000 births in neighboring Virginia (Patrick et al., 2019). Updated data can be retrieved online from the National Center for Health Statistics (https://www.cdc.gov/nchs/nvss/vsrr/drug-overdose-data.htm).

10.2 Engagement

Engaging with a client following the death of a loved one requires that the social worker acknowledge the pain of the loss. Pain may also be accompanied by anger, depression, or confusion. Nonetheless, the narrative approach to recovering from grief suggests that the practitioner quickly unites with the client on a journey of healing, as seen in Box 10.1.

Box 10.1: Practice Example: Parental Opioid Misuse, Janet, and the Child Welfare System

Malinda was a social worker at a state-sponsored foster home. She had been assigned to work with Janet Taylor, a 12-year-old middle schooler who had just been placed in foster care because her single mother, Beverly, had died of an opioid overdose 3 months ago. Janet, who was making all A's in school, was not talking to anyone at the home. Her Aunt Cassie visited her every other day. However, Janet pretended to ignore her. Malinda, who had long tried to engage Janet, decided to reach out to her again to involve her in the home's storytelling project.

The storytelling project is based on the postmodern idea that an individual can resolve the grief that follows the death of a significant attachment figure by engaging in a meaning-making process. It also requires "recruiting ongoing support and validation from other familiar figures in one's social world or from those who have experienced similar losses" (Neimeyer et al., 2009, p. 454). As seen in the interview in Box 10.2, Malinda's attempt to engage Janet was finally successful.

Box 10.2: Practice Example: Janet Starts Her Story

Malinda:	Remember I said I would come by to see you again. I want to tell you about the home's storytelling project. It is an English class project. The three winners receive an A in English for the year. There is also a list of prizes.
Janet:	Okay! What do I have to do to get an A? I could get one anyway. What are the prizes?
Malinda:	Here is the list. What do you want to win?
Janet:	No question there. I will win the fingernail design manicure. What do I have to do?
Malinda:	You have to write the best family narrative.
Janet:	What is that?
Malinda:	The history of your family in this county.
Janet:	Oh, gee. I guess I may have to talk to Aunt Cassie.

10.2.1 Practice Example Analysis: Steps Taken

The stress that results from grief can be reduced by lowering risk and bolstering protective factors. Malinda started that process as she addressed Janet's self-isolation. Malinda hoped that Janet would re-enter some form of social life while living at the foster home. Malinda was also aware that for Janet to begin to resolve the death of Beverly, her mother, Janet needed to seek new meaning in life that was grounded in her own action plans (Armour, 2010).

10.3 Multiple Systemic Loss

10.3.1 Collective Stress

Loss does not just affect the individual who has lost a loved one. Rather, loss is a multisystemic collective phenomenon connected to people's sense of others and place (Abramovitz & Albrecht, 2013). When people lose the sense that they can depend on others and that their community is safe, is receptive, or serves as an anchor for them, family and community connections seem to disappear.

Events like epidemics create shared experiences that disrupt people's sense of safety and security and cause confusion and uncertainty. However, according to Neimeyer et al. (2010), the narrative "organizes the 'micro-narratives' of everyday life into a 'macro-narrative' that consolidates our self-understanding, establishes our characteristic range of emotions and goals, and guides our performance on the stage of the social world" (pp. 73–74). Said another way, the person in mourning comes to see that his or her "personal lifestory is nested in a set of larger stories," as seen in Box 10.3 (Kenyon & Randall, 2001, p. 17).

Box 10.3: Practice Example: Janet and Malinda Recruit Aunt Cassie

Malinda:	Are you ready to start writing your story?
Janet:	I am looking up facts on the Internet. But I want to give a first-hand account. That way, I am even more likely to get an A.
Malinda:	Doesn't Aunt Cassie come today? She may know something.
Janet:	She should be here any minute. Maybe we can convince her to help. There she is now.
Aunt Cassie:	Did I hear my name? That's unusual!
Janet:	I need a favor. I want to win the storytelling project, and I need information about the family.
Aunt Cassie:	No problem. I may have some interesting old stuff in the attic you can use.

10.4 Assessment

10.4.1 Sociocultural Historical Context

Individual and family narratives consist of sociocultural and historical information. Janet Taylor learned that her family had been part of Logan County for more than 100 years. Logan County was founded in 1824 and became part of the then-new state of West Virginia in 1864. This Appalachian area was home to multiple coal mines that produced coal and coal slurry, a combustible mixture of fine coal particles suspended in water sold as low-grade fuel. Mountain top mining was also done in the area to obtain coal above ground. Surface mining involved altering the topography of the countryside by removing hills or ridges to retrieve buried coal seams (see Box 10.4).

10.4.2 Practice Example Analysis: Steps Taken

As Janet experienced the past events recounted in her family narrative, Malinda introduced additional strategies to help Janet mourn her mother. These included looking at photographs of family reunions to discover her mother as a child. Malinda and Janet then reflected on the fact that Janet was coming to appreciate the benefits of looking at family photographs (see Box 10.5).

Box 10.4: Practice Example: Great-Grandpa Taylor, the Coal Mines, Labor Abuses, and Ecological Degradation
Great-Grandpa Taylor and his family lived in Logan County, West Virginia. The family consisted of Great-Grandma Taylor and six grown children. Coal miners were divided between union and nonunion workers. Great-Grandpa Taylor was a nonunion worker. If he joined the union, he could face immediate termination from his job and eviction from his company-owned home. In 1921, Logan County was the scene of the Battle of Blair Mountain, the largest labor uprising in U.S. history, in which up to 100 people were killed. Great-Grandpa Taylor fought on the side of the nonunion organizers along with his brother Jester, who was killed during the battle. Great-Niece Frances had kept the *Washington Post* newspaper account of the event, which Aunt Cassie found in her attic and brought to the foster home for Janet to read. Aunt Cassie also found old family photographs of barbeque reunions.

10.4.3 *Creating an Assessment Profile: Balancing Risk and Protection*

The content in the narrative interview leads to a client assessment profile and to an intervention plan mutually developed by the client and social worker. The goal for Malinda was to set in motion a change process to help Janet revise negative meanings of events, find solutions, and develop a greater sense of agency (Greene, 2008). To facilitate this process, Malinda invited Janet to reflect on three questions that contributed to her assessment profile (see Box 10.6; see also Table 5.2 in Chap. 5):

1. What was it like living in Logan County during the opioid epidemic?
2. What was Janet's reaction to the stress of the crisis?
3. How did Janet's family react to Beverly's addiction and death?

Box 10.5: Practice Example: Janet Explores Her Thoughts About Her Mother Beverly

Malinda: What did you think of the pictures Aunt Cassie brought in for us to see?
Janet: I never thought my mother looked so much like me.
Malinda: Do you want to say how that makes you feel?
Janet: I guess we were really close. But she made me so mad with all those drugs.
Malinda: Do you want to write a letter to her about it?
Janet: I do and I don't. I also feel so sad. I cry late at night so no one can hear me.
Malinda: Would you be surprised that a lot of people feel just like you do?
Janet: Well, they seem to just walk around minding their business.
Malinda: You would hear those feelings a lot if you attended Dr. Cantor's Monday night group on grief ceremonies.
Janet: I would rather put it all in my letter and bring it to you next week.

Box 10.6: Practice Example: Establishing an Assessment Profile and Goals

Malinda: I see you are ready to have a conversation about some serious things.
Janet: Yes, I want to be part of the goal-setting process. The staff should know what I think.
Malinda: That's great. We want to know what you have in mind. Let's start with the news reports about the epidemic. Did you follow them?

(continued)

Box 10.6 (continued)

Janet: Yeah, our gym teacher put us on to it. I then watched the news on TV. I was watching the reporter and thought she was wonderful. Maybe I will try to be a journalist now that I am an award-winning writer.

Malinda: You could begin by journaling about your stay here.

Janet: What is journaling?

Malinda: It's when you write about what we do here and what you think about it.

Janet: Do I get to expose it like the reporter on TV?

Malinda: It's not the same, but if you decide to you could come to one of our staff meetings.

Janet: That sounds scary.

Malinda: Why don't you decide what you want to share and with whom.

Janet: Maybe I'll test you out first.

Malinda: That sounds good. What else do you want to share about the opioid crisis and your family?

Janet: When Mom got addicted, we barely had enough money for food. The family in Logan started to ignore us. The only family I care about is Aunt Cassie. But I don't know what she thinks about me.

Malinda: Would you want to invite her to a family meeting with us?

Janet: Let's think about it.

Box 10.7: Practice Example: Janet Reflects on Death

Malinda: Do you want to comment on your assessment chart? It is only a draft until you add what you want.

Janet: I don't think people realize how frightening it is to watch your mother just get worse and worse. I didn't know what to do.

Malinda: I feel like it would be almost impossible to know what to say or do.

Janet: Right. You are just afraid. And then my family just walked away. Maybe Great-Grandpa Taylor who fought in the battle would have been brave.

Malinda: Do you think he was a family hero?

Janet: He must be if Aunt Cassie kept the newspaper all these years.

Malinda: You may be making sense of an old family story.

Malinda told Janet about the foster home's policy of inviting the residents to write their own progress notes and goals. As seen in the conversation in Box 10.7, Janet was encouraged to read and comment on her person–environment assessment profile (see Table 10.1).

Table 10.1 Person–environment (P-E) assessment chart: the Taylor family

P-E dimension	Indicator
Consequences of time and place	Janet experienced the death of her mother Beverly during the opioid epidemic
Response to the stress of past critical events	Janet and her mother overcame difficult financial times until Beverly became addicted
Reaction to disruption of biopsychosocial and spiritual processes	Beverly began to take drugs for recreational purposes. She quickly became addicted and was increasingly less able to function
Family response to adversity or change	Once Beverly became addicted, her extended family avoided her and Janet.
Consequences of social supports	Janet felt estranged from her family until Aunt Cassie provided encouragement
Significance of favorable environments	The county in which the Taylors lived was on the decline, as restaurants and other businesses closed and were boarded up
Effects of strong cultural identity	The Taylors stopped having holiday celebrations as the older generation died
Effects of human rights violations	Janet became familiar with the human rights abuses of the coal industry. She joined an online protest movement
Concerns about insufficient resources and services	As Janet's mother became increasingly addicted, the family had insufficient resources. Aunt Cassie dropped off care packages but did not say hello
Response to degradation of ecosystems	Coal mining had a severe impact on individual health and the degradation of the Logan County ecosystem

10.5 Intervention

10.5.1 Situational Meaning-Making

Situational meaning is the meaning given to a particular stressful environmental event. A narrative approach to grief work creates an opportunity for clients to revisit and rewrite their stories by describing an occurrence and its foreseeable outcome. The conversations between social workers and clients help clients recognize that a problem can have environmental influences and sociocultural and historical meaning. For example, as the interviews progressed, Janet gained a new context in which to frame the meaning of her mother's death. She increasingly saw her mother's death as an outcome of bad influences she could not have prevented. Janet's appraisal of her mother's death involved overcoming seeing the event as controllable and beginning to envision ideas for her future. This personal growth meant that she was learning how to see the problem outside herself and was becoming someone who could carry the weight and move forward from her distress (Gillies & Neimeyer, 2006).

10.5.2 Reconstructing a Narrative

As Janet saw new meaning in the forces that accounted for her mother's death, she was able to reconstruct her story of grief. This turning point—the restoration of meaning—eventually led to a reconstructed narrative and a positive evaluation of future events.

10.6 Evaluation

Janet appeared to use her time with Malinda to get to know better and reexamine her attitudes about her intergenerational family. As meaning was transformed, Janet decided she would consider a meeting with Aunt Cassie to reflect on her living situation.

10.7 Summary and Conclusion

As Janet reflected on her personal feelings within a family collective sociocultural, societal context, she was able to gradually construct her story of loss. Her story illustrates that when a social worker and a client coconstruct a micro- and macro-level narrative, this process contributes to the client's recovery in bereavement.

Summary of Learning Outcomes
Keep in mind the following:

- Social workers can help clients mourn through mutual reflection on their narratives.
- Social workers help clients resolve grief as they reconstruct narratives and social connections.

Discussion Questions

1. What were the benefits of Malinda and Janet exploring Janet's family history?
2. How would you define collective grief?

Chapter Exercise
Write a letter to a significant person in your life to whom you did not get to say goodbye.

Glossary

Attachment figure A person with whom another person has a special bond or relationship.
Bereavement The process of coming to terms with losing someone important.
Collective grief The effects of wide-scale group, community, or societal loss.
Collective stress A multisystemic, collective response to risk or stress connected to people's sense of others and place.
Grief Sorrow over an important person's death.
Grief therapy A range of helping techniques that help a person come to terms with grief.
Journaling The process of writing down thoughts and feelings about critical and/or daily events.
Loss The absence of someone important to one's life scheme.
Mourning Expressing feelings associated with a loss within a cultural context.
Resilient trajectory A developmental path that consists of strong protective factors.

References

Abramovitz, M., & Albrecht, J. (2013). The Community Loss Index: A new social indicator. *Social Service Review, 87*(4), 677–724. https://doi.org/10.1086/674112
Armour, M. (2010). Meaning making in survivorship: Application to Holocaust survivors. *Journal of Human Behavior in the Social Environment, 20*(4), 440–468. https://doi.org/10.1080/10911350903274997
Bonanno, G. A., & Diminich, E. D. (2013). Annual research review: Positive adjustment to adversity—Trajectories of minimal–impact resilience and emergent resilience. *Journal of Child Psychology and Psychiatry, 54*(4), 378–401. https://doi.org/10.1111/jcpp.12021
Bonanno, G. A., Wortman, C. B., Lehman, D. R., Tweed, R. G., Haring, M., Sonnega, J., Carr, D., & Nesse, R. M. (2002). Resilience to loss and chronic grief: A prospective study from preloss to 18-months postloss. *Journal of Personality and Social Psychology, 83*(5), 1150–1164. https://doi.org/10.1037/0022-3514.83.5.1150
Bonanno, G. A., Galea, S., Bucciarelli, A., & Vlahov, D. (2006). Psychological resilience after disaster: New York City in the aftermath of the September 11th terrorist attack. *Psychological Science, 17*(3), 181–186. https://doi.org/10.1111/j.1467-9280.2006.01682.x
Dowell, D., Arias, E., Kochanek, K., Anderson, R., Guy, G. P., Jr., Losby, J. L., & Baldwin, G. (2017). Contribution of opioid-involved poisoning to the change in life expectancy in the United States, 2000–2015. *Journal of the American Medical Association, 318*(11), 1065–1067. https://doi.org/10.1001/jama.2017.9308

Feder, A., Fred-Torres, S., Southwick, S. M., & Charney, D. S. (2019). The biology of human resilience: Opportunities for enhancing resilience across the life span. *Biological Psychiatry, 86*(6), 443–453.

Flesner, J. M. (2013). A shift in the conceptual understanding of grief: Using meaning-oriented therapies with bereaved clients. *VISTAS Online*, Article 25. https://www.counseling.org/knowledge-center/vistas/by-year2/vistas-2013/docs/default-source/vistas/a--shift-in-the-conceptual-understanding-of-grief%2D%2D-using-meaning-oriented-therapies-with-bereaved-clients

Ghertner, R., Waters, A., Radel, L., & Crouse, G. (2018). The role of substance use in child welfare caseloads. *Children and Youth Services Review, 90*, 83–93.

Gillies, J., & Neimeyer, R. A. (2006). Loss, grief, and the search for significance: Toward a model of meaning reconstruction in bereavement. *Journal of Constructivist Psychology, 19*(1), 31–65. https://doi.org/10.1080/10720530500311182

Greene, R. R. (2008). *Human behavior theory and social work practice* (3rd ed.). Aldine Transaction Press.

Kenyon, G. M., & Randall, W. (2001). Narrative gerontology: An overview. In G. Kenyon, P. Clark, & B. de Vries (Eds.), *Narrative gerontology* (pp. 3–18). Springer.

Kübler-Ross, E. (1969). *On death and dying*. Scribner.

Maciejewski, P. K., Zhang, B., Block, S. D., & Prigerson, H. G. (2007). An empirical examination of the stage theory of grief. *Journal of the American Medical Association, 297*(7), 716–723.

Neimeyer, R. A., Pennebaker, J. W., & van Dyke, J. G. (2009). Narrative medicine: Writing through bereavement. In H. M. Chochinov & W. Breitbart (Eds.), *Handbook of psychiatry in palliative medicine* (2nd ed., pp. 454–469). Oxford University Press.

Neimeyer, R. A., Burke, L. A., Mackay, M. M., & van Dyke Stringer, J. G. (2010). Grief therapy and the reconstruction of meaning: From principles to practice. *Journal of Contemporary Psychotherapy, 40*(2), 73–83.

Patrick, S. W., Frank, R. G., McNeer, E., & Stein, B. D. (2019). Improving the child welfare system to respond to the needs of substance-exposed infants. *Hospital Pediatrics, 9*(8), 651–654. https://doi.org/10.1542/hpeds.2019-0106

Quast, T., Storch, E., & Yampolskaya, S. (2018). Opioid prescription rates and child removals: Evidence from Florida. *Health Affairs, 37*(1), 134–139.

Rasouli, O., Unni Karin Moksnes, U., Trude Reinfell, T., Odin Hjemdal, O., & Eilertsen, B. (2022). Impact of resilience and social support on long-term grief in cancer-bereaved siblings: An exploratory study. *BMC Palliative Care, 21*, Article 93. https://doi.org/10.1186/s12904-022-00978-5

Supplemental References

Antonovsky, A. (1987). The salutogenic perspective: Toward a new view of health and illness. *Advances, 4*(1), 47–55.

Bonanno, G., & Kaltman, S. (1999). Toward an integrative perspective on bereavement. *Psychological Bulletin, 125*(6), 760–776.

Calhoun, L., & Tedeschi, R. (Eds.). (2006). *Handbook of posttraumatic growth: Research and practice*. Erlbaum.

Daley, D. C., Smith, E., Balogh, D., & Toscaloni, J. (2018). Forgotten but not gone: The impact of the opioid epidemic and other substance use disorders on families and children. *Commonwealth, 20*(2–3), 93–121. https://doi.org/10.15367/com.v20i2-3.189

Frankl, V. (1959). *Man's search for meaning*. Beacon Press.

Janoff-Bulman, R., & Franz, C. (1987). The impact of trauma on meaning: From meaningless world to meaningful life. In M. J. Power & C. R. Brewin (Eds.), *The transformation of meaning in psychological therapies: Integrating theory and practice* (pp. 91–106). Wiley.

Lazarus, R., & Folkman, S. (1984). *Stress, appraisal, and coping*. Springer.
Park, C. (2010). *Making sense of the meaning literature: An integrative review of meaning making and its effects on adjustment to stressful life events*. American Psychological Association.
Taplin, S., & Mattick, R. P. (2015). The nature and extent of child protection involvement among heroin-using mothers in treatment: High rates of reports, removals at birth and children in care. *Drug and Alcohol Review, 34*(1), 31–37.
Winstanley, E. L., & Stover, A. N. (2019). The impact of the opioid epidemic on children and adolescents. *Clinical Therapeutics, 4*(9), 1655–1662.

Chapter 11
Facilitating Community Development Following Disruption

Roberta Greene, Nancy Greene, and Connie Corley

Learning Objectives

This chapter discusses environmental influences stemming from past and current oppressive societal critical events that may disrupt the intergenerational transmission of resilience and interfere with client or constituency social functioning. When social workers recognize the intersection of historical and structural oppression and present-day concerns, they are better able to help clients resist discrimination-related stress and to support the transmission of personal and collective resilience. On completing this chapter, you should better understand how group affiliation and personal identity are intertwined and can be strengthened using micro to macro level skills from the resilience-enhancing stress model (RESM). You should be prepared to answer the following questions:

- What is the connection between historical critical events and current individual and collective discrimination-related stress or risks?
- What is the role of culture in bolstering resilience?
- How does a social worker use a grand narrative to foster group affiliation and resilient social functioning?
- How is resilience transmitted across generations?

This chapter discusses the use of the RESM narrative method with members of oppressed communities who may face chronic discriminatory risk. Although every person's story is unique, the narrative method of interviewing has the potential to

R. Greene
Steve Hicks School of Social Work, The University of Texas at Austin, Austin, TX, USA
e-mail: rgreene@utexas.edu

N. Greene (✉)
Ethelyn R. Strong School of Social Work, Norfolk State University, Norfolk, VA, USA
e-mail: nagreene@nsu.edu

C. Corley
Fielding Graduate University, Santa Barbara, CA, USA
e-mail: conniecorleyphd@gmail.com

R. Greene et al. (eds.), *Resilience Enhancement in Social Work Practice*,
https://doi.org/10.1007/978-3-031-38518-6_11

reveal social and cultural life meanings that can be tapped to enhance resilience at both the personal and community levels. The social worker's clinical interview is therefore expanded from a narrower focus on personal concerns to broader historical and sociocultural factors. This shift in practice focus involves social workers synthesizing narrative assessment data that can then be used to ameliorate personal, community, and societal distress.

To inform skills and to help social workers accomplish these practice goals, this chapter is divided into two sections. The first section describes narrative skills that can be used to address historical trauma related to the past long-standing US government practice of forcibly removing tribal nation children from their homes and relocating them in boarding schools. The ways in which Indigenous tribal nations have resisted the effects of this negative critical event and transmitted resilience from generation to generation are described. The second section discusses how citizens of New Orleans's Ninth Ward struggled with environmental racism associated with their experience during Hurricane Katrina in 2005. The ways in which their mutual aid efforts dovetailed with their inherent resilience are explored.

11.1 Historical Trauma: Indigenous Boarding Schools

11.1.1 The RESM and Responding to Stress

Resilience is people's capacity to deal with stressors and sustain, maintain, or reconstruct functional competence (Greene, 2014). Stress may be acute or arise from a sudden event. Stress may be chronic or stem from the wear and tear of ongoing everyday life, or it may have historical origins that are related to past adverse critical events.

According to Strumpfer (2002), the process of "resiling" starts when someone perceives a challenge or threat. He contended that resilience can be an individual or collective response and can be manifested during life transitions, in the aftermath of natural disasters or war, or during experiences of discrimination or persecution.

11.1.2 A Person–Environment (P-E) Shift

11.1.2.1 Interacting Ethnosystems and Institutions

Ecological theorists suggest that stress is the result of an imbalance between a person and the environment. From this point of view, a social worker's role is to increase clients' understanding of and resistance to such stress and to help them strengthen their functional capacity.

The shift in emphasis in resilience-enhancing practice to an all-encompassing P-E point of view can further the social worker's capacity to enhance resilience as a multilevel phenomenon. The perspective also expands the reach of the narrative interview to an examination of macrolevel forces that allow social workers to examine the history of unjust interactions between a particular ethnic subpopulation and larger US societal institutions.

Understanding the United States's many ethnosystems as a group bound together by their shared, unique historical and cultural ties, with each group exerting a relative degree of societal power, can provide insight into how the group has interacted with mainstream society over time (Solomon, 1976). Has the group had equal opportunity to participate in society and an equitable distribution of goods and services? Do its members now experience a sense of local control?

Unfortunately, ethnic groups may bear the brunt of prejudices that limit their members' full participation in society. These oppressive prejudices may restrict their political power and limit environmental justice, and they may be manifested in environmental and structural racism. (Brulle & Jenkins, 2005; Brulle & Pellow, 2006). This prejudicial environmental context places a responsibility on social workers to use anti-oppressive practice strategies.

Using an anti-oppressive process necessitates having knowledge of historical and current social policies and services and the role of policy in service delivery through a rights-based, anti-oppressive, and anti-racist lens (Council on Social Work Education, 2022, p. 10). Basic terms and processes (Table 11.1) and timelines of critical historical events experienced by Indigenous (Table 11.2) and African American (Table 11.3) ethnic groups illuminate factors that may help inform resilience-enhancing practice from an anti-oppressive point of view.

11.1.3 Understanding Multiple Levels of Resilience

As social workers cocreate and reconstruct client and constituency narratives at a sociocultural societal level, their clinical attention is focused on stressors at all levels of resilience:

The personal level of resilience encompasses how an individual perceives a critical event (e.g., discrimination). It involves ascertaining clients' inner meaning of events and fostering their competence under difficult conditions.

The interpersonal level of resilience refers to interactions among family and friends. It encompasses facilitating clients' formation of nurturing relationships that provide support during adverse situations.

The sociocultural level of resilience refers to the social meaning associated with experiencing adversity while living in a certain society in a particular time and place. Clients' sociocultural resilience is enhanced when they participate in their culture of origin as well as learn about others.

Table 11.1 Basic terms and processes

Term	Definition	Process
Environmental justice	Environmental justice is the fair treatment and meaningful involvement of all people regardless of race, color, national origin, or income with respect to the development, implementation, and enforcement of environmental laws, regulations, and policies	"Environmental justice occurs when all people equally experience high levels of environmental protection and no group or community is excluded from the environmental policy decision-making process, nor is affected by a disproportionate impact from environmental hazards" (Council on Social Work Education, 2015, p. 20)
Environmental racism	Environmental racism refers to policies, practices, or directives that differentially affect or disadvantage individuals, groups, or communities based on race or color (Bullard, 2004)	Environmental racism occurs when communities of color or those with less income are exposed to higher environmental risk
Oppression	Oppression is the withholding of power by the dominant group(s) in society	Oppression occurs when a dominant group(s) imposes a negative value on others and assumes greater political, economic, and social power over them (hooks, 1984). Although power exists in most societies and is inherent in social interaction, when power is abused, it constitutes a risk to the human condition (Goldenberg, 1978)
Structural racism	Structural racism refers to "any policy, practice, or directive that differentially affects or disadvantages individuals, groups, or communities based on race or color" (Chavis, 1993, p. iii)	Structural racism occurs when there is "the normalization and legitimization of an array of dynamics—historical, cultural, institutional and interpersonal—that routinely advantage white people while producing cumulative and chronic adverse outcomes for people of color" (Lawrence & Keleher, 2004). Structural racism has been and remains a fundamental cause of persistent disparities in access to resources and services (Churchwell et al., 2020)

The societal/structural level of resilience encompasses social policies, power relations, and economic conditions that affect institutional structures in which clients participate. It also involves clients being able to obtain resources such as housing, education, and health care.

Large-scale ecological resilience involves the stability and well-being of habitats in which people, many species of animals, and plants live. A classic definition of *ecological resilience* is a "measure of the persistence of systems and of their ability

Table 11.2 Timeline: Historical and sociocultural events experienced by US tribal nations

16,000 BCE	The Indigenous populations of the United States migrate across the Bering Strait to North and South America. They eventually build large city-states known for their expansive architecture and governing bodies (Mann, 2005)
1492	The Native population of North America north of the Rio Grande totals 7–10 million. Indigenous people group themselves into approximately 600 tribes and speak diverse dialects
1492–1775	Materials are traded between Natives and Europeans
1622–1924	The American Indian Wars are waged by European colonialists and later the US government against tribal nations across what is now the United States. Between 1800 and 1900, American Indians lose more than half their population, and their proportion of the total US population drops from 10.15% to 0.31%
1830	President Andrew Jackson signs the Indian Removal Act, which claims the lands east of the Mississippi River where tribal nations are located and forcibly resettles the inhabitants in lands west of the Mississippi
1838	President Andrew Jackson ignores the U.S. Supreme Court decision that overturned the relocations, enforcing his Indian Removal Act of 1830. The Cherokee people are forcibly moved from their homeland and relocated to Indian Territory, now Oklahoma. This is known as the Trail of Tears
1869–1960s	Hundreds of thousands of Native American children are removed from their homes and families and placed in boarding schools operated by the federal government and churches
1887	The Dawes Act authorized the US president to break up Indian land
1890	Sitting Bull, a Teton Dakota tribal leader of rebellions, is assassinated; the Wounded Knee Massacre occurs
1934	The Indian New Deal abolished the land allotment act of 1887
1924	The Indian Citizenship Act is passed into law
1968	The Indian civil Rights Act recognized tribal nations self-government
1978	The Indian Child Welfare Act is passed to oversee the placement of indigenous children in foster care
2015	The U.S. Army Corps of Engineers approves a route for the Dakota Access Pipeline that passes through Standing Rock Sioux tribal nation land. The tribe holds demonstrations to protect their land, which is a valuable cultural resource
2021	The U.S. Department of the Interior releases a historic investigative report on the federal Indian boarding school system

to absorb change and disturbance and still maintain the same relationships between populations" (Holling, 1973, p. 14). Disruption in habitats, such as erosion caused by climate change, can have a negative ripple effect throughout all social systems in which people interact.

The practice example in Box 11.1 describes the consequences of a sociocultural and societal crisis among tribal nations that involved the US government forcibly removing tribal nation children to boarding schools for the purpose of acculturation or "reeducation."

Table 11.3 Timeline: historical and sociocultural events experienced by African Americans

1619	The first African slaves are brought to Virginia. Chattel slavery is first recorded as a legal system that makes free African people property
1704–1845	During the era of slavery, slave patrols and night watches made up of adult White males are created to monitor the movement of slaves. Slaves who attempted to escape are severely punished. Chattel slavery plays a key role in the development of large plantations in the South
1787	The Constitutional Congress legislates the three fifths compromise, according to which an enslaved person is counted as three fifths of a human being
1793	A federal fugitive slave law is enacted
1830s	Most southern states forbid the teaching of reading to enslaved people
1837	Cheyney University of Pennsylvania is established as the first historically Black college or university
1863	President Abraham Lincoln issues the emancipation proclamation, freeing all slaves in areas of rebellion
1865	The Thirteenth Amendment to the U.S. Constitution officially abolishes slavery
1868	The Fourteenth Amendment to the U.S. Constitution provides equal protection under the law
1870	The Fifteenth Amendment to the U.S. Constitution prohibits any government in the United States from preventing people from voting based on race
1896	Jim Crow laws, which segregate Blacks from Whites, are made constitutional, enabling the government to legislate where Blacks are allowed to eat, live, drink, and go to school
1909	The National Association for the Advancement of Colored People (NAACP) is founded and begins to act for political and social change
1954	The U.S. Supreme Court declares school segregation illegal in *Brown v. Board of Education of Topeka*
1960–1970s	Three presidential commissions make recommendations for changes in policing. Research and training eventually lead to the community policing movement, which is based on improving community contact, forming trust, and enhancing communication
1964	The Civil Rights Act is passed, which prohibits discrimination in public places, provides for the integration of schools and other public facilities, and makes employment discrimination illegal
2013	The hashtag #BlackLivesMatter begins to circulate in response to the extrajudicial killings of 313 Black people by police, security guards, and vigilantes
2020	George Perry Floyd, Jr., an African American man, is murdered by police in Minneapolis, Minnesota, during an arrest

Box 11.1: Practice Example: Personal Is Political: Returning to the Sacred Path

It is not uncommon for members of tribal nations who experience behavioral health issues to first seek out help from their tribal elders. Therefore, Mr. and Mrs. River, and their 12-year-old son Nova ("chaser of butterflies") met with tribal elders to discuss their worries about Nova's difficulties in school. In addition, Mr. River relayed that he was having flashbacks of his confinement in a US government boarding school during the late 1960s. (The reaction to this wounding, which Brave Heart, 1998, called the *historical trauma response*, often includes survivor guilt, depression, symptoms of posttraumatic stress disorder, physical symptoms, psychic numbing, anger, suicidal ideation, and fixation to trauma.)

The elders discussed plans to help the family "return to the sacred path," a balanced place of peace found through the enactment of tribal customs and rituals. As they sat together in a healing circle, the elders and the River family shared information about Indigenous healing ceremonies. The family was encouraged to use traditional tribal healing techniques such as spiritual songs, dance, and meditation to reduce Mr. River's feeling that he was personally responsible for undoing a painful historical past. The family was also referred to a group intervention program on resolving grief and reducing collective group trauma. The program, which was held at a local clinic, was specially designed to incorporate Indigenous cultural beliefs.

11.1.4 Practice Analysis: Steps Taken

11.1.4.1 From Historical Trauma to Posttraumatic Growth

Maria Brave Heart (1998), a licensed clinical social worker and member of the Lakota tribal nation, was among the first to call practitioners' attention to the concept of historical trauma in clinical practice with Indigenous people. She recommended an evidence-based approach to practice that embeds information about a client's or constituency's cultural heritage into the narrative helping process.

There is increasing evidence that this perspective on trauma strengthens ethnic group membership and cultural ties, which serve as protective factors, buffering people from the negative effects of trauma and supporting resilient functioning across generations. This is in tune with research that suggests that most people who have undergone trauma rebuild their lives and that some experience posttraumatic growth (Bonanno, 2012; Greene et al., 2009; Janoff-Bulman, 1992, 2004). The concept of posttraumatic growth suggests that many people who have experienced trauma may encounter new possibilities or find anchors in their lives and then move forward to create positive change (Goldfein, 2004).

11.1.5 Practitioner Readiness: Adopting a Theoretical Framework

To help ameliorate trauma and help an Indigenous family return to the sacred path, social workers may want to adapt their practice to fit the cultural context of the family. To do this, practitioners who work with populations experiencing discriminatory stress may turn to Terry Cross's (1998) relational view of the development of the self. The relational view holds that the development of the self is shaped by the collective in which one lives, connecting community, clan, culture, and social history.

In addition, personal identity involves the characteristics of mind, body, and spirit:

Mind encompasses a person's thoughts, memories, knowledge, and emotional processes.

Body includes all physical aspects of the person.

Spirit incorporates metaphysical and innate factors.

As seen in the practice example in Box 11.2, Ronald, the social worker at the local behavioral health agency, began to apply these concepts to better understand how past critical events had become rooted in the River family's present-day grand narrative.

Box 11.2: Practice Example: Family Communication: Returning to the Sacred Path

Ronald:	Hello. I am proud to know that the elders sent you to us. I am hoping to start to get to know you today. What can you tell me?
Mr. River:	I am not sure why the elders sent us here. Many years ago, I returned to the reservation to work after finishing trade school. I am proud to say that I have held down a job ever since. My wife, who is a teacher's aide, is much younger, and we have a wonderful son, Nova.
Ronald:	What else should I learn about you all?
Mrs. River:	I think we are good parents. We tell our son about the sacred path. I don't know why he doesn't get along at school.
Ronald:	I hope you are willing to spend several meetings with me to learn just what that is about. I have found that such conversations create a family story.
Nova:	I wouldn't mind doing that. I knew nothing about the boarding school business before we met with the elders.
Mrs. River:	We didn't think telling you would be a good thing. Why do you want to know?
Nova:	My teacher says we should know our history and be proud.
Mr. River:	Why be proud? We were rounded up, driven miles away, thrown into a school, and pushed around.
Nova:	Maybe that is why you have bad dreams and I can't sleep?
Mrs. River:	Don't tell me you are one of those boys who sleeps in class?
Ronald:	I think you have set the topic for our conversations at our next meetings. Does that work for you three?
Mr. River:	If the two of them listen carefully.
Ronald:	Okay then. Why don't I give you some homework to help you with that. Can you each bring a letter of introduction that you write about yourself to our next meeting? We can read them together.
Mr. River:	Sounds like a place to start.

11.1.5.1 Practice Analysis: Steps Taken

The amelioration of the negative lingering effects of historical trauma in the River family began when the family met with the tribal elders. It was followed up by Ronald at the behavioral health agency. Both helping processes emphasized the effects of the separation of families and the forced assimilation of the boarding school experience that had led to acculturative stress. It became clear that the negative feelings Mr. River was experiencing had begun when he had been forced to incorporate the values, beliefs, language, and customs of the dominant society at boarding school.

11.1.6 Engagement

As can be seen from this practice example, building a RESM relationship necessitates an understanding of the historical and sociocultural factors of the organizations, communities, and people for whom practice has been designed. Therefore, resilience-enhancing social workers take a learning stance and, when possible, first engage with and learn from local leaders.

Engagement also means demonstrating transparency about wanting to attain an anchored understanding of the community to be served. Achieving an anchored understanding requires having the knowledge and skills to comprehend the space that other people occupy. In the practice example of the River family, social worker Ronald drew on tribal grand narratives to uncover local knowledge related to historical legacies, spiritual ceremonies, and prayers, all of which was intended to help the family heal. A third space is developed when "a client and social worker from different cultures negotiate and communicate to co-create new meanings and relationships" (Yan & Wong, 2005, p. 186).

11.1.7 Assessment: Coconstructing a Grand Narrative

The cocreated narrative is composed of intertwining strands that come together to create a grand narrative or master plot. Thus, it can be said that a narrative is both personal and political and shapes how people see themselves and their world. According to Kenyon and Randall (2001), this perspective on the narrative leaves the door open for it to be "re-storied" or transformed and increases the storyteller's capacity to grow.

Assessment from a RESM perspective involves social workers listening to constituencies' voices and learning about critical historical events. Practitioners then chart clients' P-E dimensions and develop an assessment profile. They also turn to concepts associated with the relational self to learn about the balance among mind, body, and spirit (Brave Heart et al., 2011).

11.1.7.1 Listening to Voices

Listening to the grand narratives of ethnic minority communities is a means of understanding the multiple losses expressed across generations of oppressed people that often shape individual and collective identity. Unfortunately, the voices of the oppressed are often silenced (Bruner, 1986). However, when social workers engage in cocreating a client narrative, the storyteller and story listener become partners in the helping process (White & Epston, 1990). In other words, therapeutic conversations are a form of action or "personal liberation" (Anderson & Goolishian, 1992, p. 25).

11.1.7.2 Learning About Critical Historical Events

A RESM assessment allows a social worker to learn how a client or constituency has made meaning of critical events as well as how they have mustered their personal and collective resources to deal with overwhelming demands (Gutheil & Congress, 2000). Practitioners hopefully tap these resources and assets as they work with oppressed groups. The skills in Box 11.3 may be useful in this regard.

11.1.7.3 Mapping P-E Dimensions: The Assessment Profile

11.1.7.3.1 P-E Dimensions

Ronald conducted a RESM assessment that began with mapping 10 P-E dimensions (Chap. 5, Box 5.3) as they related to the River family's risks and protective factors. The mapping of the River family's P-E dimensions appears in Table 11.4 and reveals the close connections among personal, tribal, and historical critical events. Identifying and affirming these important social links acted as healing factors that contributed to Mr. River's and his family's return to their sacred path.

11.1.7.3.2 Mind, Body, and Spirit Balance

Ronald's assessment in collaboration with the River family also involved reflecting on mind, body, and spirit. This revealed that Mr. River's thoughts and memories of his boarding school days dominated the family narrative.

Box 11.3: Skill Box: RESM Interview Skills for Societal Inclusiveness

Skill	Definition
Diffusing power differentials	Partnering with clients in the helping process
Challenging stigmas	Confronting false personal and collective images
Building on cultural beliefs	Learning about and encouraging local values and views

Table 11.4 Person–environment (P-E) assessment chart: the River family

P-E dimension	Indicator
Consequences of time and place	The Sioux tribal nation took part in a healing network prompted by Maria Brave Heart's mental health initiative for Indigenous people
Response to the stress of past critical events	Mr. River experienced historical trauma stemming from his experience of forced attendance at a boarding school
Reaction to disruption of biopsychosocial and spiritual processes	The River family sought help to return to a sacred path—a balance of mind, body, and spirit
Family response to adversity or change	The River family banded together and sought help from their tribal elders as well as a behavioral health agency
Consequences of social supports	The social support structures of the River family's tribal nation served as a buffer against risk
Significance of favorable environments	Although the tribal nation was nurturing, oppressive larger scale institutional structures often were not
Effects of strong cultural identity	Strong cultural ties acted as protective factors for the River family
Effects of human rights violations	There have been lingering effects of historical trauma on members of tribal nations. The abuses may contribute to posttraumatic stress, suicide, and depression
Concerns about insufficient resources and services	Resources and services are often insufficient for tribal nations. Many people live below the poverty line
Response to degradation of ecosystems	Tribal nations feel the ripple effects or repercussions of mainstream government projects that degrade local habitats

11.1.7.3.3 Assessment Profile

Although historical trauma can be transmitted from generation to generation, so too can resiliency. When reflecting on the River family's assessment profile, the social worker and client family turned to solutions that encompassed strong family and cultural bonds that acted as powerful healing factors.

11.1.8 Intervention

Interventions to resist societal structural inequities can encompass family therapeutic services and larger scale interventions that mobilize social change, develop innovative programs, and take congressional action.

11.1.8.1 Uniting Therapeutic Techniques

As was the situation with the River family, tribal nation child welfare facilities can combine traditional healing methods with behavioral mental health techniques. According to Brave Heart and Deschenie (2006), behavioral interventions may involve individual, family, and group therapy; telepsychiatry; parent support groups;

coaching and training; emergency mental health support; and case management. Traditional healing methods rooted in cultural understanding and traditional practices of childrearing can include being in nature, storytelling, planting, traditional song and dance, beading, and horseback riding.

11.1.8.2 Mobilizing Social Change

Child welfare programs for Indigenous children have not always been under local control. One initiative that has led the way in empowering community members and creating child welfare systems of care congruent with local practices (Blackstock & Trocmé, 2005) is the National Indian Child Welfare Association (NICWA). Led by executive director Terry Cross, a clinical social worker and member of the Seneca tribal nation, NICWA has spearheaded a movement of organizational change to return the auspices of child welfare services to local communities. As can be seen in the practice example in Box 11.4, NICWA works with communities to better match services with community needs and resources, deepen relationships and partnerships, and strengthen cultural ties. As this knowledge is disseminated and adopted locally, resilience is enhanced.

11.1.8.3 Actualizing Innovation

In the spirit of local control, the Cheyenne River Sioux tribe has developed a first-of-its-kind intentional community of foster care for Indigenous families and their children. In 2020 the Sioux tribal nation built a children's village called Simply

Box 11.4: Practice Example: Community-Based Advocacy and Sociocultural History

To advance social change, NICWA conducts local research forums with Indigenous tribal nations and people of color who are interested in cultural sensitivity and increased local control. The movement attempts to redress the historical fact that in 1860, when the US government's Bureau of Indian Affairs established the first boarding school, traditional childrearing practices were severely disrupted. The purpose of the boarding schools, which were usually located far from local communities, was to educate or acculturate Indigenous children in the United States with White mainstream values and culture (Bureau of Indian Affairs, 2021). Parents who resisted could be imprisoned, and children could be removed from their homes by force. This practice continued into the late 1960s.

Advocacy activities conducted by NICWA are shaped by the knowledge that Indigenous families and communities originally based their systems of child care on their cultural practices, laws, and traditions. It is hoped that children can once again be viewed as gifts from the creator and that parents, extended family, and the clan can be responsible for fostering the spirit of the child.

Smiles on their reservation in La Plant, South Dakota. The children's village was built with the collaboration of the Department of Social Services, tribal elders, and Native foster parents and can house up to 18 children. The priorities of the Simply Smiles children's village include providing mental health services when needed, keeping sibling groups together, and supporting the reunification of children with the biological family.

11.1.8.4 Continuing Advocacy

The legacy of the forced assimilation of Indigenous children in government-run boarding schools remains today. In 2021, under the direction of Deb Haaland, President Joe Biden's Secretary of the Interior and the first Native American to serve as a US cabinet secretary, the Department of the Interior released a historic investigative report on the federal Indian boarding school system (Bureau of Indian Affairs, 2021). According to Haaland,

> We continue to see the evidence of this attempt to forcibly assimilate Indigenous people in the disparities that communities face.… It is my priority to not only give voice to the survivors and descendants of federal Indian boarding school policies but also to address the lasting legacies of these policies so Indigenous peoples can continue to grow and heal. (Scherer, 2022, paras. 5, 35)

11.1.9 Evaluation

The practice strategies devised to return members of tribal nations to their sacred path have been evaluated by Maria Brave Heart and her team at the Takini Network. The Takini Network is a collective of Lakota, Sioux, and other Native natural, grassroots helpers and human service professionals whose mission is to improve the quality of life for Indigenous people by helping them transcend and heal from historical trauma. *Takini* is a Lakota word meaning "survivor or one who has been brought back to life."

Researchers from the Takini Network have found that participants in various locally run, culturally sound programs have a reduction in feeling responsible for undoing a painful historical past; experience less shame, stigma, anger, sadness; and have decreased guilt, increased joy, an improved valuation of their true self and of the tribe, and an increased sense of personal power.

11.2 Historical Trauma: Hurricane Katrina

This section of the chapter expands the perspective on resilience to an examination of large-scale ecological resilience. It explores how disruption in the ecology or habitat of the Gulf Coast surrounding New Orleans has had a negative ripple effect across the region. The remainder of the chapter describes the effects Hurricane

Katrina had on human functioning as well as the discriminatory stress that resulted from the sustained social inequality experienced by citizens of New Orleans's Ninth Ward. The manner in which residents of New Orleans's Ninth Ward manifested their inherent resiliency is also explored.

11.2.1 New Orleans's Ninth Ward: A Disenfranchised Marginalized Community

Some communities experience a long-standing pattern of neglect. Such a pattern may emerge more frequently in communities in which there has been inequality and discrimination (Blundo, 2012). This was true of New Orleans's Ninth Ward, where over the years low-income African American residents received proportionately fewer goods and services. According to the U.S. Census Bureau Data Center (2022), as of 2022, 91% of New Orleans's Lower Ninth Ward was Black, and 71% of its population lived below the poverty line (see Box 11.5).

Box 11.5: Practice Example: Hurricane Katrina, the Mississippi River, and Environmental Justice

The Ninth Ward, the poorest neighborhood in New Orleans, was once home to barbershops, banks, churches, and family homes. Then Hurricane Katrina made the problems of environmental racism and the need for environmental justice a stark reality. For years before Hurricane Katrina, scientists, journalists, and emergency officials worried about what would happen if a major hurricane were to hit New Orleans. In addition, it was well known that the Ninth Ward was in a flood zone with poorly structured levees.

Issues related to a proper response to the degradation of the surrounding ecosystem prevailed. A rise in sea levels and climate change put the region at environmental risk. To further compound the ecological damage, Mississippi wetlands were drained. Oil and gas companies contributed to the disruption by digging canals and burying pipelines. This caused nearby land to erode and wash away. By 2003, much of the area around New Orleans was 4.92–9.84 ft below sea level (U.S. Geological Survey, 2003).

The erosion of the Mississippi River was exacerbated by the fact that the levees that protected New Orleans had not been properly maintained by the U.S. Army Corps of Engineers, which administers the system of levees and floodwalls. As a result, Katrina resulted in more than 50 failures of the levees and floodwalls protecting New Orleans and caused flooding in 80% of the city. "In particularly hard-hit areas, like the Lower Ninth Ward, the water reached depths of up to 15 feet" (Pruitt, 2020, para. 4).

Hurricane Katrina did not just disrupt the ecology of the region; it caused hard-hitting damage to all social systems, including schools and hospitals. The practice example in Box 11.6 illustrates how the storm threatened the lives of residents.

Box 11.6: Practice Example: Hurricane Katrina, Sally Moore, and Her Family

Hurricane Katrina was one of the deadliest and costliest hurricanes to hit the United States. An estimated 1833 people died in the hurricane. The flooding that followed caused approximately $161 billion in damage, and millions of people were left homeless (Mohr & Powell, 2007).

Just before Katrina hit, Sally Moore, a 50-year-old African American grandmother with diabetes, her daughter and her husband, and her two grandchildren drove around the Ninth Ward, a low-income neighborhood in New Orleans, trying to find a shelter that was not full. None were available. They returned to sleep at Sally's home in the Ninth Ward.

By two or three in the morning, the floodwaters, which had risen precipitously, were flooding the house. The family went across the street to the roof of a five-story apartment house, where they called 911. There was no response. They then tried to signal several helicopters circling them, but they were never airlifted.

By the next morning, Sally Moore and her family determined that the floodwaters were too high for them to remain on the roof and that they needed to get to the Louisiana Superdome taking shelter on their own. They took a camper top from a nearby truck and created a little boat for the children. Sally was put on a floating air mattress. Sally's daughter and son-in-law swam and pushed the makeshift boat and mattress to the bridge near the Superdome. There they encountered the Louisiana National Guard armed with tanks and pointing rifles. Sally yelled, "Don't scare the children! Put the rifles down!" The family was finally allowed to enter the Superdome.

After 2 weeks in the Superdome, Sally Moore was bused to a temporary shelter in Texas, where a social worker found her a home in a new high-rise apartment donated by a local philanthropist. Sally was referred to a doctor and attended church services and soon adjusted to her new environment. However, she told the social worker that she hoped to someday return to the Ninth Ward, where she could be reunited with her family, hang up her clothes on the outdoor clothesline, and say hello to her neighbor. Sally's social worker assessment profile appears in Table 11.5.

Table 11.5 Person–environment (P-E) assessment chart: Sally Moore and her family

P-E dimension	Indicator
Consequences of time and place	Sally Moore and her family lived in the Ninth Ward of New Orleans during Hurricane Katrina. They experienced widespread devastation and discrimination
Response to the stress of past critical events	The Moore family was tightknit and over the years family members helped one another during adverse events
Reaction to disruption of biopsychosocial and spiritual processes	The Moore family responded quickly to the disruption caused by Hurricane Katrina
Family response to adversity or change	The Moore family met the disruption caused by Hurricane Katrina with innovative problem-solving solutions
Consequences of social supports	The Ninth Ward was known for enduring hardships and struggles (Lee, 2006)
Significance of favorable environments	Although the Moores' immediate environment was nurturing, oppressive larger scale institutional structures often were not
Effects of strong cultural identity	Sally Moore longed for her neighborhood after being relocated following Hurricane Katrina
Effects of human rights violations	The Moore family experienced human rights abuses during Hurricane Katrina that were exacerbated by living in the Ninth Ward
Concerns about insufficient resources and services	Citizens of the Ninth Ward had insufficient resources and services well before Hurricane Katrina
Response to degradation of ecosystems	The degradation of the habitat surrounding New Orleans had disastrous effects on the city and region

11.2.2 Rebuilding a Naturally Resilient Community

It took 17 years for New Orleans's Ninth Ward to begin to show signs of recovering from the widespread destruction of the hurricane. Insufficient resources and services compounded the stress of rebuilding. But on August 27, 2022, the Ninth Ward community held a celebration of what was termed their *inherent resiliency*. A local pastor was quoted as saying the following:

> I think it showcases it [resiliency] to the highest level. When we came back from Katrina, there was nothing here. We have twenty feet of water where we stand. To see that people are coming back, now let me be perfectly clear. It's work, to rebuild this community and to bring it back to a level where people can understand and respect this community again. (Brand, 2022)

11.2.3 Phases of RESM Recovery

Social workers are often involved in recovery efforts following disruptive events such as Hurricane Katrina. They may work with the American Red Cross, FEMA, or international organizations such as the World Bank. The application of RESM practice principles is briefly described below.

11.2.3.1 Pre-engagement

Creating disaster recovery plans is a cardinal rule of disaster management. Such plans spell out the actions that must be taken by all major stakeholders before, during, and after a natural or human-made adverse critical event.

11.2.3.2 Engagement

Engagement following natural and human-made disasters is best accomplished through community development efforts that identify and bring together community stakeholders and local officials. Social work planners identify and reach out to vulnerable groups. Agendas for meetings should be transparent and reflect the needs of various subpopulations of the community.

11.2.3.3 Assessment

Social workers who collaborate on planning a risk assessment assist in outlining the parameters of the large-scale infrastructure and geographic location of the potential critical event. Equity in setting priorities and goals is paramount. Social workers practicing with individual clients and families such as the Moore's assess the critical event from an interpersonal person-environment perspective.

11.2.3.4 Intervention

The intervention phase of a recovery plan needs to consider how different social systems and levels of resilient functioning come into play. What can contribute to recovery at the personal, interpersonal, sociocultural, societal, and larger scale ecological levels of resilient functioning?

11.3 Summary and Conclusion

Historic traumatic events reflect a group's experience with loss and pain. When appropriate, the pain needs to be distinguished as stemming from a natural disaster or an event linked to societal injustice. In this way, the transmission of traumatic historical events from generation to generation can be understood within the context of resilience and posttraumatic growth.

Summary of Learning Outcomes
Keep in mind the following:

- Social workers can identify power abuses that result in systemic oppression.
- Social workers can play a role in combating oppression by ameliorating environmental and structural racism.

Discussion Questions

1. How does culture act as a protective factor for oppressed communities?
2. How would you learn about large-scale historical factors that influence your client's situation?

Chapter Exercise
Write a reflection paper on a client who has demonstrated a natural resilience response. How was this manifested?

Glossary

Ethnosystem A group bound together by shared, unique historical and cultural ties and a relative degree of societal power.

Local control Describing a situation in which services are constructed and delivered in a manner that is congruent with the culture of the people in the community that is being served.

Posttraumatic growth Growth that results from benefiting from or transforming following adversity.

Power differential A difference in power between groups of people based on perceived differences in valuation.

Relational view of development A view of the self as shaped by the collective in which one lives.

Resiling Responding to a challenge or threat, such as in the aftermath of a natural disaster or war, or discrimination or persecution.

Return to the sacred path Indigenous ceremonies and spiritual practices performed to heal.

Sociocultural history People's lived experiences and present telling of events.

Structural racism A form of discrimination that limits people's access to goods and services based on race.

Takini A Lakota term that means "survivor or one who has been brought back to life."

References

Anderson, H., & Goolishian, H. (1992). The client is the expert: A not-knowing approach to therapy. In S. McNamee & K. J. Gergen (Eds.), *Therapy as social construction* (pp. 25–39). Sage.

Blackstock, C., & Trocmé, N. (2005). Community-based child welfare for Aboriginal children: Supporting resilience through structural change. *Social Policy Journal of New Zealand, 24*, 12–33.

Blundo, R. (2012). Resilience and mental health: A shift in perspective. In R. R. Greene (Ed.), *Resiliency theory: An integrated framework for practice, research, and policy* (2nd ed., pp. 139–158). NASW Press.

Bonanno, G. A. (2012). Uses and abuses of the resilience construct: Loss, trauma, and health-related adversities. *Social Science & Medicine, 74*(5), 753–756.

Brand, E. (2022, August 27). Lower Ninth Ward celebrates its resiliency on 17th anniversary of Hurricane Katrina. WDSU. Retrieved April 2, 2023, from https://www.wdsu.com/article/lower-ninth-ward-celebrates-its-resiliency-on-17th-anniversary-of-hurricane-katrina/41008129

Brave Heart, M. Y. H. (1998). The return to the sacred path: Healing the historical trauma response among the Lakota. *Smith College Studies in Social Work, 68*(3), 287–305.

Brave Heart, M. Y. H., & Deschenie, T. (2006). Resource guide: Historical trauma and post-colonial stress in American Indian populations. *Tribal College Journal, 17*(3), 24–27.

Brave Heart, M. Y. H., Chase, J., Elkins, J., & Altschul, D. B. (2011). Historical trauma among Indigenous peoples of the Americas: Concepts, research, and clinical considerations. *Journal of Psychoactive Drugs, 43*(4), 282–290. https://doi.org/10.1080/02791072.2011.628913. PMID: 22400458.

Brulle, R., & Jenkins, J. (2005). Foundations and the environmental movement: Priorities, strategies, and impact. In D. Faber & D. McCarthy (Eds.), *Foundations for social change: Critical perspectives on philanthropy and popular movements* (pp. 151–174). Rowman & Littlefield.

Brulle, R. J., & Pellow, D. N. (2006). Environmental justice: Human health and environmental inequalities. *Annual Review of Public Health, 27*, 103–124.

Bruner, J. (1986). *Actual minds, possible worlds*. Harvard University Press.

Bullard, R. D. (2004). *Environment and morality: Confronting environmental racism in the United States* (Identities, Conflict and Cohesion Program Paper #8). Retrieved April 2, 2023, from https://www.csu.edu/cerc/documents/EnvironmentandMorality-ConfrontingEnvironmentalRacismInTheUnitedStates-Bullard2004.pdf

Bureau of Indian Affairs. (2021). *United States federal Indian boarding school initiative investigative report*. Bureau of Indian Affairs.

Chavis, B. (1993). Foreword. In R. D. Bullard (Ed.), *Confronting environmental racism: Voices from the grassroots* (p. iii). South End Press.

Churchwell, K., Elkind, M. S. V., Benjamin, R. M., Carson, A. P., Chang, E. K., Lawrence, W., Mills, A., Odom, T. M., Rodriguez, C. J., Rodriguez, F., Sanchez, E., Sharrief, A. Z., Sims, M., & Williams, O. (2020). Call to action: Structural racism as a fundamental driver of health disparities: A presidential advisory from the American Heart Association. *Circulation, 142*(24), e454–e468.

Council on Social Work Education. (2015). *Educational policy and accreditation standards*. Retrieved April 3, 2023, from https://www.cswe.org/getattachment/Accreditation/Standards-and-Policies/2015-EPAS/2015EPASandGlossary.pdf

Council on Social Work Education. (2022). *Educational policy and accreditation standards*. Retrieved September 22, 2022, from https://www.cswe.org/getmedia/94471c42-13b8-493b-9041-b30f48533d64/2022-EPAS.pdf

Cross, T. (1998). Understanding family resiliency from a relational world view. In H. I. McCubbin, E. A. Thompson, A. I. Thompson, & J. E. Fromer (Eds.), *Resiliency in Native American and immigrant families* (pp. 143–158). Sage.

Goldenberg, I. I. (1978). Oppression and social intervention. Nelson Hall.

Goldfein, J. S. (2004, January/February). The stages of trauma recovery: Principles of effective treatment. *Psychotherapy Networker*, pp. 47–55.
Greene, R. R. (2014). Resilience as effective functional capacity: An ecological-stress model. *Journal of Human Behavior in the Social Environment, 24*(8), 937–950. https://doi.org/10.1080/10911359.2014.921589
Greene, R. R., Cohen, H., Gonzalez, J., & Lee, Y. (2009). *Narratives of resilience and social and economic justice*. NASW Press.
Gutheil, I. A., & Congress, E. (2000). Resiliency in older people: A paradigm for practice. In E. Norman (Ed.), *Resiliency enhancement: Putting the strength perspective into social work practice* (pp. 40–52). Columbia University Press.
Holling, C. S. (1973). Resilience and stability of ecological systems. *Annual Review of Ecology and Systematics, 4*, 1–23.
hooks, b. (1984). *Feminist theory: From margin to center*. South End Press.
Janoff-Bulman, R. (1992). *Shattered assumptions: Toward a new psychology of trauma*. Free Press.
Janoff-Bulman, R. (2004). Posttraumatic growth: Three explanatory models. *Psychological Inquiry, 15*(1), 30–34.
Kenyon, G. M., & Randall, W. (2001). Narrative gerontology: An overview. In G. Kenyon, P. Clark, & B. de Vries (Eds.), *Narrative gerontology* (pp. 3–18). Springer.
Lawrence, K., & Keleher, T. (2004, November 11). *Chronic disparity: Strong and pervasive evidence of racial inequalities* (Paper presentation). Race and Public Policy Conference, Berkeley, CA, United States.
Lee, S. (2006). *When the levees broke*. HBO Film.
Mann, C. (2005). *1491: New revelations of the Americas before Columbus*. Knopf.
Mohr, C. L., & Powell, L. N. (2007). Through the eye of Katrina: The past as prologue? An introduction. *Journal of American History, 94*(3), 693–876.
Pruitt, S. (2020, August 27). *How levee failures made Hurricane Katrina a bigger disaster*. Retrieved April 3, 2023, from https://www.history.com/news/hurricane-katrina-levee-failures
Scherer, K. (2022, May 19). DOI report details disgraceful unconstitutional federal Indian boarding school history. *West River Eagle*. Retrieved April 2, 2023, from https://www.westrivereagle.com/articles/doi-report-details-disgraceful-unconstitutional-federal-indian-boarding-school-history/
Solomon, B. B. (1976). *Black empowerment: Social work in oppressed communities*. Columbia University Press.
Strumpfer, D. J. W. (2002, September). *A different way of viewing adult resilience* (Paper presentation). 34th international congress on military medicine, Sun City, Northwest Province, South Africa.
U.S. Census Bureau Data Center. (2022). *Analysis of local employment dynamics*. U.S. Census Bureau Data Center.
U.S. Geological Survey. (2003). *Inclusive coastal science and engineering for resilient communities*. U.S. Geological Survey.
White, M., & Epston, D. (1990). *Narrative means to therapeutic ends*. Norton.
Yan, M., & Wong, Y. (2005). Rethinking self-awareness in cultural competence: Toward a dialogic self in cross-cultural social work. *Families in Society, 86*(2), 181–188.

Supplemental References

Albert, M. A., Slopen, N., & Williams, D. R. (2013). Cumulative psychological stress and cardiovascular disease risk: A focused review with consideration of Black-White disparities. *Current Cardiovascular Risk Reports, 7*(5), 318–325.
Brave Heart, M. (2017). *Historical trauma and unresolved grief: Implications for clinical research and practice with American Indians and Alaska Natives* (Paper presentation). Smith College, Northampton, MA, United States.

Jaramillo, C. (2019, May 23). Incinerators in Camden, Chester among nation's most polluting, report finds. *WHYY*. Retrieved April 2, 2023, from https://whyy.org/articles/incinerators-in-camden-chester-are-among-the-nations-most-polluting-report-finds/

Kleinhans, R., & Bolt, G. (2014). More than just fear: On the intricate interplay between perceived neighborhood disorder, collective efficacy, and action. *Journal of Urban Affairs, 36*(3), 420–446.

Laveist, T. A. (2003). Racial segregation and longevity among African Americans: An individual-level analysis. *Health Services Research, 38*(6), 1719–1733.

National Ocean Service. (n.d.). *Hurricane Katrina: Ten years later*. Retrieved April 2, 2023, from https://oceanservice.noaa.gov/news/aug15/katrina-ten-years-later.html

Pringle, H. (2011, November 1). The first Americans: Mounting evidence prompts researchers to reconsider the peopling of the New World. *Scientific American*. Retrieved April 2, 2023, from https://www.scientificamerican.com/article/first-americans-researchers-reconsider-peopling-new-world/

Templeman, S. B., & Mitchell, L. (2004). Utilizing an asset-building framework to improve policies for rural communities: One size does not fit all families. In T. L. Scales & C. L. Streeter (Eds.), *Rural social work: Building and sustaining community assets* (pp. 196–205). Brooks/Cole.

Chapter 12
Interactional Resilience for Aging Out of Care: A South African Example

Adrian Du Plessis van Breda

Learning Objectives

This chapter introduces and presents a wide range of research from South Africa supporting an interactional approach to resilience. In addition, it focuses on a particular group of at-risk people, namely, young people aging out of foster care. On completing this chapter, you should have a good understanding of the interactional processes of resilience involving interactions between personal, relational, and systemic protective resources. You should be prepared to answer the following questions:

- What is the difference between protective factors and protective processes?
- What can at-risk individuals interact with to build their resilience?
- What are the most important protective processes for young people transitioning out of care?
- What can a social worker or a social service organization do to build the resilience of young people transitioning to adulthood?

12.1 Introduction and Background

Transitions are a ubiquitous feature of life (Meleis et al., 2000). As we grow up, we transition through a series of developmental stages. As children, we change caregivers, grades, schools, friends, and subject choices. As adults, we transition into and out of relationships, jobs, homes, communities, and health statuses. Although many transitions are planned and anticipated, others, such as being fired or sustaining an injury, are unexpected and potentially traumatic. Some life or work contexts, such as working for the military, which require personnel to repeatedly deploy away from home, are transitional in nature, leading to frequent family transitions (Van Breda, 1999).

A. D. van Breda (✉)
Department of Social Work & Community Development, University of Johannesburg, Johannesburg, Republic of South Africa
e-mail: avanbreda@uj.ac.za

R. Greene et al. (eds.), *Resilience Enhancement in Social Work Practice*,
https://doi.org/10.1007/978-3-031-38518-6_12

A category of transitions that has received much attention in the literature is that of *youth transitions*, which refers to the transition from adolescence to young adulthood, corresponding roughly to the period of 15–25 years, which Arnett (2019) termed "emerging adulthood." In their book *Key Concepts in Youth Studies*, Cieslik and Simpson (2013) placed "Youth Transitions" second in their table of contents, after "Defining Youth," which indicates the prime place it occupies in youth studies. They wrote, "Youth transitions remains [*sic*] one of the most prominent and important concepts in the context of youth studies" (p. 8).

Youth transitions are multifaceted, including the transitions from school to work, from parental housing to independent (or peer) housing, from singlehood to some kind of relationship, from dependence toward independence, through a series of part-time or temporary jobs, through periods of rebellion and identity formation (Furlong & Cartmel, 2006). In the Global North, researchers are seeing an extension of the period of youth transitions up to the late 20s and even beyond (Arnett, 2015; Furlong & Cartmel, 2006).

In South Africa, youth transitions are complicated by adverse conditions for youth. In particular, the exceptionally high unemployment rate among young adults, which exceeds 63% (Statistics South Africa, 2022), limits opportunities for young people to transition from school into the workplace. Despite South Africa being more than two decades into a non-racial democracy, educational, employment, and housing options for youth remain meager. This is particularly true for Black and female youth, both globally and in South Africa (Cieslik & Simpson, 2013), because society continues to be inequitably structured along the lines of race and gender. In such conditions of structural disadvantage, youth must rely primarily on personal agency (such as effort, drive, and determination) to leverage social resources (such as relationships, opportunities, and small amounts of cash) to facilitate their transition toward young adulthood (Furlong & Cartmel, 2006).

Among the broader population of transitioning youth are various subgroups that have unique challenges and needs. These include youth with disabilities, LGBTQI+ youth, as well as youth transitioning out of the care system. It is this last group that is the focus of this chapter. Children are removed from their families because of a wide range of issues, such as child neglect or abuse, parental substance addiction, mental illness or crime, and child behavioral problems. These children are then placed into some form of alternative care, such as foster care or residential care. Although some children are returned to their families within a year or two, many remain in care until they reach adulthood (defined in many countries as age 18; Strahl et al., 2021). At that point, these youth age out of care, which means they leave care because they have reached the age at which they must do so. Aging out of care is thus defined by age, and not by readiness to leave care. We call these youth who age out of care *care-leavers* and this process of transitioning out of care *care-leaving*.

Globally, studies of care-leavers suggest that this is a group of highly vulnerable youth in transition, which has led some researchers (Mendes et al., 2011, p. 1) to refer to care-leavers as "one of the most vulnerable and disadvantaged groups in society" and one of the most socially excluded (Stein, 2006). Care-leavers often have poorer outcomes than their peers who did not enter the care system in relation to education, employment, crime, substance abuse, finances, and mental health.

Notwithstanding this rather bleak view of youth transitions and care-leaving, not all care-leavers succumb to these structural disadvantages. Stein (2006), for example, seminally divided care-leavers into three groups: victims, who struggle to transition and have poor developmental outcomes; survivors, who grapple with the transition out of care and have mixed outcomes; and those who move on, who appear to be well prepared and supported in their transition and who adjust well to adult life.

It seems, then, that although transitions can be challenging and may lead to negative outcomes, this is not universally the case. Transitions often become opportunities for growth, new beginnings, and new opportunities. These differences in outcomes raise questions about the resilience of youth in transition. What is it that enables some care-leavers to transition well—in Stein's (2006) terms, to "move on"—when others do not?

Research on care-leaving in South Africa similarly shows that although some youth struggle with the transition out of care, others appear to do quite well—continuing with their education, finding work, establishing intimate relationships, avoiding drugs and crime, and maintaining good levels of health and well-being. Understanding what enables these outcomes, in the contexts of multiple layers of adversity and vulnerability, may generate important clues for providing effective support to all care-leavers and potentially also to all youth in transition.

Research my student researchers and I have undertaken on the resilience of families, organizations, care-leavers, and youth in transition is leading to the conclusion that the foundation of resilience among care-leavers is interactional. Although there are aspects of resilience that are personal and aspects that are in the social environment around youth, much of what appears to foster better outcomes in the transition out of care seems to take place in the interaction between youth and their social environment. There is, however, not a great deal of research focusing on this interaction—most research focuses on personal resilience and/or resilience resources in the environment, not on what happens in the interactions between these. This chapter, therefore, uses the term *protective processes* rather than the more familiar *protective factors* to emphasize that it is the interactive process between systems or people that protects. *Resilience* is thus a verb (a doing word or process) more than an adjective or noun (which describes a resource or a characteristic).

This chapter draws on South African research to argue that the interaction between people and their environment appears to be the foundation of the resilience of care-leavers. Resilience theory itself is not reviewed, as this book already provides a thorough account of resilience theory. *Resilience* is defined here as "the multilevel processes that systems engage in to obtain better-than-expected outcomes in the face or wake of adversity" (Van Breda, 2018a, p. 4). The following section provides a brief introduction to care-leaving. Then several studies that foreground the interactional foundation of care-leaver resilience are reviewed. Based on that, the chapter concludes with a model of interactional resilience for care-leavers and other youth in transition and makes suggestions for practice.

12.2 Care-Leaving

Care-leavers are young people who were placed in alternative care as children. In South Africa, children enter the care system according to the procedures set out in the Children's Act (Republic of South Africa [RSA], 2005). Children may enter care for a variety of reasons, including because they have been orphaned, abused, or neglected or because they have behavioral problems that their parents or caregivers are unable to deal with adequately. In all instances, the "best interests of the child" are central in the decision to remove a child from their family and place the child in care (RSA, 2005, section 7). This standard applies both to the decision to remove a child and to the decision on where to place the child.

The Children's Act makes provisions for a variety of placement options when a child is removed, including temporary safe care while work is being done with the family to enable them to take their child back; foster care, in which a child is placed with relatives (kinship care) or nonrelatives for a time-limited or indefinite period; residential care, in which a child is placed in a child and youth care center or group home, officially for 2 years but typically for much longer, and often until age 18; or adoption, in which a child becomes the legal child of other parents (RSA, 2005). This chapter focuses on residential or group care.

Ideally, children transition back into their families within 2 years because the issues that led to their removal and placement have been resolved (RSA, 2005, section 157). This is referred to as *family reunification* (Department of Social Development, 2012). However, evidence suggests that family reunification is underdeveloped and inadequately implemented in South Africa (Jamieson, 2014; Mamelani Projects, 2013; Potgieter & Hoosain, 2018; Sauls & Esau, 2015).

Because family reunification is limited and because it is often in the child's interests to remain in care, many young people leave care when they reach the age of 18. This is termed *aging out of care*, because the reason for leaving care is not that the child or the family is ready for the child to leave care but simply that the child has reached the age of majority. In South Africa, children are required to leave care at the end of their 18th year, thus at the end of the school year. Application can be made for an extension of placement up to age 21 if the young person continues with schooling or education, but this is uncommon.

The United States (Courtney, 2009) and the United Kingdom (Dixon et al., 2015) have adopted policies of corporate parenting, which means that when the state decides to remove a child from parental care, it takes over the parental role and does what a "good" parent would do, including continuing to provide care to the young person far beyond age 18 (Van Breda et al., 2020). Such a principle does not exist in South Africa, where care (and child-directed social security) is, to a large extent, terminated when the child becomes an adult at age 18. Extensions are possible only when these young people continue in education, and even then they are not evenly applied by the welfare system.

The vulnerability of care-leavers (Mendes et al., 2011) stems from a pileup of vulnerabilities over both time and context rather than merely as a result of the actual transition out of care, as evidenced by a growing body of research in Africa (Frimpong-Manso, 2020; Luboyera, 2014; Mhongera & Lombard, 2016; Nshinyimana, 2014; Roeber, 2011; Sekibo, 2020; Takele et al., 2021; Ucembe, 2013). This pileup begins in childhood, through exposure to adversity in the family origin, which ultimately leads to the child's removal from parental care. This removal is itself an adversity, involving a fracturing of the child's relationship with the family system and often a wider community and cultural system. While in care, some children continue to experience adversity through abuse by caregivers, multiple changes of placements, and the stigma of being in care. The transition out of the care system is yet another fracturing of a caregiving relationship, involving the abrupt loss of parental figures and siblings as well as the structure and opportunities of the care system (in particular residential care). After these young adults leave care, they continue to be vulnerable, because they are not eligible to receive child welfare services and there are few if any provisions for aftercare social services or social security for care-leavers.

Research on care-leavers from Girls and Boys Town South Africa (GBTSA), a national nongovernmental organization offering a range of child and family services, including residential care, in South Africa, points to less than ideal outcomes at 1 year out of care (Dickens, 2018). A quarter (25%) of participants in this research had one change of home during that year, whereas a third (31%) had two or more moves. A third (35%) of participants were not in employment, education, or training despite all care-leavers having a plan to either pursue education or take up employment at the time of leaving care. "Two thirds of participants (67%) who were not in their final year of school at disengagement were not studying a year later" (Dickens, 2018, p. 562). Three-quarters (79%) of participants were earning below a livable monthly wage (R1600, $88). Although most participants (87%) were not abusing drugs or alcohol at the time of data collection, a quarter (23%) had been involved in some kind of criminal activity or conflict with the law in the past year.

Over time, however, we see improvements in many of the care-leaving outcomes of care-leavers, as shown in a longitudinal study in South Africa (Dickens & Van Breda, 2021). For example, providing their own accommodation increased from 30% at 1 year out of care to 42% at 7 years out of care. The percentage of participants not in employment, education, or training dropped from 39% to 27%; the percentage working increased from 32% to 73%; and the percentage earning a livable income increased from 21% to 78%.

These findings suggest the presence of resilience processes among South African care-leavers enabling the achievement of better-than-expected outcomes over time. This prompts the resilience question: What protective processes enable these resilient outcomes among South African care-leavers? Furthermore, the finding that among South African care-leavers there is wide variation in outcomes—with some doing quite well and others doing quite badly—prompts a further resilience question: What enables some to do better than others?

12.3 Lessons for Interactional Resilience from Research on Care-Leavers in South Africa

I have been conducting research on care-leavers and the care-leaving process in South Africa together with several student researchers and research associates (Van Breda, 2018b). Key findings drawn from these studies provide support for the argument that the foundation of the resilience of care-leavers in South Africa is interactional. Among the many interactional protective processes that emerge are strong interpersonal skills, empathy, supportive relationships, social services, rites of passage, mentoring, mobilizing others toward helpfulness, reading and responding to one's environment, taking responsibility to care for others, teamwork, and social activities. These protective processes are shown to enable resilient outcomes like good health and well-being, stable and self-supported accommodation, low rates of substance abuse and crime, greater engagement in education and work, and stronger relationships.

12.3.1 The Agency–Structure Debate

The debate between agency and structure, or micro and macro, has been ongoing in sociology since the 1970s (Sztompka, 1994) and continues into present times (Delva et al., 2021). On the one hand, there is an emphasis on the power that individuals exert over their lives, making free choices based on personal preference; on the other hand, there is an emphasis on the structural forces in society that constrain and direct the choices of individuals. Theory development to address this debate is ongoing (Dépelteau, 2018). The developmental social welfare approach in South Africa has also picked up on this debate, calling for a harmonization of both micro and macro approaches to social welfare (Patel, 2015).

I did a content analysis of the constructs that emerged in five studies on care-leaving in South Africa (Van Breda, 2016). The constructs were not exclusively resilience oriented but also included a focus on interventions and care-leaving outcomes. Constructs relating to both agency and structure emerged in the analysis in equal numbers (24 of each). Agency constructs included alcohol and drug use, having goals, and a sense of identity, whereas structure constructs included the availability of a mentoring program, staff turnover, and poverty. It seems, then, that both agency and structure are important yet distinct aspects of care-leaving.

In addition, however, an equal number of constructs that were neither strictly agency nor strictly structure emerged. These constructs involved both agency and structure or were located in the space between agency and structure and constituted interactions (Van Breda, 2016). These included community involvement, being heard by others, and engaging in teamwork. Relationships with people are, perhaps, quintessentially interactional. However, relationships, which are typically categorized as environmental protective processes (and thus located in the macro or structure domain), involve not only another person in the environment but also the care-leaver. A relationship exists only when both parties engage in a reciprocal relationship through their interactions with each other. Thus, it appears that it is the actual interaction between the care-leaver and another person that facilitates resilient outcomes rather than either the young person (agency) or the other person (structure) alone.

In addition to constructs that are interactional, there were also numerous instances of the interaction between an agency construct and a structure construct. For example, Tanur (2012) described "how a rites of passage intervention (which constitutes structure, because it is a service that exists in the environment independently of the care-leaver) creates a space within which care-leavers can explore and reconstruct their selves (agency)" (Van Breda, 2016, p. 47). This suggests that structure on its own is insufficient to effect change; there is a need for agency as well, enabling a translation from macro to micro and potentially from micro to macro also. This further supports the importance of interaction in care-leaving, because it is only as the care-leaver engages with the structural resource that resilience is enabled, as illustrated in the practice example in Box 12.1.

Box 12.1: Practice Example: Mobilizing Personal Agency to Change the Environment

Bongani, a social worker, is interviewing Cynthia, a young person preparing to age out of care. Bongani is keen for Cynthia to take increasing responsibility for her life, as she is soon to become independent of the care system. But it seems she is anxious or reluctant to do so. Bongani uses focused exploratory questions to help Cynthia describe situations in which she was able to direct her own life while in care. It emerges that Cynthia has had very few such opportunities—more often than not her choices are constrained by care legislation, policy, and procedures. Bongani helps Cynthia recognize that although she is keen to exercise agency, the structure of her social environment has not allowed it. They agree that they will collaboratively approach the manager of the residential facility to make the care system more flexible, thus relaxing the structure, so Cynthia has a real opportunity to exercise agency. The first opportunity involves Cynthia negotiating with her case worker to spend a long weekend with a school friend out of town. Bongani coaches Cynthia in thinking through what she wants. They role-play how she will advocate for it. He accompanies her to the manager to coach her, when needed, during their conversation. In the end, Cynthia has a great weekend with her friend.

12.3.2 Journey to Independent Living

In 2011, I led a study on the care-leaving journey toward independent living (Van Breda, 2015; Van Breda et al., 2012) with two colleagues from GBTSA. We interviewed nine young men who had left GBTSA's care several years previously. Using grounded theory methods (Charmaz, 2014), we generated a theory of care-leaving that emphasized young people's agency in shaping their social environment. The theory of leaving comprised four interactional resilience or protective processes (Van Breda, 2015):

1. *Striving for authentic belonging:* building deep, meaningful relationships that satisfied the need for attachment. For example, Andre had had a history of broken relationships before coming into care. While in care, he worked to build a tight circle of friends who cared for and stood up for one another. He felt a deep sense of belonging in this group, fully accepted for who he was (Van Breda et al., 2012).
2. *Networking people for goal attainment:* mobilizing people in their social environment, including those they did not know well and even strangers, to help them achieve short- and long-term goals. Thabo had left care a few years before. He described how he had the "gift of the gab" and could talk anybody into anything. For example, he applied for a job and "talked the manager at the time into giving me a job." Another time he was arrested by a police officer, but when he used his "gift of the gab" the officer said, "You look like a bright kid" and let him go with a warning (Van Breda et al., 2012, p. 29).
3. *Responding to context:* reading their social context to identify and leverage opportunities while minimizing or avoiding risks. Germaine, who grew up in care, befriended a drug merchant who ran a gang. This relationship gave him safety, protection, and belonging. But by observing other gang members in his context, he realized that this relationship was going to lead him into crime, so he responded by leaving. He said, "All that sounded nice [car, money, rings, clothes] but I knew at the end of the day what's going to happen, because I saw how he treated his people… I knew that's the time I had to get myself out, so I disappeared" (Van Breda et al., 2012, pp. 31–32).
4. *Building hopeful and tenacious self-confidence:* working persistently to develop hope for a better future and believe in themselves. Christopher, for example, was able to rewrite his story, saying, "Well the positives that I've experienced are that a person does have will power. You can make up your mind to do something or not to do something. Like I've made my mind up that I'm going to go on my own and my target is to make it while I am on my own, and I believe I'm going to make it. I know as well I had my downfalls, I've learnt from my mistakes and ja [yes]. The mistakes I made I will not make again" (Van Breda et al., 2012, p. 37).

Three of these four resilience constructs can be regarded as interactional, in that they involve not only the care-leaver or the social environment but rather the reciprocal interactions between them. First, striving for authentic belonging (Van Breda, 2015), which appeared central in participants' constructions of a successful transition from care, is about establishing meaningful and enduring relationships with others that generate an experience of belonging. Participants typically constructed these relationships as familial in nature, even when they were not actually family (e.g., teachers or a crime lord). This striving for authentic belonging was a protective process because it facilitated better transitional outcomes, while at the same time it was an outcome because it was toward such belonging that youth were striving.

Second, networking people for goal attainment (Van Breda, 2015) also involves interactions with other people, but not in a typically relational manner. Here others are viewed as potential resources that can contribute to the young person's transitional goals. The resilience process involves using networking strategies to mobilize a person into a helpful stance and to leverage resources from the person. In most instances, these people are strangers or acquaintances, which Granovetter (1983, p. 201) referred to as "weak ties." Weak ties are typically overlooked in resilience research, as the focus is primarily on sustained and meaningful relationships. However, weak ties are often a better route to new information or opportunities than strong ties, because they tap into social networks to which care-leavers and their strong ties are not connected. Weak ties, however, only become part of a protective process when the care-leaver networks with and mobilizes them.

Third, with responding to context (Van Breda, 2015), care-leavers observe their social context, read the opportunities and threats that the context presents to them, and then respond in ways that are contextually appropriate and that preserve or advance themselves. This involves cognitive processes of observing, assessing, and anticipating future outcomes and also the capacity to intervene in changing one's social environment.

Box 12.2: Practice Example: Constructing New Narratives for Perceived Failures

Ntombi is a social worker providing aftercare support to women who have transitioned out of care. Kwesi, one of her clients, informs her that she is pregnant. Kwesi shares that many of the people in her social environment have been very critical of her pregnancy, judging her for being irresponsible and defining her as a failure. Kwesi is hurt by this, as she views her pregnancy as a gift and as an opportunity to be a better parent to her child than her parents were to her. Ntombi helps Kwesi fill out this narrative of becoming a mother as an opportunity to grow, develop responsibility, take care, and express her love. This positive narrative inspires Ntombi.

12.3.2.1 Implications for Practice

Social or care workers can listen carefully to a young person in or leaving care describing his or her interactions with other people. When they hear one of these four processes being used, they could ask the young person to describe that interaction in more detail, in particular what the young person did to improve the situation. They could name it with the young person. Moreover, they could explore other times the young person has used this same skill. In so doing, the young person gains confidence in social interactions and skills and further develops them for future use.

12.3.3 Women's Journey Toward Independent Living

The previous study (Van Breda, 2015; Van Breda et al., 2012) focused on only young men, because they were the only care-leavers GBTSA could track. This, however, raised the question of whether this theory of care-leaving was relevant only for men and what it meant for female care-leavers. A student researcher thus replicated the study with female care-leavers. She found that all four resilience enablers listed previously were clearly present in the narratives of woman care-leavers (Van Breda & Hlungwani, 2019). This appears to confirm that these care-leaving processes are gender neutral.

However, she also found two new protective processes that were not apparent or prominent in the men's narratives (Hlungwani & Van Breda, 2020). These were *taking on responsibilities* and *embracing motherhood*; the latter can be regarded as a specific and highly prominent instance of the former. Female care-leavers' journey toward independent living was enabled by a heightened sense of responsibility for others, including peers who left care around the time they did; other children still in care; and their own siblings, friends, and other family members. By aspiring to take on responsibility for these others, these female care-leavers adjusted well to independence and established themselves as capable role models.

Similarly, these female care-leavers embraced motherhood. Five of Hlungwani's nine participants had a child, and the other four all planned to have a child (Hlungwani & Van Breda, 2020). Motherhood was a prominent theme among these women, who spoke passionately of the desire to create a life for their children that they themselves did not have as children, as illustrated in Box 12.2. Thus, having or desiring a child was a protective process because it motivated the journey toward independent living.

These protective processes are both interactional. They reflect an internal motivation among these women, rooted in a present and future view of the self as taking care of others and raising a happy child, that was expressed in their actual interactions with others (in all cases) and with their child (for those who had a child). They are thus not merely self-representations but also interactions with others in their social environment.

12.3.4 Protective Processes in the Growth Beyond the Town Study

My primary research project, called *Growth Beyond the Town*, is hosted at GBTSA. It is a longitudinal study of young people leaving GBTSA's care and transitioning toward young adulthood and independent (or, more accurately, interdependent) living (Dickens & Van Breda, 2021). Dr. Lisa Dickens, a former student researcher, did her doctoral research on this project (Dickens, 2016, 2018; Van Breda & Dickens, 2015). In 2021, we published findings on the contribution of resilience to the 7-year transitional outcomes of care-leavers (Dickens & Van Breda, 2021) with a sample of 176 care-leavers. Figure 12.1 summarizes these findings by showing the main protective resilience processes on the left that contribute to main transitional or resilient outcomes on the right over the first 7 years out of care.

The protective processes were measured with the Youth Ecological-Resilience Scale, which was designed and validated for this study (Van Breda, 2017). They were structured according to the person-in-environment framework, which is one of the foundational frameworks in social work theory (Van Breda, 2022b). Variables were thus categorized as personal, interactional, relational, environmental, and in-care. Figure 12.1 depicts the resilience processes that predicted three or more transitional outcomes over the first 7 years out of care. Box 12.3 provides an example of how the scale can be used in practice to consolidate existing protective processes and build new protective processes.

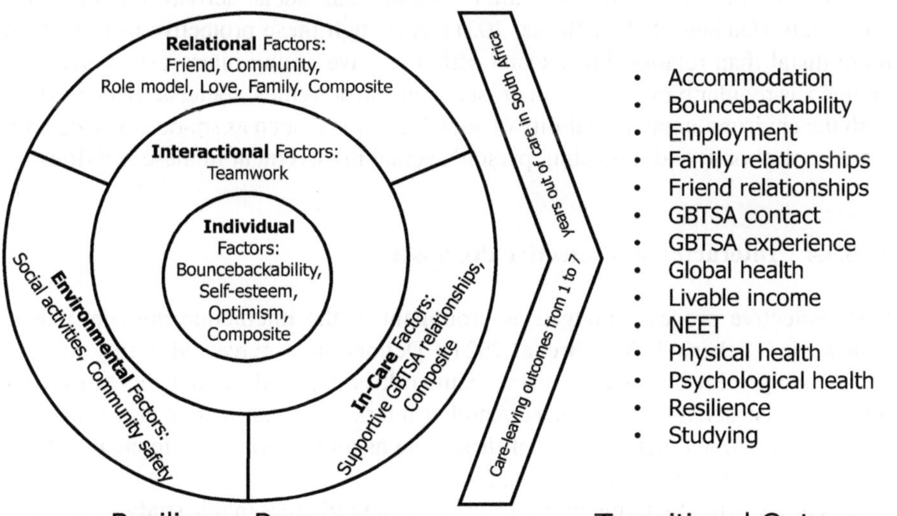

Fig. 12.1 Contribution of resilience to care-leaving outcomes (Dickens & Van Breda, 2021). (Adapted from Van Breda & Dickens, 2017, Copyright 2017, with permission from Elsevier). *NEET* not in employment, education, or training

12.3.4.1 Relational Protective Processes

Six of the protective processes are relational: relationships with friends, community members, role models, lovers, and family and a composite measure of relational resilience (which includes relationships with teachers; Dickens & Van Breda, 2021). As has been argued previously, although these relationships are in the social environment, they are inherently interactional, because their resilience-enabling properties emerge as the care-leaver interacts with these people. Merely having people in the environment is insufficient to facilitate transitional outcomes; it is through the interrelationship between them that resilience is enabled (Van Breda, 2022a).

12.3.4.2 In-Care Protective Processes

In-care processes, notably having supportive relationships with staff at GBTSA, also emerged as prominent protective processes (Dickens & Van Breda, 2021). These relationships are important because although they appear similar to the relationships mentioned previously, they are formal relationships with paid professionals in the childcare context.

12.3.4.3 Environmental Protective Processes

Another two protective processes are environmental: social activities and community safety (Dickens & Van Breda, 2021). Although these protective processes are more distal than relationships, social activities have strong interactional elements. Defined as regular participation in prosocial group activities, social activities require both the environmental availability of social activities (such as sports clubs, dancing classes, or choirs) and the young person's actual involvement in these activities.

12.3.4.4 Interactional Protective Processes

One protective process emerged as prominent in the interaction domain, that is, teamwork (Dickens & Van Breda, 2021). Defined as a perceived ability to work productively with others in a team, teamwork is explicitly about the capacity to interact constructively with others. Another interactional protective process, empathy, emerged in another analysis of these data as an important component of long-term resilient outcomes (Van Breda, 2022a).

It is noteworthy that nine of the 15 prominent predictors in this study have strong interactional elements (Dickens & Van Breda, 2021). Only four predictors emerged at the individual level. This suggests that greater attention should be given to understanding resilience at the interface between people and other people and systems.

Box 12.3: Practice Example: Utilizing Resilience Measures to Identity Strengths and Growth Areas
Anthony, a social worker, helps young people in care identify their protective processes. He asks them to complete the Youth Ecological-Resilience Scale and then works through the scores with them. He shows the young people the resilience processes on which they score higher than most other young people. By eliciting examples from the young people of how they exercise these resilience processes, he builds up their confidence in their interactions with the world around them. Later, he also identifies that resilience processes that are less strong and explores ways that these can be strengthened. In so doing, Anthony helps consolidate existing strengths and build new strengths for sustainable resilience.

Box 12.4: Practice Example: Building Social Skills
Khanyi is a social worker working with foster families. She helps foster parents identify and develop the social skills of the children in their care. For example, a simple skill is greeting—saying "hello" to a stranger. Khanyi guides the foster parents to first explain what the greeting skill is and why it is useful—we are always meeting strangers, and learning to connect with them will help open up opportunities for us. She also teaches the parents a step-by-step approach to teaching the skill to their foster children: first describe the steps, then demonstrate the steps with the child, then ask the child to use the skill with them, and a bit later practice the skill with a stranger in a safe space (such as at a youth club). She also helps the parents give positive feedback to the child on the child's use of the skill (e.g., "You did so well when you looked the adult in their face. That showed confidence!") and suggestions for improvement (e.g., "Perhaps you could have smiled a bit more? You have such a lovely smile. When you smile at others, they just want to smile back at you. It makes both of you feel happy.").

12.3.5 Transfer of Social Skills

Another former student researcher, Dr. Fatima Mmusi, investigated how GBTSA care-leavers transferred the social skills they had learned while in GBTSA's care into young adulthood, several years after leaving care (Mmusi, 2013; Mmusi & Van Breda, 2017). These skills were acquired through daily interaction with staff in the child care system, as illustrated in Box 12.4, and constituted protective processes that facilitated better life outcomes.

Mmusi found that care-leavers continued to use the skills they had learned in their post-care lives in their interactions with other people, which suggests that these were interactional skills. More important, she found that they adapted these skills to suit the particular contexts in which they found themselves. These skills, therefore, were not merely something care-leavers had as a personal resource but were tools that they used to facilitate or mobilize their social environment. Thus, these skills were inherently interactional, as they played out in contexts and took on different forms depending on these contexts.

12.3.6 Narratives About Possible Selves

Another former student researcher, Dr. Sue Bond (2017), conducted her doctoral research on the development of possible selves and resilience in youth transitioning out of care. Possible selves (Markus & Nurius, 1986; Van Breda, 2010) are narratives about one's self in the future that motivate current behavior. There are two principal classes of possible selves: those that are hoped for and those that are feared. Hoped-for possible selves drive people toward a desired future, whereas feared possible selves drive people away from an undesirable future (Bond, 2022).

Bond (2017) found that the possible-selves narratives of adolescents preparing to transition out of care were rooted in their interactions with other people. These included families of origin, peers, role models, turning point people, activities, and social services. Some of these sources of possible selves are clearly relational, involving strong ties with family and friends, whereas others are only marginally relational, involving weak ties with role models and turning point people, who are often encountered only once or twice. Other sources of possible selves are related to structures in the social environment with which the care-leaver engages, that is, social activities and social services. Thus, the narratives about one's future or possible selves emerge in people's interactions with people and structures in their social environment. Furthermore, possible selves and resilience processes are mutually reinforcing patterns of development (Bond & Van Breda, 2018). The use of possible selves in practice is illustrated in Box 12.5.

Box 12.5: Practice Example: Activities to Build Up Possible Selves
Nyeleti, a social worker, uses an activity called the *Possible Me Tree* (Bond, 2022) to help Musa, who is preparing to leave care, to construct a narrative of the life she wants to live in the future. The tree exercise helps Musa identify and describe in some detail the person she aspires to be as well as the person she fears becoming. Through this exercise, Musa develops a clearer vision of her future self. Nyeleti works with Musa to determine what actions she needs to take now to achieve that future self. Musa feels quite excited that this possibility could become a reality and so invests time and effort in making it so.

12.3.7 Social Policy

Finally, in line with contemporary notions of multisystemic resilience (Theron & Van Breda, 2021), Pinkerton and Van Breda (2019) argue that social policy provides a macro framework of resilience enabling that holds and supports organizations, communities, and families as they provide a social ecology that fosters the resilience and resilient outcomes of care-leavers. It is the constructive interactions across a set of nested systems that enable the resilience of young people leaving care.

12.4 Conclusion and Implications

South African research on care-leaving is foregrounding the interactional foundation of resilience. It appears that many protective processes that we currently think of as personal or environmental may in fact be interactional, involving a set of transactions between people and other people or social structures and systems. It appears, then, that resilience is not primarily qualities or capabilities of individuals or primarily the availability of protective resources in the social environment. Rather, interaction between people and systems appears to be the mechanism whereby these personal and environmental resources become resilience enabling.

12.4.1 A Model of Interactional Resilience for Care-Leavers

Fostering the resilience of care-leavers, therefore, requires far more than teaching children skills or placing resources in their environment. It requires a more integrative approach that considers various interactive layers of the social environment. Based on the findings presented in this chapter, Fig. 12.2 is a proposed model of interactional resilience for care-leavers. This model may indeed be of relevance to all youth in transition, not just those transitioning out of the care system.

A set of *structures* is required in the social environment to serve as possible resources for youth in transition. These may include formal systems (e.g., social services, foster placements, child and youth care centers, churches, and clubs) as well as relational resources with family, peers, teachers, and mentors and unregulatable encounters with strangers (weak ties). A resource-rich social environment is an important platform for youth in transition, providing a varied network of resources from which they can select that which is most suitable for their needs and preferences. Although some structures do require funding, many are indigenous and informal, requiring no infrastructure or funds.

As a foundation for such structures, youth need to be equipped with *agency*. Although many agential competencies are natural and emerge through life, in particular through adversity, these are also competencies that can be nurtured,

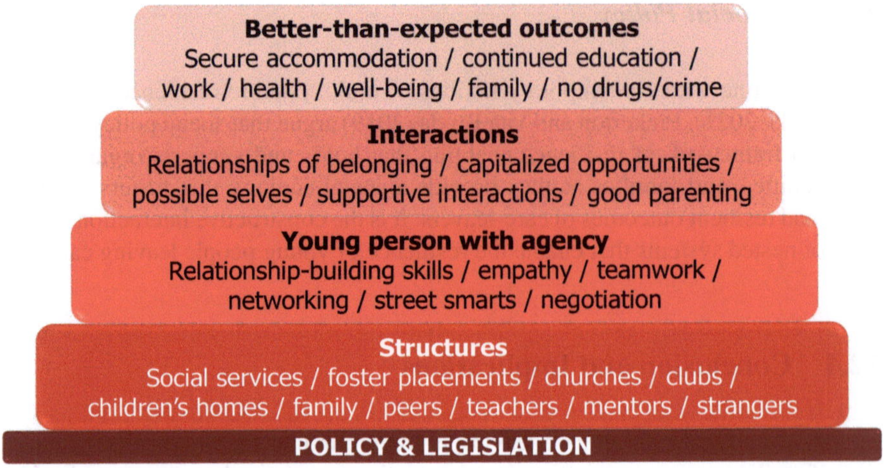

Fig. 12.2 A model of interactional resilience for care-leavers

modeled, and learned. GBTSA's social skills program is a good example of this: A range of social skills are available, tailored to the needs of each child in care, and taught through intensive coaching and mentoring in real-world contexts. The skills necessary for youth agency include relationship building, empathy, teamwork, networking, street smarts, and negotiation. These provide young people with a set of skills to interact with the people and structures around them.

Drawing on these skills, young people need to *interact* with their social environment. This may involve youth building intimate relationships that satisfy a need for belonging (building strong ties), reading their social environment and capitalizing on opportunities presented to them (and avoiding, neutralizing, or transforming threats and risks in their social environment), and developing hoped-for and feared possible selves that motivate their interactions with others toward their goals. These interactions also require the structures in the young person's life space to provide supportive responses to young people, including both initiating reaching out to a young person and reacting constructively to the young person's initiative. Good-enough parenting by parents and other parental figures is an ongoing need, not only in childhood but also in young adulthood.

From these interactions between supportive structures and an agential young person, *better-than-expected outcomes* are likely to result. For young people leaving care, and indeed for all youth in transition to young adulthood, these outcomes may include secure accommodation, continued and completed education that sets the young person up for employment, lack of involvement in substance abuse or criminal activities, stable and rewarding employment, good health and well-being, and a contented family life. It is to such outcomes that all parents aspire for their children.

This entire model rests on a foundation of *social policy* and legislation. Without this foundation, it is unlikely that all the elements required for successful transitioning from care or childhood toward independent living will occur. Moreover, policy

Table 12.1 Implications of interactional resilience for practice with care-leavers

Drawing on indigenous knowledge and heritage, it may be useful to think of resilience as a form of *ubuntu* more than as personal growth, knowledge, or a set of discrete skills. *Ubuntu* refers to the relational and interactional nature of human life, that we are who we are through other people (Van Breda, 2019). Our identity is not merely our own but rather is located in our relationships and interactions with others.
Social services need to mobilize existing *structures* in the social environment or put in place new structures that can serve as a crucible for growth and development. This will involve not merely reacting to crises when they present themselves but rather engaging in macro processes to strengthen communities and to capitalize on resources and processes already available but underutilized, thereby cultivating a resource-rich environment for care-leavers.
Social service practitioners working with children in care need to develop in them a range of *relational skills* to establish loving relationships that foster the experience of belonging (strong ties). These may include active listening, empathy, and conflict management.
Social service practitioners working with children in care need also to develop their skills to build *functional networks* (weak ties) that enable youth to achieve their goals. These may include meet-and-greet skills that provide confidence to approach and engage strangers, skills for ingratiating oneself (such as paying compliments and aligning oneself with the interests of the other), and skills in negotiation.
Social service practitioners working with children in care need to create opportunities for children to implement these interactional processes in the *real world*, not merely in the counseling room or the safety of the children's home. In particular, as children in care transition through adolescence, there is an increasing need to allow them to take developmentally age-appropriate risks in the world outside their home.
Social services need to develop *policy* to support these activities, both mandating and enabling them, in particular in contexts of high numbers of children and low numbers of professional staff.

is needed to leverage the financial resources necessary to provide some of the structures and services mentioned here.

12.4.2 Implications for Social Services

All these insights regarding interactional resilience and the model of interactional resilience in Fig. 12.2 have several implications for practice, as set out in Table 12.1.

12.5 Summary and Conclusion

Social work's notion of person-in-environment argues that practitioners must consider both the environment around people and the interactions between people and their environment. This approach, which harkens back to the earliest days of social work (Van Breda, 2022b), is central to what makes social work social work. This chapter has argued that an interactional approach to resilience, which focuses on the interactions between people and the systems around them, is key to a holistic and effective resilience practice. An interactional approach to resilience promises to generate useful insights into the actual processes involved in achieving better-than-

Summary of Learning Outcomes
Keep in mind the following:

- Interactions between multiple systems are more helpful for building resilience than protective resources in just one system.
- Resilience is more about processes (acting, doing, interacting—verbs) than about the qualities of a person (characteristics, resources, strengths—nouns and adjectives).
- A variety of micro, meso, and macro interventions can build the resilience of young people transitioning out of care.

Discussion Questions
1. How does the notion of interactional resilience link with the resilience-enhancing stress model's focus on risk and resilience, systems, ecology, and narrative?
2. Which of the lessons for interactional resilience in this chapter do you connect with the most? Why? How can you use this in your own life?

Chapter Exercise
Write a one-page reflection paper on the interactional resilience processes that facilitated, are facilitating, or could facilitate your transition from adolescence to adulthood.

expected outcomes in the face or wake of adversity, leading to improved services for those experiencing adversity. For young people leaving care, this promises to increase their chances of a successful transition toward independent living.

Glossary

Agency The capacity and belief in one's ability and resources to influence one's environment.

Aging out of care The process of transitioning out of foster and other forms of alternative care toward independent living as a result of turning 18 years or another legally required age for leaving care; also called *care-leaving*.

Better-than-expected outcomes Outcomes of individual or other systems that are better than might be expected given the adversities faced or better than average or better than the person or system had expected.

Interactional resilience An approach to resilience that is "not so much about what is inside the young person, nor what is in the world around them, but rather what takes place in the interaction between young people and other people and the social environments that surround them" (Mushonga & Van Breda, 2021, p. 427).

Multisystemic resilience An approach to resilience that focuses on the "complex, reciprocal relationship between the many systems that influence … people's capacity to thrive" (Ungar et al., 2023, p. 1).

Possible selves "Individuals' ideas of what they might become, what they would like to become, and what they are afraid of becoming … [that] thus provide a conceptual link between cognition and motivation" (Markus & Nurius, 1986, p. 954).

Protective processes The actions that people and other systems engage in, in contexts of (or following) adversity, that facilitate better-than-expected outcomes.

Resilience "The multilevel processes that systems engage in to obtain better-than-expected outcomes in the face or wake of adversity" (Van Breda, 2018a, p. 4).

Social policy The plans that institutions (from small institutions like a local church through to large institutions like a country's government) put in place to achieve the flourishing of human society.

Social skills Any techniques or competencies, both verbal and nonverbal, that people use in their interactions with other people to build productive relationships or achieve mutually desired outcomes.

References

Arnett, J. J. (2015). *Emerging adulthood: The winding road from the late teens through the twenties* (2nd ed.). Oxford University Press.

Arnett, J. J. (2019). Foreword. In V. R. Mann-Feder & M. Goyette (Eds.), *Leaving care and the transition to adulthood: International contributions to theory, research and practice (pp. xiii–xx)*. Oxford University Press.

Bond, S. (2017). *The development of possible selves and resilience in youth transitioning out of care* [Unpublished doctoral thesis]. University of Johannesburg.

Bond, S. (2022). What are possible selves and how do we find out about them? The revised Possible Me Tree model. *Child Care in Practice*. Advance online publication. https://doi.org/10.1080/13575279.2022.2071218

Bond, S., & Van Breda, A. D. (2018). Interaction between possible selves and the resilience of care-leavers in South Africa. *Children and Youth Services Review, 94*, 88–95. https://doi.org/10.1016/j.childyouth.2018.09.014

Charmaz, K. (2014). *Constructing grounded theory* (2nd ed.). Sage.

Cieslik, M., & Simpson, D. (2013). *Key concepts in youth studies*. Sage.

Courtney, M. E. (2009). The difficult transition to adulthood for foster youth in the US: Implications for the state as corporate parent. *Social Policy Report, 23*(1), 1–19. https://doi.org/10.1002/j.2379-3988.2009.tb00058.x

Delva, J., Forrier, A., & De Cuyper, N. (2021). Integrating agency and structure in employability: Bourdieu's theory of practice. *Journal of Vocational Behavior, 127*, 103579. https://doi.org/10.1016/j.jvb.2021.103579

Department of Social Development. (2012). *Guidelines on reunification services for families*. Department of Social Development.

Dépelteau, F. (2018). *The Palgrave handbook of relational sociology*. Springer.

Dickens, L. F. (2016). *The contribution of resilience to the 12-month transitional outcomes of care-leavers in South Africa* [Unpublished doctoral thesis]. University of Johannesburg.

Dickens, L. F. (2018). One-year outcomes of youth exiting a residential care facility in South Africa. *Child & Family Social Work, 23*(4), 558–565. https://doi.org/10.1111/cfs.12411

Dickens, L. F., & Van Breda, A. D. (2021). *Resilience and outcomes of South African Girls and Boys Town care leavers seven years on*. Girls & Boys Town South Africa and University of Johannesburg.

Dixon, J., Lee, J., Stein, M., Guhirwa, H., Bowley, S., & Catch22 NCAS Peer Researchers. (2015). *Corporate parenting for young people in care: Making the difference?* Catch22. Available at https://eprints.whiterose.ac.uk/86665/2/CparentSum.pdf

Frimpong-Manso, K. A. (2020). Stories of care-leaving: The experiences of a group of resilient young adults on their journey to interdependent living in Ghana. *Emerging Adulthood, 8*(1), 16–25. https://doi.org/10.1177/2167696818807114

Furlong, A., & Cartmel, F. (2006). *Young people and social change* (2nd ed.) McGraw-Hill International.

Granovetter, M. S. (1983). The strength of weak ties: A network theory revisited. *Sociological Theory, 1*(1), 201–233.

Hlungwani, J., & Van Breda, A. D. (2020). Female care-leavers' journey to young adulthood from residential care in South Africa: Gender-specific psychosocial processes of resilience. *Child & Family Social Work, 25*(4), 915–923. https://doi.org/10.1111/cfs.12776

Jamieson, L. (2014). Children's rights to appropriate alternative care when removed from the family environment: A review of South Africa's child and youth care centres. In P. Proudlock (Ed.), *South Africa's progress in realising children's rights: A law review* (pp. 213–251). Children's Institute.

Luboyera, F. (2014). Unsettled youth: Examining the life experiences of resettled youth raised under institutional care in Uganda. International Institute of Security Studies.

Mamelani Projects. (2013). *Transitional support: The experiences and challenges facing youth transitioning out of state care in the Western Cape*.

Markus, H., & Nurius, P. (1986). Possible selves. *American Psychologist, 41*(9), 954–969. https://doi.org/10.1037/0003-066X.41.9.954

Meleis, A. I., Sawyer, L. M., Im, E., Messias, D. K. H., & Schumacher, K. (2000). Experiencing transitions: An emerging middle-range theory. *Advances in Nursing Science, 23*(1), 12–28.

Mendes, P., Johnson, G., & Moslehuddin, B. (2011). *Young people leaving state out-of-home care*. Australian Scholarly Publishing.

Mhongera, P. B., & Lombard, A. (2016). Poverty to more poverty: An evaluation of transition services provided to adolescent girls from two institutions in Zimbabwe. *Children and Youth Services Review, 64*, 145–154. https://doi.org/10.1016/j.childyouth.2016.03.013

Mmusi, F. I. (2013). *Description and assessment of care leavers' application of social skills into independent living* [Unpublished master's dissertation]. University of Johannesburg.

Mmusi, F. I., & Van Breda, A. D. (2017). Male care-leavers' transfer of social skills from care into independent living in South Africa. *Children and Youth Services Review, 81*, 350–357.

Mushonga, S., & Van Breda, A. (2021). Nonhuman systems as a source of interactional resilience among university students raised by alcohol-abusing caregivers in Lesotho. *Social Work/Maatskaplike Werk, 57*(4), 425–442. https://doi.org/10.15270/57-4-967

Nshinyimana, B. (2014). *Experiences of children regarding the care received at Windhoek residential child care facilities* [Unpublished master's thesis]. University of Namibia.

Patel, L. (2015). *Social welfare and social development* (2nd ed.). Oxford University Press.

Pinkerton, J., & Van Breda, A. D. (2019). Policy as social ecological resilience scaffolding for leaving care: A case study of South Africa. In V. R. Mann-Feder & M. Goyette (Eds.), *Leaving care and the transition to adulthood: International contributions to theory, research and practice* (pp. 87–104). Oxford University Press. https://doi.org/10.1093/oso/9780190630485.003.0006

Potgieter, A., & Hoosain, S. (2018). Parents' experiences of family reunification services. *Social Work/Maatskaplike Werk, 54*(4), 438–451. https://doi.org/10.15270/54-4-671

Republic of South Africa. (2005). *Children's Act, No 38 of 2005*. Government Printers.

Roeber, E. (2011). *A fair chance to life: Young care-leavers in Kenya*. Kenya Network of Care Leavers.

Sauls, H., & Esau, F. (2015). *An evaluation of family reunification services in the Western Cape: Exploring children, families and social workers' experiences of family reunification services within the first twelve months of being reunified.* Department of Social Development Western Cape, Directorate Research, Population and Knowledge Management.

Sekibo, B. (2020). Experiences of young people early in the transition from residential care in Lagos State, Nigeria. *Emerging Adulthood, 8*(1), 92–100. https://doi.org/10.1177/2167696818822232

Statistics South Africa. (2022). *Quarterly labour force survey: Quarter 1: 2022* (P0211). Retrieved February 17, 2023, from https://www.statssa.gov.za/publications/P0211/P02111stQuarter2022.pdf

Stein, M. (2006). Research review: Young people leaving care. *Child and Family Social Work, 11*(3), 273–279.

Strahl, B., Van Breda, A. D., Mann-Feder, V., & Schröer, W. (2021). A multinational comparison of care-leaving policy and legislation. *Journal of International and Comparative Social Policy, 37*(1), 34–49. https://doi.org/10.1017/ics.2020.26

Sztompka, P. (1994). Introduction. In P. Sztompka (Ed.), *Agency and structure: Reorienting social theory* (pp. ix–xvi). Routledge.

Takele, A. M., Kotecho, M. G., & Mendes, P. (2021). The poverty of policy: Examining care leaving policy in Ethiopia. *Institutionalised Children Explorations and Beyond, 8*(2), 206–271. https://doi.org/10.1177/2349300320982399

Tanur, C. (2012). Project Lungisela: Supporting young people leaving state care in South Africa. *Child Care in Practice, 18*(4), 325–340. https://doi.org/10.1080/13575279.2012.713851

Theron, L. C., & Van Breda, A. D. (2021). Multisystemic enablers of sub-Saharan child and youth resilience to maltreatment. *Child Abuse & Neglect, 119*(2), Article 105083. https://doi.org/10.1016/j.chiabu.2021.105083

Ucembe, S. (2013). *Exploring the nexus between social capital and individual biographies of "care leavers" in Nairobi, Kenya: A life course perspective*. Institute of Social Studies.

Ungar, M., Theron, L., & Höltge, J. (2023). Multisystemic approaches to researching young people's resilience: Discovering culturally and contextually sensitive accounts of thriving under adversity. *Development and Psychopathology*. Advance online publication. https://doi.org/10.1017/S0954579423000469

Van Breda, A. D. (1999). Developing resilience to routine separations: An occupational social work intervention. *Families in Society, 80*(6), 597–605. https://doi.org/10.1606/1044-3894.1774

Van Breda, A. D. (2010). Possible selves: Group work with young people in a South African township. *Practice: Social Work in Action, 22*(3), 181–192. https://doi.org/10.1080/09503153.2010.485678

Van Breda, A. D. (2015). Journey towards independent living: A grounded theory investigation of leaving the care of Girls & Boys Town South Africa. *Journal of Youth Studies, 18*(3), 322–337. https://doi.org/10.1080/13676261.2014.963534

Van Breda, A. D. (2016). The roles of agency and structure in facilitating the successful transition out of care and into independent living. *Social Work Practitioner-Researcher, 28*(1), 36–52. https://doi.org/10.25159/2415-5829/1349

Van Breda, A. D. (2017). The Youth Ecological-Resilience Scale: A partial validation. *Research on Social Work Practice, 27*(2), 248–257. https://doi.org/10.1177/1049731516651731

Van Breda, A. D. (2018a). A critical review of resilience theory and its relevance for social work. *Social Work/Maatskaplike Werk, 54*(1), 1–18. https://doi.org/10.15270/54-1-611

Van Breda, A. D. (2018b). Research review: Aging out of residential care in South Africa. *Child & Family Social Work, 23*(3), 513–521. https://doi.org/10.1111/cfs.12431

Van Breda, A. D. (2019). Developing the concept of *ubuntu* as African theory for social work practice. *Social Work/Maatskaplike Werk, 55*(4), 439–450. https://doi.org/10.15270/55-4-762

Van Breda, A. D. (2022a). The contribution of supportive relationships to care-leaving outcomes: A longitudinal resilience study in South Africa. *Child Care in Practice*. Advance online publication. https://doi.org/10.1080/13575279.2022.2037516

Van Breda, A. D. (2022b). Person-centred approaches to social work practice. In D. Hölscher, R. Hugman, & D. McAuliffe (Eds.), *Social work theory and ethics: Ideas in practice* (pp. 1–26). Springer Nature Singapore. https://doi.org/10.1007/978-981-16-3059-0_8-1

Van Breda, A. D., & Dickens, L. F. (2015). Educational persistence and social exclusion among youth leaving residential care in South Africa. *Nuances: Estudos sobre Educação, 26*(1), 22–41.

Van Breda, A. D., & Dickens, L. (2017). The contribution of resilience to one-year independent living outcomes of care-leavers in South Africa. *Children and Youth Services Review, 83*, 264–273. https://doi.org/10.1016/j.childyouth.2017.11.009

Van Breda, A. D., & Hlungwani, J. (2019). Journey towards independent living: Resilience processes of women leaving residential care in South Africa. *Journal of Youth Studies, 22*(5), 604–622. https://doi.org/10.1080/13676261.2018.1523541

Van Breda, A. D., Marx, P., & Kader, K. (2012). *Journey towards independent living: A grounded theory*. Retrieved February 17, 2023, from https://www.girlsandboystown.org.za/portfolio-item/gbt-uj-2012-journey-towards-independent-living/

Van Breda, A. D., Munro, E. R., Gilligan, R., Anghel, R., Harder, A., Incarnato, M., Mann-Feder, V., Refaeli, T., Stohler, R., & Storø, J. (2020). Extended care: Global dialogue on policy, practice and research. *Children and Youth Services Review, 119*, Article 105596. https://doi.org/10.1016/j.childyouth.2020.105596

Supplemental References

Doucet, M. M., Greeson, J. K. P., & Eldeeb, N. (2022). Independent living programs and services for youth 'aging out' of care in Canada and the U.S.: A systematic review. *Children and Youth Services Review, 142*, 106630. https://doi.org/10.1016/j.childyouth.2022.106630

Frimpong-Manso, K. (2022). Residential care-leaving in the Global South: A review of the current literature. In M. Israelashvili & S. Mozes (Eds.), *Youth without family to lean on* (pp. 165–178). Routledge.

Gray, M., & Lombard, A. (2022). Progress of the social service professions in South Africa's developmental social welfare system: Social work, and child and youth care work. *International Journal of Social Welfare*. Advance online publication. https://doi.org/10.1111/ijsw.12562

Hlungwani, J., & Van Breda, A. D. (2022). Affording managed opportunities for independence to build looked-after young people's resilience: Perceptions and experiences of care workers. *Journal of Children's Services, 17*(2), 137–151. https://doi.org/10.1108/JCS-10-2021-0044

Keller, S., Oterholm, I., Paulsen, V., & Van Breda, A. D. (Eds.). (2023). *Living on the edge: Innovative research on leaving care and transitions to adulthood.* Policy Press.

Theron, L., Murphy, K., & Ungar, M. (2022). Multisystemic resilience: Learning from youth in stressed environments. *Youth & Society, 54*(6), 1000–1022. https://doi.org/10.1177/0044118x211017335

Van Breda, A. D., & Theron, L. C. (2018). A critical review of South African child and youth resilience studies, 2009-2017. *Children and Youth Services Review, 91*, 237–247. https://doi.org/10.1016/j.childyouth.2018.06.022

Epilogue

Resilience, the powerful human capacity to withstand adversity, is amplified when narratives of resilience are *shared*. This epilogue tells the story and legacy of Erica, a participant in a 2010 study of resilience and survivorship among 133 Holocaust survivors living in the United States funded by the John Templeton Foundation (Greene, 2010a).

Erica endured the Holocaust in hiding in Hungary during the last year of World War II and found ways to creatively avoid being sent to the ghetto or the inferno (Corley, 2010a). During the Holocaust and throughout her life course, she demonstrated creativity and ingenuity—the core elements of the narrative of her century-long life, during which she engaged many people through her storytelling (Corley, 2010b). Although Erica experienced multiple medical challenges, she was committed to sharing her life story of survival through speaking and art as well as writing.

As Greene (2010b) noted in an examination of family life in the Templeton study, survivors built on protective factors and assets in their family lives and careers, often noting that having children contributed to their legacy. Although Erica's great-grandchildren, both younger than 5 at the time of her death, may have limited memories of her as they grow into their own resilient lives, Erica's writing, art, and recordings are a repository of her life for her son, grandchildren, great-grandchildren, and many others.

At age 70, Erica moved to America to marry her long-lost fiancé, who had left Hungary just before the start of World War II. Ten years after leaving Hungary, she wrote a memoir. Her memoir is archived at the Museum of the Holocaust in Los Angeles, the city where she lived to age 100.

The Epilogue from Erica's memoir, written as a legacy for her grandchildren, epitomizes what Viktor Frankl stated in *Man's Search for Meaning*: "Our greatest freedom is the freedom to choose our attitude" (Frankl, 1969, p. 147). Meaning-making is central in Holocaust survivors' capacity to thrive across the life course. According to Armour (2010), in meaning-making, "the intense pursuit of what matters creates a sense of continuity because the accumulation of individual acts about

R. Greene et al. (eds.), *Resilience Enhancement in Social Work Practice*,
https://doi.org/10.1007/978-3-031-38518-6

what matters provides the creation of an ongoing history from the time of the trauma to the present" (p. 440).

Armour (2010, p. 441) went on to say that meaning is the basis for constructing a coherent narrative and creates an internal experience that "I go on." One way Erica made meaning of her experiences was by painting scenes from Hungary that had been devastated in the war to offer positive images to override the trauma. Another way she expressed meaning is seen in the following quote:

> I wrote my memories for my grandchildren.... I want them to remember that there is hope always in life. There is music and nature—in these you will never be disappointed. Life is full of wonderful things along with the tragic ones.
>
> You just have to discover the beauty and love in life. There is no sunshine without shade. And no shade without sunshine. Everything is gray when we don't have both of them.
>
> We cannot enjoy constant happiness. We're only aware of the difference when we compare it with our troubled times. The shell has to suffer to produce the pearl—and so it is with our soul. Suffering makes it valuable.
>
> Many times, what seems to be bad—turns out to be for our benefit. We just have to wait and see.
>
> Connie Corley, Los Angeles, California, USA

Selected Museums with Extensive Educational Resources and/or Testimonials

Holocaust Museum LA (https://www.holocaustmuseumla.org/)
United States Holocaust Memorial Museum (https://www.ushmm.org/)
Yad Vashem (https://www.yadvashem.org/)

References

Armour, M. (2010). Meaning-making in survivorship: Application to Holocaust survivors. *Journal of Human Behavior in the Social Environment, 20*(4), 440–468.
Corley, C. (2010a). Creative expression and resilience among Holocaust survivors. *Journal of Human Behavior in the Social Environment, 20*(4), 542–552. https://doi.org/10.1080/10911350903275325
Corley, C. (2010b). A tale of three women: Survivorship through creative expression. *Journal of Aging, Humanities and the Arts, 4*, 262–275.
Frankl, V. E. (1969). *Man's search for meaning*. New American Library.
Greene, R. R. (2010a). Family dynamics, the Nazi Holocaust, and mental health treatment: A shift in paradigm. *Journal of Human Behavior in the Social Environment, 20*(4), 469–488. https://doi.org/10.1080/10911350903275010
Greene, R. (2010b). *Studies of the Holocaust: Lessons in survivorship*. Taylor & Francis.

Supplemental References

Carlberg, I. (2017). *Raoul Wallenberg: The heroic life and mysterious disappearance of the man who saved thousands of Hungarian Jews from the Holocaust*. MacLehose Press.
Frank, A. (1993). *The diary of a young girl*. Bantam.
Gilbert, M. (2018). *The Holocaust: The human tragedy*. Rosetta Books.
Keneally, T. (1982). *Schindler's list*. Simon & Schuster.
Levi, P. (2007). *Survival in Auschwitz: If this is a man*. Orion Press.
Luri, L. G., & Lurie, R. (2010). *Bending toward the sun: A mother and daughter memoir*. Harper Perennial.
Szpilman, W. (2002). *The pianist*. Picador.
Wiesel, E., & Wiesel, M. (2017). *Night*. Hill and Wang.

R. Greene et al. (eds.), *Resilience Enhancement in Social Work Practice*, https://doi.org/10.1007/978-3-031-38518-6

Index

R. Greene et al. (eds.), *Resilience Enhancement in Social Work Practice*,
https://doi.org/10.1007/978-3-031-38518-6

MIX
Papier aus verantwortungsvollen Quellen
Paper from responsible sources
FSC® C105338

If you have any concerns about our products,
you can contact us on
ProductSafety@springernature.com

In case Publisher is established outside the EU,
the EU authorized representative is:
Springer Nature Customer Service Center GmbH
Europaplatz 3, 69115 Heidelberg, Germany

Printed by Libri Plureos GmbH
in Hamburg, Germany